TALES FROM THE
BLACKBOARD

TALES FROM THE BLACKBOARD

True Stories by Australian Teachers

edited by
AMANDA TATTAM

First published 1998 in Pan by Pan Macmillan Australia Pty Limited
St Martins Tower, 31 Market Street, Sydney

Copyright © Amanda Tattam introduction and selection 1998
Copyright © in individual stories remains with the authors 1998

All rights reserved. No part of this book may be reproduced or
transmitted in any form or by any means, electronic or
mechanical, including photocopying, recording or by any
information storage and retrieval system, without prior
permission in writing from
the publisher.

National Library of Australia
cataloguing-in-publication data:

Tales from the blackboard: true stories by Australian
teachers

ISBN 0 330 36100 7.

I. Teaching – Australia. 2. Teachers – Australia. I.
Tattam, Amanda.

371.10994

Typeset in 11/13 pt Bembo by Midland Typesetters
Printed in Australia by McPherson's Printing Group

Every endeavour has been made to
contact copyright holders for permission to
use extracted material in this book.
Any person who may have been
inadvertently overlooked should
contact the publisher.

In memory of my parents:
Richard (Dick) Tattam who died while still employed as a teacher at Melbourne High School.
Dad, you honoured the work.

Valerie Tattam whose teaching career and passion to impart knowledge was tragically cut short by cancer.

ACKNOWLEDGMENTS

This volume of stories is a creation made possible by the enthusiasm and support of many people.

I offer particular thanks to the Australian Education Union and Independent Education Union of Australia who have endorsed this project and offered feedback on stories, especially federal office staff Sharan Burrow, Lynne Rolley, Susan Hopgood, Rob Durbridge and Sharon Gibbard.

The views of Olivia Tattam, and her assistance with administration is especially appreciated. Thanks to Ursula Tattam, Emma Tattam, Angelique Jansen, Anne Minos, Linda Fabb, Sarah McKinna, the Victorian and NSW Writers' Centres and the scores of others who promoted this project to teachers and writers.

Julie Hamston, Lecturer in Language and Literacy Education, Faculty of Education at Melbourne University; Ian Coffey, Director of Curriculum at Padua College, Mornington; Victoria and Marlene Drysdale, Senior Lecturer and Director, Koorie Studies Centre, Monash University Gippsland Campus, provided valuable insight on story content. The enthusiasm, support and advice of Pan Macmillan staff Amanda Hemmings, Alexandra Mohan, Paul Kenny, Phil Lawson, Katie Williams and Lisa Grigg is appreciated.

To any of my good teachers who read this book, I appreciate the fact that you believed in me – someone who 'could-do-much-better-if-she-didn't-talk-so-much-in-class-and-improved-her-concentration'. In particular I cherish the memories of my English teacher at Richmond High School, Linda James (née Parker).

My special thanks go to all teachers who submitted contributions and to John Marsden for taking the time to reflect on the power of their work. It has been a real privilege to read the stark and grim, plus the lighthearted tales from people with obvious talent as teachers, writers and human beings.

Amanda Tattam, Editor

The editor and publishers wish to acknowledge the following in the compiling of this book: 'When It's Fun You Learn' by Jenni Satrapa and Janet Rickwood, both from Canberra, is referred to in *Write for Life*.

Best Before March 1 is reproduced with permission from 'Education', the newspaper of the NSW Teachers' Federation.

He's Our Boy was first published in 'The Education Magazine', Education Department of Victoria, Vol. 36, No 3, 1979.

The following texts are referred to in *Feral Line Five:* 'Teacher and Child', H. Ginott, Macmillan, New York, 1972.

'Fully Human, Fully Alive', J. Powell, Argus Communications, Illinois, 1976. Random lines from poem, 'I'm here' by T. Roethke, 1956.

FOREWORD BY JOHN MARSDEN

I was a teacher for thirteen years. There were times when I felt murderous, suicidal, frustrated, cynical. There were times when it seemed like the worst job in the world.

And yes, OK, there were times when I was stimulated, inspired, uplifted, enchanted.

Before going into teaching I'd tried two dozen different jobs. They included cleaning offices, collecting blood, looking after a mortuary at nights, working on a side-show, and guarding Australia's oldest house from vandals.

At the age of twenty-eight I found myself sitting in an office in Rydalmere, Sydney, having reached the dizzying heights of Administration Manager of a group of transport and storage companies, a title which sounds impressive but meant bugger-all. It was a job where there was almost literally nothing to do: I spent half an hour each morning on paperwork and the rest of the time reading magazines and doing the crossword.

Perusing the newspaper one day, filling in the idle hours at what I'd laughingly learned to call work, I came across an advertisement for a teaching course at Mitchell College Bathurst. It sounded interesting, and I liked the idea of living in the country again. I applied and was accepted.

From the first day I knew I'd found something extraordinary. Maybe I was just lucky that the Primary Education faculty at Mitchell was progressive and intelligent. Whatever, I raced through the course, and got a job as an English teacher at All Saints' College Bathurst.

My life's never been the same since. I've learnt infinitely more as a teacher than I ever did as a student.

In a time when the morale of teachers is often low, and the profession is attacked almost daily, a book like *Tales from the*

Blackboard is pretty damn important. It reminds us that teachers are so often the conscience of our society, that they're often brave and passionate and funny, and that although many are defeated by the insidious enemy – cynicism – in many the idealism burns as bright as ever.

A teacher has to be like a priest or a prostitute, and fall in love in a hurry with anyone who comes along.

In one way or another, every story in this collection reminds us of that truth.

Contents

INTRODUCTION
xiii

Choose Your Own Adventure: Don't We All?
KATHRYN HARRISON
1

Rubicon
JEAN MROZIK
9

Slippery, the School Mascot
DON SMITH
17

To Ms With Love?
MAREE HERRETT
29

He's Our Boy
EDEL WIGNELL
37

Kultitja
LINDA WELLS
44

Red Corner, White Corner
GRAHAM McLENNAN
52

The Wasp in the Soccer Socks
RHODES GARWEN
57

Lesbeans
LAURA DERIU
62

Archery Delinquents
SHARYN LAWRENCE
69

Best Before March 1
ROBERT YEN
76

A Fine Line
GREG BOGAERTS
80

The Hill School
HELEN WAKEFIELD
85

The Three Microphones
PETER HOWE
91

Out of Uniform
SUE UTTING
95

The Key
BEV McGREGOR
105

Why Do I Keep Teaching?
GORDON HOLDER
120

Walls and Bridges
SUSAN LANE
125

Reunion at the Star Hotel
SUSIE ARMILLEI
129

A Winter's Tale
ROBBY WRIGHT
135

The Pole
JAMES JOHNSON
147

Write for Life
CHRISTINE MELICAN
152

Her Master's Voice
MICHAEL SMALL
161

How Yellow Changed to Gold
JOY PRICE
168

The Great Greasy Pig Chase of 1967
RUSSELL JAMES
179

The Lesson
SHEILA DUKE
187

A Place for the Living
WENDY RATAWA
192

Acting Up
LYNDALL HOUGH
202

If No One Cares for Me
HELEN GORDON
208

Feral Line Five
ROSEANNE WILDMAN
216

Antony
PETER COX
224

Mars Bars and Lawson
LYN CHATHAM
232

An Inquiring Mind
VIC O'CALLAGHAN
238

Neville
PINO SACCARO
252

Sometimes We Forget!
RON SKIDMORE
256

NOTES ON THE CONTRIBUTORS
261

INTRODUCTION

We've all been there. We think we know what goes on, even years after leaving the place. Parents with memories from school become experts on contemporary education standards once their children enter a classroom. Public figures and the media claim to have particular insight and they use rhetoric to generate debate, often for political ends. Headlines about low morale and status are depressingly common and misconceptions such as this, are given regular airing:

'Teaching is, broadly speaking, a low tech, low risk profession with quite low intellectual demands . . .'[1]

The 1997 Senate Inquiry into the Status of Teachers sought to find out why the profession is regarded so poorly by the community and what can be done to address societal perceptions. This book is part of the ongoing process of explaining the nature of schools and teaching so that the community appreciates the role and status of teachers.

Society relishes being able to pass judgement about schools, teachers and teaching because in part it feels ownership over institutions which are symbols of our past and our future. Schools are blamed for almost every human foible, but how often do teachers get the chance to provide the community with their personal views in a form that is accessible and informative?

In August 1997, Australian teachers from pre-school, primary and secondary sectors took up an invitation to write stories – not didactic accounts of their teaching careers – but true narratives about the challenges and triumphs of school life.

---

[1] (Christopher Bantick, *Courier Mail*, 4 March 1997, p 15, as quoted in 'The Status of Teachers' report by the Australian Education Union, 1997)

With the backing of the Australian Education Union, and the Independent Education Union of Australia, teachers were encouraged to write about memorable events, colleagues, classes, students; their experiences of dealing with children with unusual behaviours or disabilities; different cultural expectations, bullies and stress. Over the following four months, teachers submitted 320 stories: the task of choosing the thirty-five for this volume was an awesome one, but those that appear represent a cross section of voices, issues and dilemmas facing teachers.

The aim of this book is to reflect the complex nature of teaching within contemporary and some historical realities from a broad range of experiences. Despite the overwhelming emphasis on the challenges, rather than triumphs, the stories are not universally bleak and some are very funny, while being poignant. Not surprisingly, the things that stick in authors' minds tend to be the watershed experiences – a sequence of events, an episode, a class, student or teacher who changed the teacher forever. Some teachers reflect on their own journeys, by writing in the first person; others opt for the third person to explain events or people that have shaped their lives and careers. Several stories are written from a student's perspective. Characters and events have been altered to protect anonymity of the authors or people associated with the story.

How teachers cope (or otherwise) with discipline problems or uncontrollable students is the most popular topic. Teachers' most enduring memories of students tend to focus on badly-behaved, attention-seeking boys. I would love to have the luxury of exploring this trend further, but unfortunately it is not within the scope of this book to analyse why boys seem to absorb so much time and effort – on the part of male *and* female teachers. There is ample research on the complexities of gender in teaching and millions of people (mainly women) have spent their lives trying sort out the phenomena of 'the naughty boy' and are none the wiser! Seriously, I believe the qualitative material contained in these stories will provide rich material for an academic intent on exploring this and other issues of importance to teachers.

The authors are also deeply affected by the experience of dealing with discipline problems. Their stories speak of the desperation of trying to resolve disruptive influences while at the same time trying to help conscientious class members, who want to learn, and yet are disadvantaged by the behaviour of a minority of students. Even in classes where teachers eventually gain control, attitudes towards them are often characterised by foul or violent language, a lack of respect and at worst, sheer contempt. This is especially the case when teachers are doing casual/emergency teaching. Maree Herrett describes this in *To Ms With Love:*

'I can see ya tits, Miss.'
I knew I shouldn't have worn that red shirt that gapes but it's my first teaching job and my wardrobe isn't exactly replete with teacher-type clothes. Apart from my shirt that doesn't meet in the middle, I'm at the distinct disadvantage of being a substitute teacher; the regular one's on maternity leave – and whether or not she was liked or loathed, she was their teacher . . .
'What's yer first name?'
Feeling very progressive and hoping to win some favour, I tell them my name is Karen.
'Yuck – that's me middle name,' Anna blurts out . . .

More often than not, teachers recognise that the child or, in some cases, whole groups of children have been damaged by profound social problems or something that was going on at home, as this extract from *The Hill School* shows:

. . . there were subtle indicators too, such as an acceptance of pain and suffering and indifference to the pain of others. One boy calmly sliced the legs off a live lizard he had inside his desk while a lesson was in progress. Behaviour which was appalling to us was everyday and commonplace to many of these children. They seemed desensitised.

Family fights overflowed into the school grounds. The grisly activities at home included hanging other people's pets, starting fires and stealing animals ...

Another prominent theme was the illustration of direct (or indirect) social problems as 'the great intruder' on safe, caring learning environments. This was dealt with in some small or large way in many contemporary and historical stories. The stories show that regardless of appalling home circumstances, teachers just get on with it, making the best of the situation.

In 1963, Michael had severe disabilities because he was bashed by a drunken father. As an older boy in a Grade 1 class he unintentionally wreaks havoc. More than twenty years later, a Year 12 English student brings a plethora of social problems into the classroom, as Roseanne Wildman writes:

I'm not sure where to begin with Cheryl. When I looked through her school records they rivalled *War and Peace*. Cheryl was tall and thin with a nose that looked like it had done many rounds with Mike Tyson. She had three tattoos on her cheek and 'F.U.C.K.' tattooed across each knuckle on both hands. Although Cheryl was only twenty, she would occasionally bring to class the youngest of her three children.

Cheryl made no bones about what she did to supplement her income. She ran a mobile brothel catering to anyone who 'had the money up front' ...

While it is not the purpose of this book to do an in-depth investigation comparing conditions in classrooms between various eras, there is a palpably different tone of voice in the pre-1980s stories. Not only were there variations in class sizes, but in the minds of teachers there seemed to be a different energy in schools. This is portrayed in *If No One Cares For Me* when Helen Gordon compares the role of a pastoral teacher to its contemporary equivalent:

> There were thirty-five of them, not two hundred. *Of course* I knew each of them better than a Year Adviser can know most of her two hundred . . .

This author is not resistant to reform, indeed in one sense she welcomes it, but she reflects on how the profession has changed and made her 'a different sort of teacher, with a crab's shell'.

It is of note that many teachers chose to be reflective when telling their stories: *He's Our Boy*; *The Wasp in the Soccer Socks*; *If No One Cares for Me*; *How Yellow Changed to Gold* and *Rubicon* are recollections of characters from the 1940s–1970s. However, it is difficult to imagine the events of *The Great Greasy Pig Chase of 1967* being played out in the 1990s school; or the 1990s Year 7 class being satisfied with small gifts of novelty pens, rulers and erasers, which was the case in the story *How Yellow Changed to Gold*.

First days at school as student teachers, new teachers, or inexperienced teachers in challenging schools is another common theme in the stories submitted. In *The Key*, the teacher has a grand vision when graduating from training college and is bursting with young arrogance and pride about how she can apply these theoretical ideas in the classroom. Instead she finds herself searching for headlice with chopsticks.

More specifically, scores of stories seek to explain the anxieties facing teachers. Such anxieties are especially potent in younger teachers, but can also affect teachers who are burnt out after years of service and others who are facing unusual teaching positions. For example, in *Kultitja*, Linda Wells sums up the lot of the new teacher going to the outback:

The Education Department had shoved a few papers in my hand, blindfolded me, spun me around three times and sent me on my merry way . . .
   'Congratulations, you've won a year of isolation and neglect smack bang in the middle of the Australian continent. How do you feel?'
   'I feel shit-scared, unsupported, nervous, excited and like good things lie ahead of me.'

The reader is left in no doubt of how vulnerable new teachers feel and how they learn lessons from students and other teachers. Fresh teachers come with high expectations but ultimately their idealism is shattered or they realise the limitations of education theory and resources. Yet, once again they get on with the job at hand.

The hidden work of teachers — not just marking and meetings, but increasing administration, counselling and work associated with educational reforms — also features in many stories. In *Walls and Bridges*, the teachers organise counselling for a victim of torture and in *Mars Bars and Lawson* Lyn Chatham grapples with feelings of helplessness when a student reveals suicidal tendencies. Most people assume teachers have some kind of counselling role, but I did not expect it to be such a dominant theme. Another surprise was the extent to which the administrative side of the work could provide such rich material for humour. Lyndall Hough has managed to do this wonderfully with *Acting Up*.

The physical state of schools is also frequently raised in stories, with some teachers recounting how ceilings collapsed near children, fires destroyed libraries or whole schools and conditions in portable classrooms on hot or cold or even temperate days were a fundamental deterrent to learning.

Finally, the school as repository for all creatures great and small is undoubtedly the most quirky subject matter. Many stories deal with snakes, dogs, cats, rabbits, pigs, spiders and wasps as invited and uninvited guests. As an animal lover, it was refreshing to read stories such as *Slippery, the School Mascot* and *The Great Greasy Pig Chase of 1967*. Both of these stories are fine examples of how animals represent a diversion and a focus for learning and *The Wasp in the Soccer Socks* is just pure fun!

Few other institutions shoulder the level of responsibility that schools do. The content of the 320 submissions for this book provides ample evidence of this and the way teachers still cherish children and young people – despite the ardour and the child and adult beings that rile them. Teachers learn about their craft from the very beings they are trying to teach. When Steve Byrne, a primary school teacher in the outer suburbs of Melbourne was on playground duty, a Prep child wanting help approached him and said: 'Are you a teacher or a person?' He replied, 'I'm trying to be both.'

Teachers *are* human – they give so much of themselves and yet society demands more and more and gives less and less, so many decide to leave. The haemorrhage from the profession is now more palpable with experienced teachers burning out, retiring or taking very un-gift-wrapped redundancy packages. In the late 1990s, the cumulative effect of years of undervaluing teachers is slapping us in the face.

The constant emphasis on high literacy and numeracy rates is all well and good, but education is much more than this. One good measure of an educated society is the value placed on educational institutions and the human resources therein. The Senate Inquiry into the Status of Teaching recommends that the value of teaching be promoted to the community;

doing this will require more than just lip service and political grandstanding. I hope readers of this book will develop a deeper understanding of the complex nature of teaching and schools, because although we've all been there, the learning never stops.

Amanda Tattam Melbourne May 1998

Reference: *A Class Act – Report on the Status of the Teaching Profession*, Senate Employment Education and Training Reference Committee, AGPS, Canberra, March 1998, ISBN 0642 251 703.

CHOOSE YOUR OWN ADVENTURE: DON'T WE ALL?

Kathryn Harrison

You trudge unobtrusively up the scuff-marked corridors. Your palms tingle, the imprint of your teaching degree still being felt. But you are not unobtrusive. This is your first day of teaching and all eyes are upon you: the kids who stare and whisper as you walk through the corridor, your parents and boyfriend waiting eagerly back home, other teachers yet unknown and the Principal as you make your way to his office.

You enter. A balding man rises from behind the desk. You smile nervously, noticing he is dressed in brown shorts and long white socks. The little vein in his temple is throbbing.

'Alison, welcome to Happy Valley High School. I'm sure you'll be very happy here. We have a very supportive staff and the kids ... Well, kids are kids everywhere, don't you agree?'

You swallow nervously and nod, contemplating whether this is a bad omen.

'Your Head of Department is Marie Jones. Ah, here she is now. Marie, take Alison down and show her to her desk. Marie should be able to help you with any problems or queries you may have. As I said before, our staff are very supportive.'

He picks up his pen and begins writing. Your mumbled 'Thank you' goes unheeded. You turn and follow the retreating heels of Marie. Over and over in your head roll the words 'this is a mistake, this is a mistake'.

Your desk is small, very small, still containing some stationery from the last occupant. It is a dark space and tucked away in the less appealing end of the staffroom. A loud sniff followed by a hawking noise is emitted from the occupant of the desk across from yours. He notices you and stares.

'Excuse me,' he says, his eyes suggestive. You smile tightly and look away. The spitting has really disgusted you.

You arrange your lessons neatly on the desk, thinking you have overprepared. You glance again at the timetable sent to you by the Principal.

'That timetable's changed,' says the Spitter. 'We're on to a green timetable now. There have been two new timetables since the pink one. The new one's over there on the bulletin board.'

Great, you think. Double Year 8 English. Talk about throwing you in the deep end. You sigh.

The Spitter hears you. 'If you need any help.'

Yeah, help for what? To take my clothes off and go and sit on your lap? You have recognised that look before.

'I'm divorced,' he continues irrelevantly. The bell goes. You giggle as the thought 'saved by the bell' comes into your head. You pick up the relevant lessons, walking to the classroom placed conveniently near the staffroom. Your teaching career has begun.

If you want to see what is happening in the classroom two weeks after you have begun, turn to (1).

If you decide to stay in teaching five years after you've begun, turn to (2).

1

You breathe deeply. It started so well when you began two weeks ago, but now the kids think they have you worked out. It is now that you struggle to recall all the advice you have been given. The main one is 'Don't smile till Easter', but it is too late. You know that you have been too nice, letting the kids get overfamiliar.

'Are you married, Miss?'
'How old are you, Miss?'
'Do you have a boyfriend, Miss?'

You walk in. The Year 9s are lounging around on the chairs and tables.

'Sit down in a chair and open your books, please.'

They are slow to respond and deliberately drag the chairs around. You turn and start writing on the blackboard. Behind you laughter erupts. A spit ball, all chewed up and damp, sticks to the board. Their laughter is louder and more malicious when they realise that you have seen. Your face has turned red and you feel a headache coming on from the throbbing in your temples. You turn to the known troublemaker and try to take control.

'Jeremy, pick up your books and move.'
'It wasn't me, Miss.'
'I've asked you to move.'
'But it wasn't me.'

Your voice is getting louder. You have become oblivious of the fact that the Principal can probably hear you. The laughter and grins around you make you more angry.

'Do I have to go and get the coordinator?'
'All right then, you stupid fucking bitch.'
'Out!' you scream. You have lost it.
'No. I'm not going.' You feel deflated, powerless and very, very close to tears. Behind you another spit ball lands on the blackboard.

You decide to leave teaching, turn to (3).

You stay in teaching, turn to (2).

2

'Hurry up, sit down and open up your books. Now. You waste my time and I'll waste yours.'

You look around the room, seeing the same old behaviour. Kids are so self-centred and at times predictable. You are pleased with this class. They have just written fantasy stories and most of them have included the elements you outlined on plot, dialogue and description.

'Kevin, I will be phoning your parents if your story is not submitted by Monday.'

You know the story will remain unwritten but you keep trying.

'Carrissa, that story was excellent. I really enjoyed reading it.'

'All right, open your novels to page 69.' You groan. Why does it seem we always stop at page 68? 'Okay Kevin, get your mind out of the gutter and start reading.'

'Miss? Miss?'

'What is it, Jeremiah? We are trying to read!'

'William smells, Miss.'

You go red. William, you remember, has the unfortunate habit of defecating in his pants. He has been examined but apparently the problem is all in his head. This is coupled with another bad habit: theft.

'Jeremiah, go with him to the toilet.'

'Ah Miss, do I have to?'

You continue reading. You are really enjoying the novel but some of the kids are bored and have begun to chatter. This makes you angry and you tell them to continue reading by themselves. The new girl sits with her head in her arms. You ask her to start reading but she raises a tear-stained face. You are aware that she is a case from Community Services, but you don't want to get involved. You don't have the energy as this is your five-on day, with yard duty.

You say to her gently, 'Do you want to go and see the welfare coordinator?' but she shakes her head and thrusts you her journal. You leave her alone because in the back corner, Jye has pushed Cindy's books on the floor.

There are some muffled announcements on the speaker, but by the time you have quietened down the class, the bell has gone.

'And push in your chairs,' you yell at their disappearing heads.

At your desk, you read the letter that your new student has written in her journal:

God, I feel like killing myself. I suppose I better tell you the story. About a month ago . . . Oops, I better start from the beginning. Three years ago, my Mum married Jake, who is my stepdad. I never liked him but I was sort of pleased coz Mum was so happy and I got to be bridesmaid. It wasn't long after that he started hitting Mum. Sometimes I couldn't stand it and would try and stick up for her but then he would hit me too.

Anyway, why CSV moved me to Smithton is because about a month ago, they were fighting worse than usual. I was holding a new pet puppy. I ran in and stood in front of Mum. Jake grabbed the puppy and twisted its neck. It was crying in pain but it died soon after. I just screamed at him, crying. I couldn't handle it any more. I ran out and rang the police. Now, here is the bit I can't stand. Mum and Jake told the police that I am lying and they won't speak to me.

You stop reading, and feel sick and upset. The bell rings. You feel too vulnerable and depressed to go to your next class, but you have no choice.

You decide to leave teaching, turn to (3).

You continue on with teaching and accept a position of responsibility after teaching for ten years. Turn to (4).

3

You have been waiting half an hour in the offices that deal with the unemployed. You have forgotten the acronym of the government department, there is a myriad to contend with. The inner walls are covered with different job descriptions. You are writing down the details, when you notice someone standing close to you. You look and it is one of your old students. What was his name? Gilbert. No, Gordon, you think to yourself and then you remember. This is the same student you had suspended for vandalising the antenna on your car. Unemployment, the great leveller. Your smile tightly and walk away.

It is Saturday and you open the paper to the Employment section. You scan the columns searching for that job which welcomes your skills. With a red pen you circle some possible options with the same force as you used to circle spelling errors.

At the Office for the Finally Fucked (you have made up your own acronym), you show your case manager the growing pile of rejection letters.

'Not even one interview!' She shrugs helplessly at you.

Back at home, you phone the Education Department.

'Excuse me, I was wondering if there are any available positions in the Loddon–Mallee region. There are? Great.'

4

You turn on the overhead projector. All staff members' eyes are upon you, most look bored.

'The new Victorian government directives dictate that we have to have all curriculum written up in a standardised document to fit in the new DSE-directed college charter.'

You see them staring at the butcher's paper and the coloured markers, each hoping they have not been chosen scribe of their group. You know how they think. You were one of them once, full of apathy, but now you are being paid to produce this Schools of the Future documentation. But you know the change is starting to get to them. Each year in the past ten years the staff have been asked to produce more jargon rather than having been left alone to put the words into action.

'Here are the groups. Nominate a scribe to report back.' You switch on the carefully prepared overhead.

'I'll go scribe.' It is the enthusiastic voice of Kenny, the first year PE teacher. He is the only first year who has been employed at your school in the last five years. You smile briefly, heartened, but then you remember the school will soon be full of a thousand Kennys. It is cheaper to employ five Kennys on a limited tenure than one of you. The school will be economising, managing its own global budget. Maybe that won't be a bad thing. The school has been top heavy and stagnant for a number of years.

'Another decision that must be made today is what former AST3 and 4 positions must be transferred to the new Level 3 and 4. You have your sheets and can clearly see that our budget is not sustainable. What position of responsibility can we combine or reduce to a payment?'

Everyone shuffles, disconcerted. This is the everyday reality of the budget cuts. Reduced time allowance, less payment for higher duties and more expected from the classroom teacher on top of their regular face-to-face duties. You stare at them and imagine that they are soldiers in the field. The image makes you smile.

'Important jobs, did you say? Looks like yours is the first to go,' our resident joker yells out and everyone laughs. Black humour features large in teaching and it is the one thing that links all staff members. Unfortunately, you know that there is truth in that comment. Jobs are linked to personalities.

You lose your position of responsibility in the new reshuffle. You have passed the learning curve and the difficulties you had when you started begin to reappear. Go back to (1) and experience the loss of control.

RUBICON

Jean Mrozik

It's been four weeks now. The tannery has become my private Rubicon. Every morning when I see the chimney, my pulse lurches, pauses, takes off. My bowels loosen. The train always seems to slow down at the tannery as if to let the stench of the settling ponds seep in to remind me that we have reached the point of no return. Lambskins stretch out on fences, row upon row, like a dead vineyard. That's how Mum would look by now, under the peppercorn trees. It only takes a couple of weeks in that heat. I look down at Mum's dress. It's the pink of peppercorns with brown polka dots and brown velvet bows on the bodice. I can hear her laughing, soft as the pink stuff of her dress. She isn't wearing the dress, of course – I am – because she's dead.

If she hadn't died, I wouldn't have got the dress. I can't help this thrilled feeling that mixes up with the cramp in my bowels. It's about being a student teacher in the city, having no mum. Being grown up. They've bombed Darwin and you can see fast girls on the arms of Americans. I'm thinking this is freedom – soldiers, dances, all that stuff – when suddenly there's a horrible noise in the carriage as if someone's let out an awful hiccup but then it turns into big, blubbering sounds that can't be coming from my mouth because that's not our way. Not in our family. Some people cry at funerals, in public. It's very embarrassing for the people standing around.

The other passengers stare hard at their newspapers or knit as if there's a whole army without any socks. They think I'm not much chop, that I've got myself pregnant to an American marine. I blush, feel mysterious as if I've got a secret baby inside me and stop crying because the idea is very grown up. Until we pull into Yarraville I imagine I've got a huge diamond engagement ring on my finger and my fiancé's in some jungle up north. But when the train groans and pulls into the station, I'm just a sixteen-year-old kid again, in her mum's hand-me-down.

I get out and walk towards the school because I'm a teacher. I see Miss O'Halloran stride out the gate in front of me and the fear of her rolls in a slow agony down my side. I run like crazy to the railway toilets and make it just in time.

But I hurry, so I'm not that far behind her. I'm hurrying because I have an appointment before school. The big bluestone school squats in front of us in a square of asphalt. Miss O'Halloran hauls her heavy body up the steps and marches along the corridor. I catch a whiff of sweat and jam sandwiches, of unwashed feet, of pencil shavings in old biscuit tins. By now I'm just behind her. The thing inside me that is revulsion and terror, that is excitement about fuchsia lipstick and stilettos, final leave and weddings, grips and twists. I stop in midstride to absorb the pain. It is an eye inside of me. We stare each other out, the pain and I. It requires my whole being.

The headmaster, Barton, pipe clenched in his teeth, darts out of his office. He nods curtly to Miss O'Halloran as his little legs fuss along on some early morning trivia.

'Good morning, Mr Barton,' she says, cooing, and bends imperceptibly to acknowledge the supremacy of the little man. She pauses as if she expects him to impart some small pleasantry to her because of her own importance, but he has gone. Only the blue smoke remains as he struts out of sight.

The pain recedes and I am free to imagine an obsequious smile unfolding from her large pink face and I see the disappointed droop of her shoulders as she plods towards her Grade 3 room. It is 8.15 am. I have fifteen minutes more freedom so I stay outside the classroom where I can watch her begin her daily routine.

She steps majestically onto the dais and with slow, deliberate movements, places her carry-all on the desk. The temperature is already climbing towards the century so she takes out a bottle wrapped in damp newspaper and places it, together with her brown paper packet of sandwiches, in the old wooden cupboard. Dimpled flesh quivering, she lifts her arms to unpin her straw hat.

For a moment she stands with her hands pressed to her temples as if she is holding them together and I think, oh please God, just this once. Let her have a dreadful headache and have to go home. Please. But I've seen it all before. I know the ritual. She opens the drawer in her desk and takes out the strap. She unrolls it and lays it along the front of the desk so it's the first thing the children will see when they file into class. Satisfied, she spreads her buttocks over the chair. She sits there looking at her watch. It's 8.29 and she's waiting for her prey. For me. And I will come to her. She's waiting to give me my lesson in blackboard writing.

'Good morning, Miss O'Halloran,' I whisper at 8.30. By the merest inclination of her head she notes my presence. I put my own brown paper bag beside hers in the cupboard and turning towards her back, hesitate. Her fingers are already drumming on the desk. I swallow and the sound in my gullet is deafening.

'Will I write the transcription on the blackboard then?' I say in my mum's timid voice, with my mum's inflection. The drumming of Miss O'Halloran's fingers ceases. She turns her moonface towards me.

'Isn't that what you always do?' Her voice is sneering, sharpened by flatulence or the pulsing in her temples. I know that I have to ask another question. The classroom clock ticks and Miss O'Halloran sits smiling a deadly little smile. Fear rolls again and the fire spreads down into my thigh.

'What will I write?'

'You will write the same as you wrote yesterday morning. It was a disgrace and with your sloppy correction, you permitted the children to make far too many mistakes. They also will repeat it this morning, Miss Jenner.'

The shame! 'This is my daughter,' Dad had said to the stationmaster at Tragowel, 'she's got a job as a school teacher in the city, you know.' But as I turn towards the blackboard with its red and blue lines, I know that my handwriting will be perfect. I see all my first prize penmanship certificates from the agricultural shows and I know that Miss O'Halloran will be pleased with me, that she will say to Mr Barton, 'What a treasure that young country girl has turned out to be.'

I am almost happy as the white chalk sweeps firmly up and down, around in magnificent loops and ovals as I commence the long passage again. 'Out of the darkness the Hobyas came, hop, hop, hopping ...' As I write, the fifty Grade 3 children file into the room, under the cold gaze of Miss O'Halloran.

Miss O'Halloran smiles as she looks at the finished script, perfect, as it had been the day before. The children sit upright, rigid, like terriers waiting for a morsel. I see Miss O'Halloran's eyes drop to my long bare legs and her mouth fold with distaste. The silvery pinkness of her neck, protected by fifty-nine summers of sensible hats, floods to an angry red as she rises. Her voice shears through the classroom.

'I see no improvement whatsoever, Miss Jenner. Kindly erase it and do it again. We will wait.' She turns regally to face the class. 'Good morning, Grade 3,' she says softly and bestows on each her frigid little smile. 'Say good morning nicely to Miss Jenner now.'

'Good morning, Miss Jenner,' they chorus, singsong, sniggering.

As the dust settles on the blackboard ledge, I start again. There is nowhere to go. 'Out of the darkness ...'

'Hands on heads!' Miss O'Halloran settles in her chair to wait.

There is a soft shurring of chalk on the blackboard and the rhythmic chant of a class reciting tables somewhere down the corridor. I write slowly so my eyes will have time to dry. I hear Miss O'Halloran open another page of her newspaper, and another, and then it is done. I turn to face her.

'That is much better, Miss Jenner,' she mocks, not bothering to look up from the newsprint. 'You may now conduct the transcription class.'

She turns another page and I do my best to emulate her crisp authority as I admonish the children from time to time. I busy up and down the rows, fuss from desk to desk, making corrections, guiding small hands. She will see my enthusiasm, my competence. The children work in a hushed silence, awed by her presence.

The acquiescence of the class calms me. The pain has almost gone. I hurry back to a small child and sit beside her, guiding her uncoordinated movements while she gazes up at me with uncomprehending delight. I have never heard of Down's syndrome.

'Will you leave that idiot child alone, Miss Jenner!' Miss O'Halloran's voice is sharp with irritation. 'Kindly stop wasting your time and concentrate on the other children.' I rat-tat on my new stilettos, up and down the aisles, frantic in my desire to please. She will see. All fifty of them will have not a single mistake. Tat-tat-rat-tat. Ratatat.

The shout erupts. Miss O'Halloran is frenzied now by her pulsing head, my grovelling subservience and the incessant rat-tat of my heels. 'Will you lift your feet, Miss Jenner!' she screams. 'The noise is hurting my head.'

'I'm sorry, Miss O'Halloran,' I whisper, humiliated that I have not heard my own feet echoing on the wooden floor. Mum would have been so ashamed. I tiptoe all through the spelling test, all through the chorusing of the tables while Miss O'Halloran reads the newspaper. Like the tip of a cat's tail, her foot twitches from time to time.

The day is searing by the time she folds her newspaper and supervises the children, 'Left, right, chins in, left, right,' out onto the asphalt to play. Tiptoeing still, I move towards the door.

'Miss Jenner,' her voice is soft, caressing, 'would you like a glass of lemonade, dear?' She pours the effervescent fluid into a glass, tempting me. I turn, wanting it to be all right to accept. I have tasted lemonade only once before. I can remember the sweet biting cold.

'Thank you, Miss O'Halloran,' I say, 'I am not thirsty.' I turn and walk across the black heat of the yard to the sour-smelling toilets seething with damp children. I snib myself into the cubicle that says 'Teachers Only' and I weep. I don't bother to pee. I lean my head against the door and weep inconsolably.

My joy at Miss O'Halloran's absence the next morning overrides any remorse I feel on account of my request to the Lord the previous day. It appears she is most unwell. I choose a text and transcribe it on the board. I am very early, so with sudden boldness, I go to Miss O'Halloran's cupboard for her coloured chalks and work with sure, swift strokes. I draw the pied piper with his robes swirling out behind him, the light glinting off his pipe. I draw the children dancing in their brightly coloured clothes. They dance across the board and in a kind of mad joy at the beauty of my creation, I continue across on to the other board. The dancers wind in and out Miss O'Halloran's tables and spelling lists until I have finished the last, sad little child who will be left behind.

I am glad I have worn Mum's dress again. It is so pretty. It matches my joy. I am a gifted teacher.

'Good morning, Grade 3,' I say in the voice my mum used to use when she was happy, all bubbly underneath with laughter. 'We'll have a little change this morning. First I'll tell you a story about a piper and the children who danced to his music.'

'Oh Miss,' they say, wriggling and grabbing at their crotches in excitement. The child with Down's syndrome doesn't understand but she rocks with laughter because there is happiness everywhere.

I take Miss O'Halloran's wooden chair from behind her big desk and bring it close to the children, right to the edge of the dais, and I begin. I can tell a yarn well. That's what we did in the evenings on the farm. The children lean forward and I feel my power. I bring the piper and the children, dancing down off the blackboard, colours blazing, down across the dais and into their drab lives. Silent, suspended in magic, they listen and I know I am a born teacher.

Suddenly the door of the classroom crashes open. Barton strides in but the children forget to stand, hardly spare him a glance. I am so proud. He struts to the back of the room and stands in the aisle in front of me. I am too modest to look directly at him but I know that at last the great man has seen me. 'A born teacher,' he will say of me to Miss O'Halloran when she returns.

The headmaster stands for a long, long time. He turns then, brusquely, and walks out of the room. The children stir uneasily as he slams the door, but I am deep in hubris, high on pride. In the distance his office door slams and I am just about to reach the river when the intercom crackles.

'Miss Jenner,' Barton's voice is like a whip crack. 'To my office immediately!'

'Ooh Miss,' the children breathe, more knowing than I. I had not expected to be called so soon. 'Be very good,' I say, 'and we will continue in a minute.'

Barton barks again when I knock on his door. As I walk towards his desk, he gives no acknowledgement of my presence. I wait. Gauche again. An Avro Anson drones in the distance, pulses heavily overhead and vanishes slowly in the direction of Mangalore. Far away down a corridor a teacher too old and tired to be in the war shouts at his class as I stand shyly waiting for my accolade.

Barton stares down at the papers on his desk. The early morning sunlight shines on the polished virility of his scalp but I have never heard of hormones. He grabs a sheaf of papers and shuffles them in frenzied activity.

'Let your dress down,' he sneers, vicious suddenly. His eyes reach no higher than the hem of Mum's dress. I blush deeply, aware that I have been coarse, that he must have seen my thighs when he stood at the back of the room. My pants! He could have seen the middle bit of my pants. I could die with the awfulness of it. I stand motionless, unable to find some place to store this knowledge until I am alone in darkness to retrieve it, to explore my shame.

'Well go on girl,' he screams, 'what are you waiting for? Get out. Go back to your class.'

'Ooh Miss,' the children shout, 'did you get into a row?'

'What did 'e say to yer, Miss?'

'Eh, she got told off by baldy,' a voice yells and the children thump each other with joy and yell until the teacher in the next classroom bangs on the wall.

I lift the chair from the edge of the dais and put it back behind Miss O'Halloran's desk. I pull out her drawer and unfurl the strap slowly while the children watch.

'Right!' I say, in Miss O'Halloran's proper teacher's voice. 'Transcription!'

SLIPPERY, THE SCHOOL MASCOT

Don Smith

The sound of the rain pelting down on the tin roof was a continual drone in my mind. Classroom conditions were arduous, with the children oppressed by tropical heat and soaring humidity. The wet season always brought with it the constant dangers of floods; where power could be cut for days, spoiling food supplies and severing all contact with the outside world. For weeks rain drummed on the school's tin roof: drumditty drumditty drum drum drum. The constant hammering was tormenting me.

'How long will this rain last?' I asked the class, shouting above the clamour of a thunderous torrential downpour.

'Only another couple of months, sir,' Carmen shouted nonchalantly. 'You city folk have to be careful. Too much rain sends you troppo if you're not used to it.'

'It's just such a pain,' I groaned. 'It's stopping us from doing all sorts of interesting things, like basketball, football and athletics.'

Johnny's hand shot up. I shot him a threatening teacher's glare.

'This is not another story about the bulls and the mares, is it, Johnny?' I asked.

'No, sir! That's Science, sir. You said we are doing Social Studies,' he answered cheekily.

'Okay, what's your question?' I asked hesitantly. In my experience, every class has a Johnny in it. They're put there just to challenge us and keep life interesting. Sometimes, though, I could do without them. This particular Johnny was very smooth at changing the direction of class discussions. When a certain look twinkled in his eyes, I became especially wary.

'Well, sir, if there's snow when it's Christmas overseas, and it's hot here in Australia, that means the calfin' time would be different because the mares wouldn't want to drop the calves in the snow.'

I shrugged in despair. Carmen raised her hand. I nodded at her to speak, attempting again to sidestep Johnny's favourite topic.

'Excuse me, Mr Smith, when Mr Dorite was the Principal, we were allowed to bring our pets into class during the wet season. It meant we had something to do at lunchtime if we had to stay inside.'

The very thought of it horrified me. 'But they would all fight and try to eat each other,' I argued, desperately trying to extricate myself from such a potential nightmare.

'Oh no, sir!' they all chorused. They looked at me dolefully, laying a big bad ogre trip on me.

'Put up your hand if you think we should have a Pet Day,' I conceded democratically.

All hands were automatically raised. A pets' day it was.

The following Monday the children brought in a diverse menagerie of animals from the rainforest that surrounded their homes. They cradled their pets to protect them from yet another downpour as they dashed madly from their vehicles into the dry classroom. Soon the room was filled with an array of unusual creatures, frenzied by the many different sights, sounds and smells.

Regardless of the species, all of them peed, pooed, plopped or pebbled. At one second past nine the classroom was a war zone; dogs barked at goats, piglets squealed at bandicoots, and cockatoos screeched at kittens.

'Quickly!' I cried above the racket. 'Save the white mouse. He's heading towards the geese.'

'I'll put the piglet in the birdcage with the pigeon,' said Carmen helpfully.

'If that's a male pigeon, and she's a female piglet, what sort of calf would they make?' asked Johnny. The familiar twinkle reappeared in his eye.

'No, Johnny!' I snapped. 'There is no chance of calfin' from either pigeons or pigs. Now grab that dog by the chain and tie it to that desk.'

For the next two hours we did battle to save victims from life-and-death struggles. My mind was on full alert, pursuing and preventing every potential disaster. Mrs Moonlight wouldn't be happy if she rocked up in the afternoon to collect her child and dearest pet lizard, only to be informed that half of it was missing after throwing its tail in a desperate bid for survival. And how would I inform Mrs Ashton that little bunny's four lucky feet were nearly tucked up in puppy's fat tummy?

Just when we finally restored some semblance of sanity into the classroom, our eyes fell on a self-invited visitor. It stopped at the front door and peered in. It sensed no danger; nor detected any movement as every animal froze. When it moved inside, the classroom reignited into a panic-stricken melee, erupting into a cacophony of bleating, barking, hooting, squawking and hissing. Pandemonium raged. It was what every teacher dreaded – a snake in the classroom.

One of the boys pelted a jogger, striking it on the back. The snake became enraged and slithered wildly, searching for an escape. The rest of the class grabbed weapons ready to hack the intruder to pieces. Someone hurled the class roll, barely missing the desperate snake. One boy raised a chair ready to smash down with the steel legs.

'No! No!' cried Carmen. 'Don't kill it. It's only a harmless python!' Harry speared the blackboard ruler, narrowly missing another child.

'Leave it alone!' I yelled, as if I had some bold battle plan.

But the children, fired up with fear and excitement, continued bombarding the snake.

'You're going to kill it!' screamed Carmen. 'Just leave it alone!' She ran forward, hurling her body over the snake, which appeared to be about half a metre long. I saw her wince in pain as someone's Maths book bounced off her head.

'Stop chucking!' I screamed. 'The next person to throw anything gets a year on toilet duty.' All missiles were quickly grounded.

Carmen rose unsteadily to her feet with the snake securely wrapped around her arm. Its head scanned our faces, searching for a place to inflict its viciousness.

'It won't hurt us, sir. Look!' Carmen thrust the reptile towards me.

'*Yikes!*' I screeched and promptly stumbled backwards over a terrified bandicoot. 'Keep it away from me.' Some of the children giggled.

'Put the snake in the birdcage with the piglet. Take out the pigeon and put it in the fish tank with the white mice,' I ordered shakily. She walked towards the cage patting the snake affectionately as she unwound it from her arm and placed it gently inside. Again some sort of order was restored. I sent Carmen to the library immediately to see if there was any possibility that our uninvited intruder was harmful, while the rest of us battled to maintain harmonious classroom dynamics. She returned quickly waving a photocopy at us, her face beaming with success.

'What has our brave Carmen found to report?' I asked fondly as a tribute to her courage.

'It is a non-venomous python,' she read emphatically. 'It is a nocturnal animal that feeds mainly on lizards and mice and can grow to over a metre in length.'

'How often does it have to eat?' asked Johnny, inquisitively eyeing off the small white mouse.

Tears welled in Rhonda's eyes.

'After a meal the snake does not need to eat for at least a week and spends most of its time sleeping,' Carmen informed us.

'Who thinks they can catch a lizard?' I asked quickly, hoping to alleviate Rhonda's fears.

Every hand in the room shot up.

We spent the rest of the day experiencing life on Noah's Ark. Only the steady clatter of rain belting on the roof shielded our ears from the cacophonous insanity. At three o'clock all the children scurried through the mud to the waiting four-wheel drives, relieving me of their pets, until only one remained – a snake in a birdcage. I watched it curiously, wondering how I could dispose of it without being strangled or bitten. It stared threateningly through its yellow eyes and flicked its tongue contemptuously. I shuddered as I contemplated its evil thoughts.

My major consideration was the children's safety, and I was determined to let it go. I decided to wait until Mrs Parson, the cleaner, had finished so I could simply inform the class that it had escaped. I didn't need a witness to expose my lie and I knew she'd be cleaning for at least another hour.

I headed through the pouring rain towards the shed to change the blades on the mower in the hope that, one day, the deluge might cease long enough to mow. It was probably more appropriate to attach floaties to the wheels in case it was washed away. I shrugged hopelessly as I emptied the water from my boots.

After I changed the blades I headed back to the comfort of the classroom and a cup of tea. I glanced at the empty cage . . . Empty? The snake was gone. It couldn't possibly have escaped through the grille. Perhaps it had lifted the cage door, or squeezed through the bars. Maybe it was a Houdini. After a frantic search I felt satisfied that it had escaped through the open door and was now safely back in the wild.

No lies were required the following day as the children accepted the explanation, some with disappointment, others with relief. I glanced at Carmen, who was visibly upset.

'Sometimes it is better when things happen this way,' I said, trying to console her.

'I thought up a good name for it last night,' she said sadly. 'We could have called him Slippery. He could have been our school mascot.'

'What's the difference between a chook and a snake?' asked Melvin.

'I don't know,' I conceded.

'We won't send you out to collect the chooks' eggs then,' said Melvin, very pleased with himself.

The morning progressed and the rain belted down. My voice had worn thin from hollering above the clatter. The littlies were playing with the puppets when a frightening shriek struck terror into our hearts. Emerging lazily from the pouch of Katie Kangaroo was the head of the snake. The children were once again ignited into panic mode, scurrying immediately for weapons. It was Carmen who again saved the day.

'No!' she screamed. 'Don't hit Slippery. Let him sleep.'

She thrust herself between the snake and the potential assailants, cradling both the kangaroo puppet and its strange intruder in her arms. Then she reached in and gently pulled the creature from the pouch.

'I'll hold his head while you pat his tail,' she announed to whoever was brave enough.

My legs were still in reverse but some of the more curious children moved forward to touch, stroke, pat or prod the reptile. Natural curiosity prevailed and their fears abated. I had never touched a snake. What I imagined to be wet and slimy was velvety smooth with hard muscle flexing beneath the incredibly patterned skin. It was fascinating.

There is no rest for the wicked and by lunchtime Slippery had taken on the role of most sought-after class member. It spent the morning being wheeled around in the pram with Katie Kangaroo, Garfield, Barbie and Ken. When not engaged in baby duties, it would wrap itself around an arm or a neck, contentedly soaking up the human warmth, endeavouring to catch another nap amid the excesses of attention. The new class member became the focus of our day's lessons.

'Can you read us a story about a snake?' asked Carmen.

'That's an excellent idea,' I replied. 'Henry Lawson wrote a wonderful story called "The Drover's Wife".'

'I have a story about a snake,' said Mabel, our Aboriginal teacher's aide.

'Yeah!' the children replied as Mabel held up the book *The Rainbow Serpent* by Dick Roughsey. They sat riveted as she read them the story of how the giant serpent travelled over the land. Where its body touched, gorges appeared and they became the rivers and streams which fertilised the earth. She also told them a snake tale from the white man's stories: how once the earth was a fantastic garden, which was not only beautiful but also generously bountiful. From the sky a snake appeared in the form of a comet. After the comet struck the earth the beautiful garden was wrecked and all who lived were forced to work hard to survive. The seas shifted and the rivers changed course, reforming the face of the earth. For that reason the snake will always be hated by human beings and reviled as a serpent – a devil in the garden.

Mabel might have been a mild-mannered speaker but when she told her stories she could raise the hair on a cat's back. The children remained spellbound. When she was finished she held up the snake.

'Just like every creature, the snake plays its part in nature. We must respect them for their role and not just kill them through fear or ignorance.'

As soon as her story was completed the children's hands shot up with a myriad of different requests.

'Sir, can we do some paintings about the snake?'

'Sir, can we write some stories about snakes on the computer?'

'Sir, can we take the snake outside with the trundle wheels and do some measuring?'

Johnny's hand waved vigorously. I motioned for him to speak.

'Well, sir, you know how a snake hasn't got any arms or legs or anything? How would they get involved in something like calfin'?' he asked curiously, the ever-present twinkle glinting in his eyes.

'Believe me, Johnny,' I snapped, 'snakes don't have calves.'

The sound of the rain had finally softened to a gentle tapping and for the first time in days it stopped. The snake had brought us luck. Mabel held Slippery under the light.

'Look closely,' she told the children. 'The snake's glassy scales reflect light, breaking it into its rainbow colours. But you have to be brave enough to come close to look.'

'Hey you can really see the colours of the rainbow,' I replied incredulously. 'It really is a rainbow serpent.'

We collected rulers, tape measures, trundle wheels and the snake and headed for the outdoors.

During our lesson, the children found out that Slippery was not only an excellent swimmer, but also an experienced climber. True to his name, Slippery slid from a child's unsuspecting grasp and slithered up a tree as fast as greased lightning. His keen sense of smell zeroed in on a bird's nest and the snake promptly polished off the eggs, much to the despair of the parent birds, which were flapping around helplessly.

We were soon driven inside by the next downpour. We had to desert Slippery, who was out of reach. But it wasn't long before he decided that the comfort of the dry classroom was the best place to be. He was eagerly attended to when he appeared in the doorway. In the afternoon, we agreed to put Slippery in the lawn mower shed overnight where he would be warm and dry. This would enable him to catch his own food, which would also be looking for a dry and comfortable place. If Slippery disappeared, then that was nature's way and something we would all have to accept.

With the new-found mascot comfortably housed and the three o'clock bell ringing, the children scurried to waiting vehicles.

The next day the class were disappointed not to find Slippery in the mower shed and had to console themselves that he had departed. After Morning Talks, we began with a handwriting lesson. A buzz of consternation rose as the children examined their tidy trays and found that all their rubbers had disappeared.

'Does anyone have a reasonable explanation as to where all the rubbers have gone?' I asked curiously.

Johnny's hand shot immediately skywards. 'Could it be UFOs, sir?' he inquired.

'That's a very good question, Johnny,' I replied, pleased that he had at least two thoughts in his head.

The level of debate woke Slippery, whose head slowly emerged from the kangaroo's pouch. He was either doing a head count or looking for somewhere different to sleep. I noticed that behind the back of his head there was a peculiar square shape caused by whatever the snake had devoured. In a flash of intuition our minds were communally enlightened.

'Slippery ate the rubbers,' stated Carmen as she moved towards the animal for a closer examination.

The children burst into laughter when they saw lumps down the full length of his back.

'Who can tell me why the snake ate the rubbers?' I asked.

Andrea from Grade 2 answered. 'Becauth the thnake thought they were googy eggth.'

'That is an excellent answer, Andrea,' I said. 'The snake is a nocturnal animal and last night it went hunting for food in the classroom. The rubbers would have looked like a good feed of birds' eggs.'

'But how do we get them back?' Toni whined disconsolately.

Carmen's hand shot up. 'If we put the snake in the birdcage it will have to regurgitate the rubbers if it wants to get out.'

'Excellent idea, Carmen.'

We placed Slippery's beloved kangaroo puppet beside the cage as an extra incentive for the reptile to escape.

The first of the rubbers appeared on the bottom of the cage just as Carmen had predicted. The snake began writhing and gyrating in a grotesque ritual, dislocating its jaw to expel the rubbers. As we watched, it became an informative science lesson that demonstrated the regurgitative powers of snakes. When Slippery was finished, he deflated his muscles and slid through the bars to the warmth and comfort of the kangaroo's pouch.

During the following days the rain poured incessantly and the weekend was a total wash-out. Apart from showing the electricians where the fuse boxes were located on the buildings, I was confined indoors.

The black dismal skies on Monday morning augured badly for those fearing rising rivers. The black gaseous soup above us clouded all indications that there was ever a sun, raising unnatural paranoia in me that I might never see it again. Perhaps I was going troppo.

At eight o'clock, I sidestepped determinedly across the playground, avoiding the muddiest puddles. A group of children stood huddled under the covered play area. Their body language warned me that, as well as the weather, I was about to face my next problem and it was still an hour before bell time. The children were weeping in despair and disbelief. I froze in horror when I saw the grisly sight. On the ground in front of them lay the mutilated body of our beloved Slippery; his head severed from his body.

'But how did this happen?' I asked.

'It was like that when we arrived,' cried Toni.

'I loved Slippery,' sobbed Janey.

'Did anyone see any strangers here on the weekend?' I asked.

'I saw the electrician's van here,' replied Andrew.

Then it all fell into place. When the electricians saw the snake they killed it and left it to warn us that there were snakes about. Oh my God! They had murdered Slippery.

'I'll take the snake and bury it,' I told them, hoping to alleviate their sorrow.

'Wait!' interrupted Mabel. 'All the children should be allowed to grieve. We must sing the spirit from the snake so that it can be reunited with the Earth's Spirit.'

I looked at their distraught faces. Mabel was right. The children needed some time to ceremoniously farewell their friend. I nodded in agreement. Mabel organised the children in a circle around the snake and handed out clap sticks for them to beat.

'This song,' she explained, 'is to tell the snake that it is no longer one of us, that its spirit must move on to the world beyond ours to the realm of flickering time.'

She began beating the sticks and chanting her strange song. The children followed her rhythm and echoed her mournful wail, harmonising their grief and expressing their sense of loss. Suddenly there was a deafening crack of thunder and a bolt of chain lightning tore through the sky with such velocity the children screamed in fear of being blasted out of existence. They huddled together as the whole area was lit by the lightning's peculiar silver haze.

At first it seemed that Slippery was moving as, momentarily, an ethereal blue mist struggled to free itself from the dead body. Suddenly the lightning stopped and what had been visible in the silver light could no longer be seen. I would normally have dismissed the sequence of events as a peculiar weather pattern, but the children would have been unconvinced of that. They stood motionless, their jaws fallen at the sight they had just witnessed. Dreading another terrifying bolt of lightning, I ordered the children inside. They were confused and frightened.

When the children turned to me for an explanation, I didn't have any answers. I was dumbfounded. All I knew was how to add up, subtract, spell and play football. I didn't know anything about the supernatural or Aboriginal folklore. Mabel understood more about what had happened than I did. Was it possible we had witnessed the Universal teacher? The circumstances were too difficult for any of us to grasp. I don't know what the others learnt from the experience, but in this instance I was like them – only a student.

TO MS WITH LOVE?

Maree Herrett

'I can see ya tits, Miss.'

I knew I shouldn't have worn that red shirt that gapes but it's my first teaching job and my wardrobe isn't exactly replete with teacher-type clothes. Apart from my shirt that doesn't meet in the middle, I'm at the distinct disadvantage of being a substitute teacher; the regular one's on maternity leave – and whether or not she was liked or loathed, she was their teacher.

'And just who might you be?' I demand, while giving a penetrating teacher stare I resurrect from my own school days.

'Anna Kanstanovis – but you can call me Anna.' She beams back at me.

'And you can call me Ms McCarthy.'

She's small, olive-skinned, fair-haired, out of uniform, scruffy and not in the least intimidated by my performance.

'What's yer first name?'

Feeling very progressive and hoping to win some favour, I tell them my name is Karen.

'Yuck – that's me middle name,' Anna blurts out. While I'm debating whether or not they can call me 'Karen', the rest of the class is calling her a liar because they all know her middle name is Theresa.

'Have ya gotta boyfriend?' She's got the whole class going now – sniggering, muttering behind their hands.

'Anna, what did I just say?'

'Oh come on, Miss, tell us about him. Have ya got a photo?'

If only she knew! The only thing steamy in my life right now is an early morning shower.

'Let's get on with it, okay? I know it's hard when a new teacher starts — '

'Tracey's got a boyfriend, haven't ya Trace?'

'Shut ya face, Anna.'

Anna seems to be in charge of the whole script and it's not just me who's unhappy with the parts we've been allocated.

'Ooo, what's the matter? Did he dump ya?'

'*Girls!* That's enough. I'm going to write my name on the board so you all know how to spell it, and then we'll start our new unit of work.' Before I even get to the little c in McCarthy, they're dissatisfied.

'Mrs Bailey didn't write like that,' says Anna, in a way that leaves no doubt that I just don't measure up.

I decide Mrs Bailey must be an uptight Neo-Fascist with a penchant for neat, regular handwriting, labelled folders, a tidy desk and everything else that I'm not.

'Why do you put Ms McCarthy? Are you married?'

'No Tracey, it's just that — '

'Who'd have her?'

'*Anna!*'

'Not you, Miss, I was telling Rania about me aunty. Rania wanted to know if she was gunna get married again.' Before I have a chance to resume, Anna's off again.

'Mrs Bailey's married. She's gonna have a baby.'

'Wonder if she's dropped it already,' laughs Tracey, recovering from her earlier sullen demeanour.

Rule Number One — I'm making them up as I go. Ignore deliberately provocative or suggestive language. Instead I try to explain the gender politics involved in adopting the new Ms title, but it's lost on 7G or whatever level of the alphabet thinly disguises that Anna's class is the lowest Year 7 stream. They're much more interested in whether or not I had sex last night.

'Anna, my private life is not a matter for class discussion, okay?'

'Mrs Bailey used to let us talk about anythink,' adds Anna, looking around the class for support. And she gets it. The Mrs Bailey fan club is formed and I'm its raison d'être.

My first few weeks of teaching are spent wishing that Mrs Bailey would fall off the face of the planet and never be heard of again. Colleagues assure me it will pass: that the students always give newcomers a hard time, and that Jenny was a hard act to follow. I hate her even more.

'I think you've found your niche,' my supervisor had said during prac teaching, 'but you'll need to work on your blackboard skills.'

Who needed blackboard skills when for twenty-two periods out of twenty-eight, they were in a windowless drama studio that lacked any of the accoutrements of a classroom – no desks, chairs, rows, order, authority or ... blackboards! My sudden switch from English to Drama teacher has more to do with timetabling needs than training or inclination. I had completed a mini drama unit in my Dip Ed, which left me with a meagre and limited repertoire of improvisations, role plays, trust exercises and cooperative games. The result is a rapid learning curve and lots of voice strain.

So the blackboard's put on hold while I work on my voice. Off to lessons (self-paid, of course) on breathing from the diaphragm, tongue twisters and other exercises to practise at home.

When 7G enters – no, when 7G surge, barge and shove their way into the drama studio – I'm ready. I have my whistle. One blow means 'get into a circle', and is used at the beginning and end of the class and sometimes in-between. The circle is the closest I come to establishing control and calm; but it says to the students that I'm one of them. So that when they have completed their trust exercises – raising each other in the air, catching each other in a circle – they naturally insist that I take my turn.

'But I've got a dress on,' I protest, ignoring the fact that the same is true for each of them.

'Doesn't matter – we're all girls,' pipes in Anna, as if we're about to jump in the bath together.

So I lie on the floor with them in a circle around me as they move steadily closer, perilously closer and ... swoop ... they've got me. I'm being raised up slowly until I'm about shoulder height above the ground. It could be a scene from the *Lord of the Flies* as they chant and steady themselves. When I'm finally vertical, I feel more like Sidney Poitier from *To Sir With Love* – breaking barriers, winning trust, respect, love in the face of overwhelming odds.

The girls have other ideas, though.

'Mum, can we go on an excursion?' asks Anna, without blinking or bothering to correct herself. It's a cry the others quickly take up. I'm twenty-two, about six weeks into my teaching career, and suddenly 'Mum' to 7G. Another role, another script.

We head for the city to watch a movie, vaguely related to whatever we're doing in English (I have 7G for English as well as Drama). I'm too young to realise the danger of such a project and happily organise permission notes and money.

It starts on the train. Shoppers headed for the city tut and sigh at the loud behaviour of the girls as they call out across a crowded carriage at each other. None is in complete school uniform, but varying combinations constitute a recognisable identity. They're clearly not private school girls. Anna moves between carriages, followed by her faithful followers. The other teacher accompanying us waits with the rest while I'm off in hot pursuit, and I realise I could lose some of the kids on this excursion. Suddenly I'm frightened.

They're just one carriage ahead.

'Give us a kiss,' Anna says to a young man in business mode. He squirms and grimaces and almost jumps off at the next station. Despite an immediate reprimand, it's a scene repeated throughout the day.

'Give us a kiss,' she says to almost every man who happens to walk anywhere near her.

I can't wait to get back to school and report her to the year coordinator, the Principal, the Director-General of Education. She's incorrigible, insufferable ... embarrassing. Now I'm Ursula from D.H. Lawrence's *The Rainbow*, and I know she'll have to be beaten into submission – not physically, but somehow made to apologise, confess, submit.

When I blurt it all out to the Mistress in Charge of Girls, a rather large woman who dresses in pink, resembling a giant muskstick, she sighs rather than fumes.

'She's a little unsettled at the moment,' she explains, as if Anna's behaviour is the result of teething or something similarly benign.

I've never been good at hiding my reactions and my look of moral outrage prompts her to tell me more.

'Look, her father's due out of jail any day – she's worried. She might be going to live with her aunty. We're not sure just yet.'

'How long's ... what's he been in for?' I don't know what to ask. It's not the answer I was expecting at all. I was ready for broken home, non-English speaking background, poverty – the usual and acceptable disadvantages.

'I can't tell you any more, Karen. You have to trust me. Go a little easy on her. She's had a tough time.'

'But what am I supposed to do with her? She's so disruptive.'

'Set the limits – both for you as well as her.'

'What'd you mean?'

'She has to know that certain behaviour is unacceptable – like today's.'

'And?'

'You can't be her friend, Karen, or her mum, no matter how much you want to help.'

'Oh, they don't mean anything by that. It's just a joke,' I suggest, trying to overcome my embarrassment that Muskstick knows what the kids call me.

'Maybe, but for some of these kids, school is the most stable part of their lives. You may be more mum than teacher to some of them.'

'But I'm only twenty-two – '

'Look, I overheard some of 7G talking in the playground. You're supposed to be taking them to the movies on a Saturday?'

'I just said that I'd meet a couple of them who were going in anyway.'

'It'd be better not to, Karen. You're still their teacher, and even if it's a Saturday you could be held responsible.'

'I know. I shouldn't have said anything. It's just that things have been getting better. They're not raving on about Mrs Bailey every five minutes. I'm really beginning to like them.'

'Just be careful – '

Before she has time to say any more, the bell's gone and the next class is about to start. I'm not sure what to make of the conversation, but think that Muskstick has probably been teaching too long and needs a break from kids. When I walk past the Principal's office I can't help but hear Anna let fly with four-letter words, and hope, at least, that the Principal's shirt meets in the middle.

The next day Anna's not at school. The Muskstick tells me she won't be back. She's changing schools and will be living with her aunty. At first I'm relieved. Apart from a few distractions when someone threatens to punch someone's face in at lunchtime, 7G is subdued and almost working. I'm starting to feel like a real teacher.

'Do y'know where Anna is?' asks Rania, about a week after Anna has left.

'Apparently she's moved. Gone to her aunty's.' I hardly turn to face Rania, who's obviously not satisfied by my answer. I clean the board, gather up books and pens, check my watch while she stares straight past me, shrugging her shoulders in disappointment. As I step down from the raised teacher platform, Rania's eyes meet mine.

'Did they tell yer about her old man?' she sneers, arms folded, leaning against my desk.

I lie and mumble something about a student I have to see.

'No one gives a shit,' she snarls, 'especially you! You're such a fake.'

At recess I search for Muskstick, suddenly glad of her garish get-up. I blurt out the scene between Rania and me.

'Ah, Rania is Anna's best friend. She probably knows.'

'Knows what?' I haven't had time to think about Anna. I'm still too devastated by Rania's accusations.

'Look, come into my office – this is not the appropriate place to discuss . . .'

Not that there is an appropriate location to discuss a father's sexual abuse of his daughter. It's twenty years before the Wood Royal Commission. Incest and paedophilia are not prime-time news items, and I am no longer Sidney Poitier or Ursula or Mum. I'm Alice, and the looking glass bewilders me.

'He's been in jail since Anna was ten. Now that he's due for release, she's acting out in various ways.'

'I didn't have a clue.'

'You weren't supposed to, Karen.'

'No – it's not just that. I mean if that's happened to Anna, what about the others? Who knows about their lives?'

Muskstick gets me some tissues because I've started blubbering about my incompetence and whether or not I've chosen the right career. The folder on my lap drops as I balance tissues and tears, and my photos of Year 7 spill out onto the floor. Images of Anna collide. Standing out in her mix'not'match uniform – smiling cheekily, rude finger gestures, a bravado that the others try hopelessly to assume. And me, centre stage: Indian-style dress left over from uni, waist-length hair, a beatific smile on my face as I embrace these children in a gesture of let's-be-girls-together and simpering-social-worker-to-the-rescue.

Although Muskstick helps gather the photos together, she says nothing about my impersonation of the Madonna in the classroom. She chuckles at the assortment of hairstyles and uniform variations, stares just a second longer at Anna than she does at the others, and says, 'You won't know them by next year.'

And she's right. It's not that I've somehow magically transformed them into the perfect class from a Hollywood movie, but because a departmental telegram instructs me to report out west among blue-eyed blondes by the following Monday. I don't even see out the year, let alone see what became of 7G.

Twenty years on, I'm still rifling through my wardrobe for something suitable to wear in case I ever teach Anna again. With fumbling fingers, I button up my shirt ever so carefully, tuck bits of self neatly away. But in spite of the different outfits I've worn, the clever lines I've delivered and the blackboard skills I've almost gained, I'm unprepared for what I might say.

She's there at the desk in front of me, registering every gap and slip in my performance. As I turn to face the blackboard, I hear her laugh.

'I can see more than ya tits, Miss.'

'I know, Anna. I know.'

HE'S OUR BOY

Edel Wignell

Crash!

Cuisenaire rods scattered in a random, gaudy pattern across the floor.

'Michael! Be careful!'

Michael surveyed the scene, then gazed contritely at Miss Piner, one pale-blue eye on her face, the other staring sideways.

'Sorry, Miss Piner. Didn't mean to,' he wheedled softly, and gripped her arm.

'I know you didn't.' Miss Piner's exasperation fell away quickly and her professional calm asserted itself. 'Never mind.'

Turning to the class, she asked, 'Who'll help Michael pack away the rods?' Several hands shot up. 'Thank you Sue, Helen and John. Everyone else go quietly to recess.'

Forty-four Grade 1 children filed out in an orderly manner. They had been well trained at the beginning of the year.

It was 1963, and Miss Piner knew that with a class of forty-eight, rigorous training in routines for independent working and movement was essential for survival. This was her seventh year as an infant teacher, and her third school. Her classes had always numbered between forty and fifty.

The projected new school in the fast-growing east of the town would not be ready for two years. Meanwhile, the central school bulged and overflowed.

'I've given you Michael,' the Infant Mistress had told Miss Piner. 'You're more experienced than the others.' She outlined his history: head injuries in infancy, caused by a drunken father; two years in prep grade, but still highly uncoordinated and unable to complete any discrimination tasks; lacking in concentration; loving and willing, the butt of children's cruelty.

'He's been tested by the Psychology and Guidance Branch,' she said. 'We'd hoped he might go into our Opportunity Grade when he's eight, but he can't make it, so he'll go into residential accommodation for mentally retarded boys.

'I've put his sister Pam in your class, too. I'm not sure whether it's a good idea or not, but her mother requested it. You can let me know in a few weeks whether we should put Pam in another grade.'

'Michael, pack the orange and blue rods, please.' Miss Piner pointed to the largest ones.

The children always left him to pack the smallest — the whites — a job which they regarded as terribly tedious. But he scattered more than he packed. Helen was nimble-fingered.

'Pack the whites, Helen. Sue and John, pack the rest. Be quick so you'll have time for play.'

'It's all right. We don't mind,' said John.

'They're kind,' said Michael. 'My friends are kind, aren't they, Miss Piner?'

'They certainly are!'

The word *kind* had become a watchword in the class. During the first weeks several of the brighter boys had gibed in Michael's hearing, trying to impress Miss Piner.

'Look, Miss Piner. I read this book right through. Michael can't even read a bubs' book, can you, Michael?'

Miss Piner reacted quickly. 'I know who I'd rather have in my grade. I'd rather have a kind boy than a good reader.'

Sometimes for emphasis she made pointed remarks about thoughtful children being an asset to the grade. Soon the boasting at Michael's expense stopped. Attention seekers had to use different tactics to gain the notice they craved.

The first thing that Miss Piner had observed in those early

weeks was the unkindness of the grade and the school in general to the inoffensive Michael. He was blamed for every disturbance in both classroom and playground.

'I didn't! I never!' he cried, time and time again. Pam was his staunch ally, defending her tall brother with a fierce motherliness belying her six years and small frame.

Miss Piner noticed that Pam's chosen role gave her neither time nor opportunity to make friends or to become involved in her schoolwork. Obviously the pattern had been established in prep. The solution she attempted sprang from this awareness, and a concern for Pam's future. She waited for an occasion when Pam and Michael were away from school.

'I was wondering why so many children in this class are cruel and rude to Michael,' she observed.

'He's dumb.'

'He can't read or anything.'

'He's stupid. He'll never learn nothin'.'

'He mucks up our games and that.'

Miss Piner listened to their comments, and said, 'I'm surprised every day when I see children being unkind to Michael. I like this class. There are so many kind children in this room – kind and thoughtful children.' She laboured the point, speaking slowly and pausing for effect. The class had nothing to say.

'Now I want you to think of all the good things about Michael.'

'He'll help you put things away – paste and scissors, and that.'

'If ya forget to take ya cricket bat out, he'll go an' get it.'

'He'll give you a sandwich.'

'He'll give you his pocket money.'

'He always helps you when you get hurt – skin your knee or something.'

'Now,' said Miss Piner. 'Listen carefully. Michael might never be able to read a book, but he's a wonderful boy because he is generous and thoughtful and kind. It's better to be a kind person than a good reader or good at sums. Do you understand?'

'Yes, Miss Piner,' they chorused dutifully.

'Michael's *our* boy. He belongs in our class. And I think that some of you aren't helping him very much. Pam helps him a lot, I know. Who else helps? Tell me all the things you do, or the things you'd like to do for Michael.'

'We could give him a turn at cricket.'

'We could stop kids from teasing him.'

'And bashing him.'

'We could ask him to sit with us at lunchtime.'

'We could let him have a turn on the slide.'

'Good! That sounds marvellous,' said Miss Piner. 'I'll be looking during the next few days to see if you remember that Michael's our boy.'

Miss Piner visited the playground often during the next few weeks and commented in general terms on the kind behaviour that she noted. Kindness that at first was ostentatious was becoming habitual, she noticed. While she felt that she had been fairly successful, she couldn't be sure what happened on the way home from school. Perhaps there was one sort of behaviour to please Miss Piner, and another to feed brutal inclinations. Was she cynical or realistic, she wondered.

The year wore on. Michael changed little. He was still a demonstrative, loving child, endlessly needing attention and contact. Perhaps he was a little less wary of his peers, though his trusting nature had never allowed much suspicion of their motives.

The classroom had three rows of eight desks with narrow aisles between. Michael knew the shortest distance between two points. He charged impulsively through the classroom when something caught his eye or his needs became imperative. Off he galloped, hips swinging and elbows flailing. Books, pencils, papers, paste and paints landed on the floor.

Art and craft sessions in the afternoons were particularly hazardous. The class learnt to cope by working in large groups at four different activities. But a restraining adult hand and a vigilant eye were needed to avert disaster in the form of Michael, the human rocket.

Sometimes Miss Piner called at the newsagent's on the way home, where the greeting was always the same. 'Hello, Miss Piner. What a life, eh? You schoolteachers have it good!'

If her day had included spilt paint or milk and broken glass, she agreed a little less enthusiastically than usual.

Pam blossomed. Her work improved and, freed from the need to watch and protect Michael, she participated in everything.

Each day began with Infant School Assembly in the two prep rooms with the double doors between them folded back. Friday was 'concert' assembly day. Each grade took a turn to present an item: a poem, a song, a play, a folk dance, or a participation story.

Michael always took part. Once he stood on top of a cupboard as a splendid tree from which apples were plucked. The Infant School appreciated his interpretation. His facial expressions and gestures were unpredictable, evoking surprise and laughter.

The next year, the two Grade 1 classes were reorganised to make two Grade 2s, and Miss Piner chose to have Michael and Pam again. She had become protective, and wanted to continue the work she had initiated.

One day in June, their mother arrived, red-eyed, after school, carrying a letter. 'You'll guess my news,' she said.

Miss Piner read the letter. She had known that Michael would get a residential place when he turned eight, or as soon afterwards as a place became available for him, but she hadn't given any thought to the reality of it.

She handed the letter back. 'Will you let him go?'

'I've always said I would. It's for the best really – he'll be with boys like himself. He's such a big boy now – nearly nine – and in a few years I won't be able to look after him, I guess. His father has no time for him, you know.'

'I suppose it's the best thing to do,' Miss Piner agreed, taking her cue from the mother's good sense.

There was a pause as Michael's mother struggled with her distress.

'He's such a loving boy. It's hard – you understand. What will happen to him? What are these places like? Will he just be a nobody among fifty other nobodies? He needs so much attention . . .'

Miss Piner didn't have any answers. She couldn't speak. She had a sudden vision of the trusting boy, rebuffed and hurt among strangers.

'I know I'll miss him,' she said. 'I'll miss him a great deal. I wish I knew how to advise you. Would you like to talk to the psychologist again?'

'No . . . No thank you. *I* have to decide. I *have* decided. I just wanted you to know . . .'

Composed now, she thanked Miss Piner and assumed a bluff, humorous tone. '*You'll* miss him! Like a hole in the head you'll miss him!' She laughed, and left.

Miss Piner knew that Michael's mother would need a great deal of courage during the next week, when the final arrangements for the boy's entry would be completed and he would be taken to the institution.

Children came and children went every year. One child fewer made little difference in a class of forty to fifty. But Miss Piner noticed Michael's absence. There was so much more time. At crucial moments she found herself ready to avert the chaos she knew he would cause. Ready with a restraining hand when he charged from his desk, when he passed the painting group, when he stepped over a classmate drinking milk . . .

In their own way, the children missed him, too.

'Isn't it funny without Michael,' they said from time to time.

About a fortnight later, when everyone had almost forgotten, Pam announced that Michael would have a birthday the next week. Suggestions came spontaneously.

'Let's send him a birthday card.'

'And a present, too.'

The children collected five pence from everyone in the class. Miss Piner took them to the toyshop where they looked at all the items they could buy for the available money. They voted and bought a drum and drumsticks. They worked out a birthday message, and everyone signed the card. An excursion to the post office completed the operation.

A few months later, Miss Piner spent a long weekend at a holiday resort. On the way home she drove through the town where Michael's institution was situated.

I'd love to call and see him, she thought. No! Better to leave him alone. By now he'll be settled. The past is probably just a blur.

She thought for a few minutes about Michael's mother and about Pam, and the huge gap in their lives. Of course no one told her she'd still remember him thirty and more years on. A child like Michael lives in your heart forever.

KULTITJA

Linda Wells

12th August 1989
Mount Larna
via Alice Springs NT 0872

Dear Meg,
How are you down there in old Melbourne town? It's incredible to be at Mount Larna. Where do I begin?

We had a great drive up. I love driving the open roads, singing at the top of my voice. Marty was great company. We went our own ways in Alice Springs. He headed for the tropics, I for the dust.

I set out from Alice one hot morning. The Education Department had shoved a few papers in my hand, blindfolded me, spun me around three times and sent me on my merry way. They invited me back in four weeks for an induction. That's big of them, isn't it? Lucky I'm the pioneering kind. But it says something about our values. When Malcolm went to the Antarctic to study the penguins, the powers-that-be interrogated him to ensure he was of strong constitution and sound mind for the job. When they send white fellas out to work with the indigenous people of this country, they'll send any maniac.

The drive out along the Tanami Highway blew my mind. They call it desert but it's not all sand and rocks and gibber plains, you know, like we learnt about in high school Geography. The land is covered in spinifex grass and mulga trees and other little herbs and bushes that have learnt to survive in this dry, hot environment.

Every now and again there's a riverbed. Not like the Yarra! They're white and sandy and dry. River red gums grow there – big old solid trees. There's always a collection of debris nestled in the forks of those eucalypts – twigs, bark, leaves, any old stuff that was washed in with the last flood. That's how you know where the water flows.

I stopped twice to change tyres that the hot, corrugated dirt road just chewed up. It was lucky that I had two spare tyres. Marty gave me one as a parting gift. You should see the roads. They're just red dust really, and wide, and they stretch eternally before and eternally behind you. As you drive along you send out clouds of red dust. Occasionally road trains appear out of nowhere and go charging past.

Remember those silly discussions we had about what road trains were? Well they're not trains that have got out of control and are now charging down the highways. They've got nothing to do with trains really, only that they have a few compartments.

I met some Yapa on the way out. Yapa is the Warlpiri word for Aboriginal. Warlpiri is the main language of the people of Mount Larna. That's the white fella name for the place called Mingarra. You roll the two r's at the end. The Yapa I met were stopped by the side of the road, about twelve of them around a battered old ute minus a windscreen. I stopped on the other side of the road and went over to them. Everyone was watching me. I felt really nervous. I'll tell you how our conversation went. It was hard for me to understand the Yapa accent. I listen very carefully and I'm always asking them to repeat themselves.

'Hello,' I called out.

'Allo.' An older man stepped forward. The other men stayed behind, near the ute. Women and children were seated by the side of the road in the shade of a mulga.

'Plat tyre, you got em tube, size thirteen?'

'No.'

'You got em patch?'

'No.'

He seemed to become serious and concerned, momentarily. 'You might get em plat.' He laughed along with all the other men. It was jolly, contagious chuckling and I joined in too. When this mob are travelling along, when they get a flat they just stop and repair it. They carry patches and pumps and tubes and all the tools, whatever else they need. Bugger that, I'll make sure I carry lots of spares.

'I've got a spare tyre,' I told him, 'but it's size fourteen.' I was disappointed because I would have liked to help but I was sort of glad too. I was all alone in the big wide Tanami Desert and it was best for me to hold on to the things that may contribute to my survival. I had no idea who these people were, I thought I'd never see them or my tyre again. As it turned out, I would.

'Where you goin'?' the man asked me.

'Mount Larna.'

'Kultitja?' I didn't get that one. I looked at him puzzled and he repeated himself, upon my request, again and again and again. My mind was stuck, I just couldn't get it. It was so frustrating.

Another man piped up. 'Kul-titja, you might be new kultitja.' The cogs in my brain finally started turning. Putting the word in context helped me to make sense of it – a good initial lesson in cross-cultural, cross-lingual education.

'Schoolteacher,' I arrived at. I almost heard the communal sigh of relief and then giggles. Although almost all of that party of folk were looking down or looking elsewhere or apparently asleep, I reckon they were totally tuned in to everything that was going on. So it is in the desert – watch, listen, wait, learn. 'Yes, kultitja.' I said it his way and that made him smile. He stepped forward to shake my hand.

'I'm Linda.'

He didn't tell me his name. He said, 'You're welcome.' It was so simple and so warm. It wasn't just a glib thing to say – you know, how we use manners in our culture. It came from his heart and it felt so beautiful, like I really was welcome.

'When you get to Mount Larna you tell Bobby.'
'Tell him you're here?'
The other man stepped forward.
'Yuwayi, you tell 'im ol' Sampson.'
'How much further is it?' This time it was old Sampson who didn't understand.
'Is it much further?' I asked, pointing up the road.
'No, you nearly there. Just round corner.'
'You got em water?' Pleased to be able to help with something I provided them with a bottle of water and some oranges which the children snatched hungrily. All eyes were on me as I drove off, leaving them waiting beneath the mulga. A lot of waiting under mulgas happens out here.

The eagles couldn't fly much more direct than the Tanami. There are no corners. After I'd driven hopefully around five slight deviations in the road, I decided there was no point in worrying about the bends. 'Just round corner' meant about forty more kilometres, straight ahead, due west. The perceptions are so different.

Finding Bobby seemed like it would be an impossible task but he was the first person I found in the community. He was sitting on the ground outside a humpy made of corrugated iron, painting dots onto canvas. I introduced myself and told him about old Sampson. Bobby laughed until he had to wipe tears from the corners of his cloudy old eyes. He laughed so much I laughed too.

'Ol' Sampson, I bin tell 'im,' he managed between snorts.

He chatted for a while. I listened mostly. I know so little and I feel like such an outsider. I've decided to do a lot of listening, at least initially. They see and do things so differently and I don't want to offend. Yapa customs are strong. I know that much. I don't know what many of them are yet but I know you can really piss people off if you say or do certain things.

One of the things is that if someone dies you mustn't say their name any more or anything that sounds like that name. Someone called Glenda died here and because Linda sounds like her name, no one here calls me Linda. They call me Kumenjay. That's the word which is used in place of the name of the dead person. There's heaps of Kumenjays here, so they call me Miss Kumenjay to distinguish me from the others.

Just as Bobby was organising a search-and-rescue party the old ute without a windscreen rolled up. Everyone cheered. They directed me to my accommodation and I went off on the next part of my adventure.

My accommodation is a silver bullet. That's like a big silver caravan but higher off the ground and squarer and more spacious. It has a bedroom, a bathroom, a kitchen and a laundry. It has all mod cons: hot and cold running water, a brand-new inner-sprung double bed, a big refrigerator which vacuum seals, a noisy air-conditioner, a table and chairs and a washing machine.

The superintendent of the Education Department in Alice Springs told me that conditions out here were rough. Rough? I haven't experienced such luxury since I left the family home. I feel like I've won on Sale of the Century. I guess the dream homes on Sale of the Century are never in the middle of the desert.

'Congratulations, you've won a year of isolation and neglect smack bang in the middle of the Australian continent. How do you feel?'

'I feel shit-scared, unsupported, nervous, excited and like good things lie ahead of me.'

The school is nothing like Mooroolbark High School and it's nothing like Ferntree Gully High School where I did my rounds. It's another big demountable van on the far side of the community. On one side of it is the community, about one square kilometre of houses, humpies, broken-down machines, rubbish, gorgeous kids and naked babies – people's lives. On the other side is the quiet old desert. It's as though the big silver caravan school was banished to that edge of the community when it arrived fifteen years ago. From there it could either prove itself to be useful and be allowed *into the community or gradually emerge as another white elephant. Then it would be banished to the other side where time and the might of the desert would consume that ephemeral construction forever.*

At the moment it hangs in limbo. I guess it's up to me, the government rep, the white fella rep, to prove beyond doubt the usefulness of Mingarra's school. I can't do that until I'm sure myself. Maybe it's just for my benefit. I reckon I've learnt more in my time here than I've taught anyone. With the learning comes questions, Meg. It seems like the more you learn the less you know. I'd love to have more people to thrash out my dilemmas with. Whenever I do talk to white fellas about the issues of being out here, no one seems to have any more answers than I do.

Anyway, I'm having a good old time, learning heaps and saving money. Maybe I'll buy a cattle station! Or a private jet! Or a flash Toyota and a house in town. That's what most bush schoolteachers seem to buy.

The kids are fantastic. They're so exuberant and loving. They were all sitting cross-legged on the mat at school the other day. It was time for English storytelling.

'Who's got a story?' I asked. They stick up their hands and put them down then stick them up then put them down, all giggly and nervous about exposing themselves.

'Yes, Rosita?' She sniffed in her snot (all the kids have heaps of snot which they always seem to sniff in before they commence speaking) then she started.

'Yes . . . ?' A few kids giggled. She squirmed.

I nodded encouragingly and smiled. 'Keep going.'

'Yeserday I went to dam.' Her tale all came pouring out of her mouth like a steam train out of a tunnel. All the kids, including Rosita, cracked up laughing. It was so dear, so simple and special and hilarious.

Rosita's beautiful. They're all beautiful but there's something incredibly lovable about Rosita. Her mum died a while back. She lives with her old grandma in the camp with the old people and the kids they look after. She looks older than her years and hungry for tucker and hungry for knowledge and hungry for something else. Maybe it's for her mother and what it is that mothers give their children.

Rosita has started to come and visit me at my camp. She often appears in the open doorway, seemingly out of nowhere. I don't know how long she's been standing there sometimes, like a little shadow. Her head is down, eyes averted, Warlpiri way.

'Miss Kumenjay,' she whispers. I want to take her in my arms and stroke her pain. Then I want to feed her and bathe her and 'talk stories' with her and put her into a clean, soft bed. I enjoy those overwhelmingly maternal feelings but of course I resist. I take her in and give her a drink and give her some strange, white fella food. She likes scones the best, with jam and cream. Sometimes we make them together. I laugh to myself, giving scones with jam and cream to 'the natives' — real colonial stuff!

At other times Rosita arrives with a little gang of the girls from school. They range from age three to fifteen. They free range, roaming the community and the surrounding bush. They're free as birds and safe, all looking out for each other.

They bowl in then, en masse. 'Miss Kumenjay, Miss Kumenjay.' I can hear them coming, like a flock of cheeky parrots. 'We want orange, we want stons (scones), we wanna see photo.' I sit down with them clambering all over me. They press my skin and squeal with delight when it changes colour, from pink to white where they were pressing. Their skin doesn't change colour when you press it. Their skin is deep red brown like the colour of the desert. I press their noses. They don't have a hard piece of cartilage running down the middle so their noses just give way and flatten onto their faces. That delights me as much as my skin colour changes delight them.

My other regular visitor is Madeleine. She's known as my assistant teacher. She's more like my teacher. She gently and

KULTITJA

patiently tells me the things I need to know — about individual kids, about the community, about culture. It's often only a couple of words she says, which are so carefully put together and so loaded that they speak reams. You must listen carefully to pick up that information. She's a young, alcohol widow and a mother of four children. Madeleine is totally focused on the kids of the community. She's like a mother duck with the flock trailing along behind her. She often turns up at school in the morning with nearly the entire school population. They're all fed and washed because they dropped in to see her before school. On days when Madeleine doesn't turn up sometimes no one else turns up either. On those days I can sit and ponder for hours, staring from my desk out the open door and into the desert. Then I do my paperwork to keep the Department happy. And I write letters to my dear friends in faraway places. Madeleine's gone to town to sell a painting. It's a welcome respite for me, to have a bit of time out, an unexpected pupil-free day. But then unexpected pupils could drop in on me at any time.

Lots of love to you, my friend. I miss you heaps but I know I've gotta be here. I love a sunburnt country . . . I hope you come to visit one day. You'd love it too.

More love,
Miss Kumenjay, kultitja.

RED CORNER, WHITE CORNER

Graham McLennan

7.25
'White or red?'
'I'll stick with the lite. Got to watch the figure, you know.'
'You look fit enough, for a man your age.'
'I'm thirty-five.'
'Sorry. What happened to the chips?'

7.37
'Great prints, eh? Didn't Van Gogh have the most vibrant sense of colour?'
'Not a bad painter, I suppose. What's his name?'
'Any more chips?'

7.42
'Looks like we're sitting here. John, is it? John, yes. This is my partner, Clair. Clair, John. John, Clair. Um . . . and this is?'
'My wife. Is that the red? I saw this at the Market Cellar. Only ten bucks a bottle. Good drop. I bought a case and laid it down. Should get me through Christmas.'
'Clair, could you pass the potatoes, please?'

7.59
'So I said to the Department Head, cut, cut, cut. We don't need half this mob. And he walked through the office just going "You, you, you, you". Should have seen the panic.'
'You're a public servant then?'
'I make policy.'
'Oh, a public servant.'

52

8.10

'*Of course, I don't get time to read any more. When you're on contract, you're busting your arse just to keep up. No punching the clock for us.*'

'You can get talking books on tape, you know. Some really good ones. We listen to lots of them when we're on car trips. The kids love them too. H.G. Wells, Garrison Keillor . . .'

'*What, people reading books on to a tape?*'

'Yes. Could I have some more vegies please? The spinach pie is great.'

8.30

'But, godammit, how can we be expected to be improving literacy in classes that are bigger than ever, where we have fewer resources, and where we have to compete with the mind-buggering bedazzlement of TV and computers . . .'

'*Oh, you're a teacher then?*'

'Yeah, I'm a teacher.'

'*Tamara and I decided to send Jocelyn and Mark to Grammar. Not easy on just a Dep Sec's salary, but we made some sacrifices. We don't go up the coast so much. But it's worth it to make sure they get a decent education.*'

'Pass the bloody spuds.'

8.45

'*White or red?*'

'Is it John, is it?'

'*Yes. Of course, I've been a Labor man all my life. So was my father. But you can't let political persuasion interfere with your appointed tasks. Not a man in my position.*'

'And that position would be? Jesus, Clair, stop kicking.'

9.15

'*These are tough economic times. They call for tough economic decisions. Everyone has to make sacrifices.*'

'What's yours, then? Mine was to stay in the classroom and teach kids. For which I get enough not to pay my bills, not to send my kids to some snobby school, not to go on holidays, and not to buy clothes. My wife shops at the local op shop. Clair, will you keep your bloody feet to yourself!'

'*Tamara works. That's how we pay for our little extras. All a question of priorities, really. Sacrifice a little, aim for the top. I buy quality. This suit, for example. Got it in Paris on that fact-finding trip last year. Should last until next season.*'

'My wife works too. She managed to get a part-time job looking after someone's kids after school.'

'*Handy that. I can't always get home in time to see the kids, so it's good to know that quality people are looking after them. Drugs, street kids, it's a worry, you know. And I blame the parents. Kids need quality care.*'

'Yeah, I've got a clue about that. I see the results in my classroom every day.'

9.50

'*The tensions are phenomenal. Six days a week, twelve hours a day. Decisions on the run. And we're on call, via the mobile. I tell you, it's easy to fall off the pace.*'

'So you're doing two people's jobs?'

'*Absolutely.*'

'So why don't they hire two people to do your job properly?'

'*My Head is great, though. A real man's man. He understands. He takes us all golfing, at his expense, every Sunday. We hit off at nine.*'

'Thank God for our day of rest.'
'*Amen, brother.*'

10.15

'*Look, be honest, the schools are failing. They are just not cost effective. A third of our kids can't read. And the schools take the biggest part of our budget.*'

'Listen, you clown. I have 300 kids a year pass through my classroom. I perform miracles with them daily, armed with a stick of chalk and a slide projector.

'In fact, I did a calculation. Each kid generates less than three dollars per head per year from government funds for teaching stuff: books, paper, anything they need. Three dollars. The same as they did ten years ago.'

'*That's why we send the sprogs to Grammar. Four thousand a term, but they get the best of everything.*'

'Jesus, Clair, will you stop kicking me!'

10.16

'Any working-class parent who sends their kids to an exclusive private school is undermining the chances of poor kids. Every kid who leaves for a private school takes over $1000 of funding with them. That money comes out of the government schools – and it never comes back.'

'*Kids who stay at government schools will stay poor. I want the best for mine, the opportunities I never had.*'

10.18

'*I'm only thirty-five. I've got years in me yet. I could be Head.*'

10.19

'Clair, let go. I'm not going to hit him.'

10.30

'*Ahem, I'm afraid we'll have to leave. Tamara has a migraine. Thank you Wayne, thank you Kaye. Lovely evening. No, no,*

must go . . . Besides, I have to be up early in the morning . . . regular golf date with the Head. We'll be discussing the education budget. Should be a good morning.'
'Looks like it's red.'

THE WASP IN THE SOCCER SOCKS

Rhodes Garwen

The hot afternoon sun glared through the classroom window. The class, 6R, was silently, soporifically, trying to concentrate on the task sheet set by Mr Rivers. Mr Rivers sat at his desk. He had piled exercise books, a globe and three papier-mâché relief maps of the Atherton Tablelands on the front of his desk and was pretending to work behind the barricade. His large hand was propped against his podgy pink cheek. He was almost asleep himself. You could tell because every so often his head would jerk up and he would stare a challenge at anyone who might be looking at him.

Mr Rivers was a podgy, flabby, florid, flatulent and bad-tempered pommy teacher, who had come out from Home to do his bit in the colonies. We hated his accent and his endless complaints about Australia, but most of all we hated his boring stories about famous English soccer teams and soccer stars we had never heard of. They held no interest for a bunch of footy-crazed Australian kids.

Rivers dressed as he thought a pukka Englishman should in the tropics. Stiff khaki shirt with epaulettes and numerous pocket, pens on parade in the top left and a neatly folded white hanky in the top right. Below his wide, highly polished, brown leather belt and covering his ample nether regions he wore British Army issue Bombay bloomers, or what we called 'crap catchers'. These were vast, wide-legged shorts reaching almost to his knees which made even his fat pink legs seem Ghandi-like as they peeped out the massive circumference of the leg holes. Long khaki cotton stockings, seams absolutely straight and kept up with tabbed garters, reached to within a centimetre of the hem of these shorts.

In November in Cairns, after a filling lunch and despite a compulsory half-hour rest, the beginning of second period of afternoon school was not the best time to be in class. Flies buzzed spasmodically against the windowpanes. Outside, the heat shimmered off the dusty red earth of the playground. Assorted birds swooped past the windows guzzling the heat-sozzled insects as they droned wearily about. Sounds throughout the classroom block were muted. The occasional weary sigh of a fellow inmate or the scratching of a pen on paper was muffled by the heat. The smell of the ink and the chalk dust floating like minuscule galaxies in the sunlight seemed to be the only things of any note in the hot, boring classroom.

Then, like a Messerschmitt 109 sweeping in from twelve o'clock high, a large wasp zoomed into the room. We knew that sound. We knew that sting. We knew those yellow and black striped legs. We knew that if we left it alone it would not harm us. But anything for a distraction. Suddenly every child in the class was fully awake and at action stations. Rulers waved. The rustle of exercise books flapping in the general direction of the wasp seemed to start instantaneously. Within seconds little paper catapults were loaded and pieces of tightly folded paper flew like flak at the lone intruder.

Rivers jerked awake.

'Stop that immediately!' he shouted.

'But, sir, it's dangerous!' rose a chorus of excited voices. The wasp increased its pace, hurtling through the barrage of flak and waving books and rulers.

'*Stop* I say!' yelled Rivers. 'It won't hurt you if you leave it alone,' he bellowed, sitting up and moving to the edge of his chair, his pink face now purple with anger.

'Watch out, sir, it's wearing black and yellow English soccer socks!'

'Yeah, sir. They're really wild, sir.'
'Leave it alone and go back to your seats immediately. It won't hurt you!'

At that very moment a desperately waved atlas hit the wasp. It ricocheted off the blackboard and landed on the floor beside Mr Rivers' desk. There the wasp lay on its back, stunned. Rivers hauled himself to his feet. He cast a disdainful glance at the wasp, then, jowls jiggling with rage, he turned on us.

'Right you lot, I've just about had it with you. Gross disobedience! You will all remain here this afternoon and miss your swimming.' Wednesday afternoon swimming for Year 6. Oh, no! Not today . . . but we knew better than to raise a 'tsk' of complaint. Rivers remained standing for a few moments, his colour fading from dangerous puce to his normal salmon pink. The class settled back to work. Rivers sank onto the front of his chair glowering down at us. The wasp lay on its back near the blackboard, its six yellow and black legs feebly stirring. Twenty-five sets of eyes peered furtively at it. Twenty-five minds cursed Rivers and wished him ill.

The wasp stirred more vigorously. One of its hind legs reached the chalky floor and pushed. The wasp rolled over on to its legs. It stayed like that for some time, moving its head from side to side like an accident victim testing joints to see how bad the damage was. It took one, then two and then more steps towards Mr Rivers' chair. It moved its wings and brushed its eyebrows with its striped forelegs. It reached a chair leg and stopped.

Now, every child in the class began to do those things that keep the teacher alert. Nothing that would get him in direct trouble mind, but just those furtive movements that keep the teacher guessing. And so the clock moved on. One minute to three. Thirty seconds to three. The bell rang. No one moved, except Rivers. He had spoken and he knew that we would obey.

He levered his behind off the chair, pushed the chair back and stood up. He would not deign to cast a glance at the wasp. He began slowly packing his books. The wasp, meanwhile, had been knocked onto its back by the shifting chair leg. This time it was on its feet in an instant, though, wings quivering with rage. One flutter and up it rose. Up, up, up. Right up into the wide, dark regions of Mr Rivers' Bombay bloomers.

Humans reactions are quick. Rivers must have heard that fateful buzz. He must have felt the light brush of wings on his fat, pink thigh. He must have seen the look of incredulous glee and fascination on our faces. He must have known that his fate was sealed! He erupted into action. Like a vast pink and khaki puppet he began to jerk about, slapping the back of his thighs, then the front of his shorts, then the sides, all the while leaping from one foot to the other, slapping with one hand and desperately trying to loosen his belt with the other. Then came the first yell of pain, then another and another. Great rasping bellows of anguish seemed to echo out of the puckered white 'O' that was his mouth as he slapped at his behind, then at his crotch and then at his thighs again.

For a moment the class sat, stunned. Then it exploded into hysterical laughter. We rolled on the floor. We clung to the walls and windows. We lay prostrate, breathless with maniacal hilarity, thumping the desks as we watched Rivers do his own version of a St Vitus-inspired Chubby Checker twist, all the while yelling like Geronimo at Custer's Last Stand.

The door and windows of the classroom darkened as children from other classes rushed to see what was happening. Rivers' dance seemed to last an age. It seemed as if the whole world was laughing. The Year 3s wet themselves with hilarity. Children collapsed, gasping breathless with choking, sobbing mirth.

Rivers leapt from the dais. One moment his Bombay bloomers were on and the next they were lying like a collapsed tent on the floor. Rivers, yelling like a whole English soccer mob, ran slapping at his huge round thighs and heaving bottom, out of the classroom. Like a one-man combination horse and jockey in pale blue silk underpants he galloped across the dusty playground slapping and yelling and clutching at his crotch.

Later, we were dismissed to go swimming by the headmaster. He told us that Mr Rivers had been taken to the local clinic and then on to the hospital. A very pale, subdued Mr Rivers returned to class a week before the end of term and left for Home in the December holidays.

Tricky things those Bombay bloomers. And to think that that wasp wore the very same colours as Mr Rivers' favourite English soccer club . . . yellow and black horizontal stripes.

LESBEANS

Laura Deriu

L-e-s-b-e-a-n. Delete. L-e-s-b-i-a-n. Enter keyword search.
Kim flicks a blonde cowlick aside, peers into the screen as if it's a crystal ball. The lunchtime library spins around her, a cubist carnival. Librarians pass on surveillance missions. She hunches around the screen.

Search Result: 0. Nervous fingers flit across the keyboard.

H-o-m-o-s-e-x-u-a-l. Enter keyword search. A medical title blips onto the screen.

Two skinners loiter in catwalk make-up and Spicegirl hair, buttoned-up blazers. They stare, all whispers and giggles.

'Fishfingers!' one spits over her shoulder.

Kim taps the ESCAPE key, pulls on her blazer, and makes herself invisible.

She wags the afternoon on the corrugated Assembly Hall roof, watching the ebb and flow of boys and girls in uniform below. She smokes and listens to kd lang on the Walkperson. Breasts appear in the clouds. When I grow up I want to be a lesbian feminist, she resolves. How old do you have to be before you really know you're gay? She wonders. She's read statistics like one-in-seven, but she feels like one-in-a-billion. Nothing known. Nothing sure. The clouds curve into a statuesque afternoon.

Period one: 11D English. Ms Perry flies to the lectern, ink-specked David Lawrence suit, Doc Martens and Caesar haircut. 'She's here!' she rasps, all Hollywood horror, and glares through her squinting tortoiseshells.

Some cartwheel to their seats; others climb down from the rafters; two slip in the door. One of those classes that's a pleasure to teach – has achieved a good standard, could do better with some collective diligence, further application, consistent punctuality and less cavalier attitudes.

Ms Perry's Shiraz-suave English teacher voice scrawls across the whiteboard, fills their heads, scribbles across their notebooks in big misspelt words.

The swots bubble with their 'Buts . . .' and 'What ifs . . . ?' as though they were already strutting the courtroom floor or slicing flesh in the operating theatre. The boyos in the back row glaze out across the leafy suburbs beyond the sealed windows, thrusting in their seats every seven minutes. Mark pouts because this is shit – he's just read Nietzsche and started doing pot. Kim listens, takes a note, and skims *Rubyfruit Jungle* under the desk for rude bits about tits and licks. Anne stares with pinpoint eyes, sedated by her parents into a society girl lest her hormones run amok and she gets into trouble. Justin watches Ms Perry cajole and stir them beyond themselves, and loves her more each day.

'Grab a partner – survey their viewing preferences,' bellows Ms Perry. 'Talk about what you enjoy watching. Why? What about a character who had a strong emotional impact on you? Fave movies, fave characters – talk about them now. Ten minutes!'

An eruption of Americanesque banter from blockbuster movies, enactments of memorable scenes, discordant strands of hit movie tunes. Dum-dum-da-da, dum-dum-da-da. Ms Perry wanders, listens. It's a diagnostic exercise – see where they're at before plunging them into a foreign film festival.

'Emotionally moving stuff!' she quips, affecting a Margaret Pomeranz drawl. 'Lovely family entertainment . . . very audience pleasing . . .'

Kim announces that her favourite two films are *Bound* and

Chasing Amy. Justin hasn't ever heard of them. Were they on at Russell or Bourke?

Seen them. Ms Perry smiles, winks an eyebrow in recognition of blockbuster queer films.

Kim blushes. She's out. Puts *Rubyfruit Jungle* onto her desk. Watches Perry glimpse the book.

'Interesting novel. Try Winterson's *Oranges Are Not the Only Fruit*.' Perry sidles off, twists a few words in the back row, argues with the brainiacs long after the bell. Kim loiters, scrawls a note, passes it to Perry and pushes off into the corridor. Period two happens.

Returning from lunch duty, Ms Perry curls around her desk and nurses essay drafts into masterpieces amid a cascade of Penguin paperbacks, dictionary allsorts and a notebook computer winking e-mail receipts. She ticks through draft after draft, Doc Martens tap Bach's 'Air on a G String'.

Beside her, Mr Godot – BA (Hons), MA, DipEd – flicks his pen into the bin, sighs and counts through his desk exercise routine. A bulbous Buddha, he flexes his fingers and pumps his legs. He lifts novels above his head – E.B.White in one hand, a tome of fairytales in the other.

Ms Perry rubs her eyes, plunges another coffee. They chortle over student bloopers. Like the one about 'the big balled Martians', or was that meant to be 'b-a-l-d'?

'I got a note from one of my students,' Ms Perry says, unfurling a piece of foolscap. Mr Godot casts an eye over the calligraphic scribble.

Dear Miss Perry. Recently, my friends dropped me. They stopped talking to me and letting me sit with them. When I asked them if I'd done anything wrong, they said that I looked too butch and didn't suit their image. I'm 17 and I know I'm a lesbian and I'm trying to come out. I can't talk to anyone my age because they already hate me for it. The problem is that no one takes me seriously. From Kim.

How to respond? A tick or a cross? A sharp red line? A question mark in the margin? An urgent 'Please see me' underlined across the bottom? Perry and Godot plunge more coffee and stir with words like 'access', 'equity', 'respecting differences', 'opportunities to celebrate differences', 'opportunities for individuality'.

They pass the sighing foolscap back and forth, its angst provoking echoing fragments of their own teenage years.

Perry laughs. 'It's not as easy as just telling her to get a buzz cut, dye it white; wear muscle tops; move to St Kilda and get a mangy dog; hang out at Girl Bar; join ten collectives, then burn out.'

Godot rumbles in his soapbox voice that the gay community is obligated to support those trying to become a part of it – show them possibilities, show them a life. Education is about possibilities and change, he rolls on, loosening his Walt Disney patterned tie.

'Teacher as tour guide, not!' Perry sniggers, and worries about blurs between discretion and indiscretion. Exclusive 'Shock! Horror! Probe!' headlines and gaping paparazzi snaps spin around her. 'The last thing gay teachers need are accusations of coercing kids into the gay and lesbian club!'

They spar about the ironies of teaching text lists containing Adrienne Rich's poetry and Malouf's prose, and the queer subtexts they unravel with their students so that they score an A+ in the final exam.

A possum-faced Year 7 boy appears at the door and shows a picture of a shaggy puppy.

'Miss Perry? Mr Godot?'

Raised eyebrows. 'Yes, Jack?'

'Would you like to buy my puppy? He's nice and he doesn't make a mess any more. I have to sell it. Dad's moving out and Mum says I can't keep it because they're tearing up the house.'

Jack sobs into Ms Perry's arms for the rest of lunchtime, and

Mr Godot fortifies him with Teddy Bear biscuits. Afternoon classes happen.

Kim pinches twenty bucks from her mother's wallet, slinks around bookshops for Winterson's novel. She blushes when she buys it – the salesman catches her eye, the spotlights catch the earring in his left ear. She spends Saturday night under the sheets in the comfort of Winterson, discovering answers in words that embrace. On Sunday afternoon, Kim re-reads Winterson and commits passages to memory. She resolves to see Ms Perry at recess on Monday, to be witty about literature and sneak in a question about that note, ask her what she thinks. Ms Perry will know what to do, Kim trusts. After all, everybody knows she's such an obvious lezzie.

Winter glow over polished boards, St Kilda terrace. Books, dogs and prints trail along the corridors. A coil of leather drips over a banister, a spray of wax across a wall. Another boring no production values alternative video squiggles into the evening. Ms Perry sprawls across the threadbare Persian rug, cuddling a fat Shiraz, watching Ms Lines push a log onto the embers.

'These girls just started kissing in a Maths class the other day,' gasps Ms Lines with a feline grin. She rolls her eyes and fast-forwards the video to another unfocused scene. 'And their teacher said it was "inappropriate behaviour". So they got all hot about it and complained to the Principal that the teacher was homophobic. They got suspended!'

'Don't they know anything? Hasn't your school got a sheltershed?' Ms Perry snaps.

They talk about protecting gay kids from the euphoria of coming out all over the place and exposing themselves to ridicule and judgement.

'In the first school I taught, this queer kid got raped with a broomstick in the boarding house. He went around with shattered eyes. Everybody knew about it – 1200 people knew about it. Nothing happened. No expulsions, no counselling,' Ms Perry murmurs. 'I corrected his essay about it. I remember bad handwriting and a line about blood trickling down his leg.'

She resolves to slip Kim a flyer for the Gay and Lesbian Switchboard Counselling Service on Monday. Kim can take it from there – it's her stuff, Ms Perry decides. Ms Perry and Ms Lines throw on some lipstick, amble down to Girl Bar and sweat out the weekend on the dance floor.

Kim hovers by Ms Perry's office, socks up and blazer on, reciting passages from Winterson. The corridor flutters with the savoury wrappings of recess and twitters of weekend scandal. Through the office venetians, Perry and Godot plunge coffee and chatter like cartoons. Mr Godot emerges; barks some rowdy skinners into silence by pointing out that they are disgracing their nation with their swearing; smiles at a senior and nods at Kim; spins and calls 'Visitor!' at Ms Perry; then plods on.

Ms Perry leans against the door, smiles 'Hi!' over her glasses.

Kim nod-nod-nods herself into a cool tone and talks to Perry's polished loafers. 'I've read *Oranges Are Not the Only Fruit*. Ace book, like I really liked the way she wrote about her feelings. And, oh yeah, some of the imagery was pretty good – it was meaningful.'

Ms Perry winces on the inside; nods professionally. 'Mmm.'

Kim shuffles, nods, sweats. 'Did you read my note?' she asks Ms Perry's watch.

'Yes. Big stuff for you, Kim,' Ms Perry says, annoyed at her neutral voice. She holds Kim's eyes. She pulls the purple flyer from her pocket, its discreet graphics belie its significance. 'I thought you might be interested in this. Good people at the other end of the line. Some answers, maybe.'

Kim takes the flyer, commits the number to memory. She wafts down the corridor. Where was the fanfare? Where was the secret handshake? Where were the open arms? She turns another corridor and wafts through the day, disappointment bruising her face.

Ms Perry lumbers to her desk, disappointed that she couldn't blow a fanfare, offer a secret handshake or show open arms.

The bell calls. Midmorning classes happen.

ARCHERY DELINQUENTS

Sharyn Lawrence

In 1981 I was in the awkward position of being known as a good but very junior teacher at my school. Because I was 'good' with problem students, the senior staff had decided that I would be perfect to supervise the naughtiest Grade 9 boys on Activity Afternoon, preferably somewhere away from the school. Because I was still junior in terms of age, experience and status, I wasn't able to say no when the Assistant Principal told me I would be supervising ten Grade 9 boys for archery every Wednesday afternoon for the rest of Term One, despite knowing nothing about archery.

'But Mike, I volunteered to take the Grade 7s for horseriding. I've organised the riding school and everything!' I said futilely.

'Yes, and a good job you've done too. Teena will be able to step in without too much bother. You see, you're good at outdoor activities and archery isn't all that different from horseriding. It's all outdoors. You will still have a small group and get to take them away from the school grounds.' The Assistant Principal looked pointedly at his watch.

'But I don't know anything about archery. I've never even picked up a bow, unless you count Robin Hood games with my brother when I was ten.'

'Don't worry about that. The president of the local archery club has agreed to come to the first session to help you get set up and show you the ropes, or should I say arrows! Get the bows and arrows from the gym storeroom. You can store the straw targets on the school farm in the barn and walk the group over to the farm after lunch.'

'Walk the group over to the farm by myself! Mike, you know they'll nick off if they get half the chance, or cause a traffic accident.' I could already see the lines of ambulances and hear the police sirens.

'Come on now, Sharyn, I don't know why you're complaining. After all, Colleen's got sixteen in her group and I think Des's group has built up to eighteen. You have to fit in if you want to stay with us, you know.'

'But Colleen's doing board games and Des is doing video watching. Hardly life-threatening activities! And look at the names on my list – Wayne Mifsud, Geoff Fitzgerald, Michael Prince, the twin Hillman hoods. I've got all the worst boys in the school in my group and they are going to be set loose with weapons that can kill!'

'Calm down, Sharyn. Those boys are certainly rather challenging, I agree, but you already teach most of them and have a good rapport with them. They like you, they don't like many other teachers, and they need to do something on Wednesday afternoons. No one else will have them. Now don't worry about the equipment. We've only got those cheap plastic bows and a few wooden arrows. They probably won't even stick in the targets, much less do any damage. The real challenge will be getting anyone to actually shoot into the straw target. Now the group will meet you next Wednesday on the steps outside the canteen. Don't be late or they're likely to wreak havoc! Only joking.' He turned and strode away, still chuckling at his feeble joke. He didn't have to take an activity group; he was the Assistant Principal.

The following Wednesday I was unpleasantly surprised to find all ten boys were present, at the designated meeting point, on time. Great, I thought, I've got at least four chronic absentees in this group but they are all here today. Just my luck.

The five minute walk over to the farm was completed without major incident, not counting one boy being pushed into a ditch, one being pelted with a dog turd and two jumping Mrs Freeman's fence to pick some late apples. The boys were very excited, eagerly discussing films they'd seen which featured death by bow and arrow and bickering over which teachers should be executed first.

The first session went surprisingly well. All the boys were keen to cooperate, dragging the heavy, pressed straw targets from the barn, setting them up on borrowed art easels and assembling behind the firing line – a skipping rope stretched on the ground. Only five could shoot at one time but there were few arguments and the group quickly accepted the discipline of waiting for the borrowed PE whistle to be blown as the signal to fire five arrows, then waiting for the second signal before running to retrieve their arrows. Then the second group moved up to the line to fire, just like the two rows of artillery I had seen in operation in old Empire films set in India or Africa. It's amazing what they'll do if they are interested and absorbed, I thought. I wonder if I can somehow weave English, Maths and Health activities into the session?

The instructor was Mr Weislaw, who was of Polish extraction, and definitely of very old age, even by my standards. Under usual circumstances the boys would have been smirking at Mr Weislaw's pronounced accent and covertly doing 'Heil Hitler' gestures, but today they sat quietly on the grass as he went through the drill of stringing the bows, fitting the arrow after checking the fletch, standing side-on to the target and the sighting of the target along the shaft. They fired questions at him, forgetting to put up their hands. But it didn't matter – Mr Weislaw was just pleased to see some enthusiasm for his beloved archery.

I sat at the side of the group, ready to use my 'death ray' glare on potential troublemakers, when Mr Weislaw called me to the front. He made me demonstrate all the skills and I felt a bit uncomfortable in front of twenty pairs of adolescent eyes as they critically scrutinised my technique. Must be what my students feel like every time I get them to read aloud or perform in front of the class, I thought. But surprisingly, I was good at it and managed to get all five arrows into the target, with two even within the yellow circle. A couple of the boys clapped and Mr Weislaw said I was a natural. Suddenly I felt as tall as the A.P.

Luckily, Wayward Wayne and Gorilla Geoff were also quite good. They even supervised the others, concerned to get through the round as quickly as possible so they could have their turn. The boys varied in attention and success. Some spent the whole session without getting a single arrow to stick in the target but most managed to hit the outer green ring, and a couple scored the inner red one, including Wayne and Geoff. I actually managed to hit the bullseye each time I had a turn and felt rather proud of myself. For once there weren't the usual sniggers about who had a red ring and who had a yellow one. In fact, the time passed quickly and I decided perhaps this activity wasn't going to be the nightmare I'd feared. The mood of the group was quite cheerful as we packed up and thanked Mr Weislaw, and the only incident on the walk back to school was a small fist fight to decide who was to have first turn next week, after me of course, as I was the best shooter!

Next week we were on our own. Mr Weislaw had had to go to hospital (or perhaps a nursing home) but it didn't matter, I decided. We would manage on our own. And we were all right until Wayne said, 'Mrs Lawrence, can we have a contest to see who can shoot the furthest?' and I said, 'Okay, but aim up the paddock because there's a bit of a slope and we won't have to look far to find the arrows.'

So all the boys lined up with an arrow at the ready, waiting for my signal, and when the whistle blew ten arrows shot high into the air, just like in a scene from *Robin Hood*. They flew high into the blue sky then curved and travelled back to earth, but far, far up the slope – so far in fact that some of them even landed in the shrubby trees at the very top of the paddock two hundred metres away. Startled white shapes erupted from the trees and raced drunkenly down the paddock. There were sheep in the paddock and one had an arrow sticking out of its side!

'Shit!' I said, as we ran up the paddock to check the sheep. Luckily the arrow was just tangled painlessly in the fleece of the victim. No other sheep had been hit, amazingly enough. The boys seemed quite concerned about the health of the sheep and were relieved to find it wasn't hurt. A bit of a surprise coming from tough country kids, I thought. But four arrows were lost and the group learned a valuable lesson about how far arrows can travel. We also learned about the dangers of shooting arrows without a target to fire into when, as we walked back to the barn to pack up, one of the Hillman twins tripped over a lost arrow which pierced his leg. 'Our first casualty,' I thought ruefully. 'It had better be our last.' We helped him to hop back to the shooting area and bandaged his leg, which was gushing blood.

The next week things went well as all boys were careful to shoot only into the straw targets. I had brought a memo book and pencil to the session and announced I would keep a tally of each boy's points. There would be a small prize for the top three shooters and the most improved. The boys seemed relieved to hear I would not be included in the contest as I was still the most consistent shooter. In fact, I had noticed that a few students had taken to calling me 'Robin' when I was on duty, and there had been a note of admiration in their voices. So perhaps it was complacency which caused the incident of the barn door that afternoon.

The other uninjured Hillman twin had just taken aim in his shooting position at the end of the line when two of the boys behind him started larking about, pushing and shoving. I was busy taking down scores and had my back turned. The wrestlers fell against the Hillman twin who lurched sideways, loosing his arrow as he fell. It flew up and back, hitting the barn wall only centimetres above the heads of two boys standing there waiting their turn. The arrow hung there, fletched end down and the arrow tip pointing upward, on the inside of the wall.

'Look, Mrs Lawrence, it's gone straight through the metal wall. That could have been my head!' said Michael Prince, looking scared for probably the first time in his life.

'Shut up, Mick. You're not hurt,' said Dwayne. 'Now you can brag that you've had a brush with death when we get back to school – but don't tell your olds, right?'

'That's it for today everyone,' I said. 'Let this be a lesson to all of us. This is a good sport but it can also be dangerous, so no more mucking around while you wait for your turn. Let's pack up.' Though I tried to sound calm my heart was thudding – it could just as easily have been a boy's skull rather than a wall.

The remaining sessions passed without further major incident. I supervised activities more closely and the boys seemed to take more care. They followed the established routines and most became quite capable shooters. The targets had been moved back an extra 15 metres and still the red bullseye was pierced. It was great to see Dwayne and Geoff being leaders in a positive way for once as they organised the turns and checked on the packing up. At the end of our last session I awarded the prizes – a certificate and a Mars Bar – to the winners, Geoff and Dwayne, and the Most Improved to a small boy nicknamed Little John.

Occasionally I did wonder about the wisdom of teaching ten of the school's most violent and disobedient students to master potentially dangerous weapons, but many of their teachers had commented on positive changes in their attitude and behaviour since Activity Afternoon began, so there seemed to be some good effects. I decided to run the activity again in Term Three when the weather should be fine, and started planning an archery display for the School Fair.

But there is a sad ending to this story. One weekend in Term Two the school was broken into and among other things, the bows and arrows were taken. School resumed on Monday to the sickening news that the equipment had been used to kill several wallabies and geese in the school animal enclosure. Although police found the bows nearby, it appeared that the victims had been stabbed to death with the arrows rather than shot. Loose arrows littered the grass. The whole school was in shock and I felt sickened and somehow responsible. After all, I had been in charge of locking away the archery equipment.

Who could have done such a thing? When I was interviewed by the police about the archery group I said I really didn't think any of the boys had done it. For one thing, the bows had been incorrectly strung by the perpetrators. Secondly, all the boys were quite capable of successfully shooting a large target like a wallaby or goose at such close range, if they had had the inclination, which I doubted. I remembered their concern when the sheep had nearly been skewered. The boys were horrified by the vicious killings and said if they found out who'd done it they would 'deal with them', and I believed them. No one was ever caught and, surprisingly, there were no rumours around the school about the perpetrators so we thought it must have been an outside group. When the time came to organise activities for Term Three, I told the Assistant Principal that I would take board games. I'd had enough of archery.

But one good thing came out of it all: those same tough boys still cross the road to say hello to me. And they still call me 'Robin'.

BEST BEFORE MARCH 1

Robert Yen

It happens around the same time every year. The middle of Term One is always marked by three naturally occurring phenomena: the arrival of autumn, the appearance of hot cross buns in the shops, and Year 7's behaviour taking a turn for the worse. Week Five is the time when the freshers overcome their initial shyness and sweet innocence, becoming all too streetwise to the workings of their big new school. And early childish fears are replaced by a greater malevolent force. Year 7 get an attitude.

For weeks now I've been priming my Gamma class (7 Gamma) constantly with praise, adopting a primary teacher's tone. 'Your behaviour's been so good this week. I'm very impressed with this class today. Excellent answer, Melanie. Great effort! Well done!' And even more so during those unbearably humid, summery days which had their place at Christmas time but not in late February.

'Year 7, I know it's hot and it's last period, but you're going to have to show me how well you can behave today, and not spoil your good record this week. I have some positive slips which I'll award to four good workers.' I can't keep this up, and soon neither will they. Damn this timetable: why do I have this class last period so often?

Like coleslaw that's been left out too long, 7 Gamma passed its use-by date last week, and went bad. Monday, period two, and I wasn't even ready for it. The kids were shoving and teasing each other when they arrived to class, some coming in late, some with laid-back expressions on their faces. I checked my watch for the date: March 1. They're really going to test me now.

'I need to go to the toilet,' yelled Adam, 'and I need to go *now*!'

'Why do you keep praising us for answering correctly?' called out Melanie. 'We're not dumb, you know.'

'What happens if we *don't* do our homework?' inquires Misty.

Well, no more Mr Nice Guy from me for a couple of days. From out of the blue, Year 7 have decided that they know all the answers now, and that adults are just bossy and uncaring squares who need to be educated. Welcome to puberty, where teens tell you their rights, where every point is debatable, and where you need to have the mental and physical stamina to match their youth. This was the start of an interesting week, a week of blood, sweat and tears. (Theirs, not mine.) Lunchtime lectures and arguments, letters and calls to parents. 7 Gamma's attitude has improved since, but sadly it'll never return to their innocent, pristine state.

'Thanks, Robert!' cried Megan in the Maths staffroom the next day. 'Now *my* Year 7 class has turned. You've jinxed me!'

'Sorry.'

'It's like last year when you predicted the return of the yoyo craze, and then we couldn't stop kids from bringing them to school. We're blaming you for that too!'

'Yeah,' supported Jane. 'Why can't you use your psychic powers for good instead of evil?'

Megan's the Year 7 Adviser, so she's given the class names a mathematical flavour, using Greek letters of the alphabet. So now we have classes like 7 Alpha and 7 Delta (shades of *Brave New World*, I know) and already the lame jokes have appeared: 7 Pi goes on an excursion to the canteen, 7 Kappa gets taught by a long-haired blond bloke in tight red shorts. Maths teacher humour. Sad.

It's not all bad. I do have another Year 7 class, 7 Zeta, the gifted and talented class of eighteen high-achieving students, including three primary kids who come over just for Maths. We're a big school (two hundred plus in Year 7), and this is our way of competing with selective and specialist high schools. From day one, I knew my new small class would be different from the rest. During an orientation activity, Linda stood up and introduced herself, listing among her likes netball and narratives. Well, I went home and looked up *narrative* in the dictionary, didn't I? And for the first couple of days, I experienced a stony, unnerving silence from these kids as they worked enthusiastically from their textbooks. I wandered around the class and tried to speak to individuals, but I felt I was intruding upon their progress.

'Does anyone need help?' I asked.

'Anybody? Please?' I pleaded.

A boy put up his hand.

'Matthew?'

'Mr Yen, how wide should we rule our margins?'

This was not a question I was expecting. This was spooky, like something out of *The X-Files*. Perhaps this class had been abducted by aliens of a superior intelligence, and now their mission was to study me.

'Um, well, two centimetres?' I replied.

Some of the class shrieked and started tearing out their pages.

'No, sorry, it doesn't matter. Do what you did in primary. As long as it's neat.'

While marking the roll, I ask, 'Does anyone know where Amanda is today?'

Silence again. I'm used to someone calling out 'She's sick' or 'She's visiting her grandma', but nobody's answering back. Then I look up and realise why. Eighteen pairs of eyes are staring at me, along with eighteen hands straight up, all waiting patiently and courteously to be granted permission to speak.

'Rebekah?' Eighteen hands drop down.

'Amanda's not feeling well today. She's experienced an allergic reaction to some medication that she's been taking.'

Such eloquence in speech and manner. Eventually, I decide 7 Zeta are not aliens after all because over time, they come out of their shells and share their warmth, character and laughter with me. Yesterday, the kids were inquisitive about my first name ('We know it begins with R') and my ethnic background, so I turn the lesson into a guessing competition. First prize: a positive slip. There was much class discussion and theorising during the period, with some students calling out 'Hey, Roger!', 'Richard Yen!' and 'Konnichi-wa!' craftily, just to test my reaction.

Sambo didn't win 'cause he guessed Rebecca. I hope he was kidding. And I looked up *konnichi-wa* in the dictionary, but it wasn't there.

A Fine Line

Greg Bogaerts

Jim Brothers could see the fox like a flame coming from the reeds of the swamp by the road. A flare of blood flat out, tongue lolling, ears back and legs pumping the close-to-the-earth slink of a body. And Jim could hear the sound coming from its throat, even through the glass of his windscreen: the hoarse, strangled sound chopped up by sick coughing. And the crimson blood coming up with each cough; red spots on the highway now. As the fox darted into the scrum of traffic.

With the town dogs, ten or more, still coming up from the swamp water. Mouths grinning open with the glee of the chase. Leaving great lines of slick slobber, from their jaws, on the cement. The pack shooting across six lanes after the red, bottlebrush tail of the fox. Every hair bristled on end from the fear.

Every dog through six bands of traffic without mishap. Seemingly immune to the impact of steel and rubber; safe, confident, arrogant in their numbers. And closing fast on the fox.

Jim Brothers, on his way to school to teach, remembered the stories, the legends about foxes he'd told in class to the Year 9s. How a fox would be set on fire and pursued by a mob through a circus or a village. And torn apart when it was caught. A story that held the attention of his students.

For once.

Jim drove across the overhead bridge and down along the flat of the main street. He could see the fox, cornered by the dogs, on the median strip in front of the main gate of the school. And the wire fence of the school ground, four-deep with boys watching the spectacle. Hoots and jeers thrown like stones at the tangle of blood and fur in the road.

Only bits of the fox left, and the dogs disappearing down a side street in pursuit of another diversion, more fun. The students drifting away from the fence, the urgent bow of weight left in the wire where half the school had pushed forward, had paused, for a few seconds, then gone back to their games of handball and Red Rover Cross Over.

Jim Brothers watched the passers-by ignore the ragged corpse, close to their feet; watched the motorists stare straight ahead, plough on over blood and bone and fur, not swerving to miss the remains. Until it was nothing; a mere stain of past life belted by rubber tyres into the black surface of the road.

Jim Brothers spilled the coffee when the bell went for first period. Hot coffee on his hands that immediately had the skin raised red and blistering. The bell for the start of the day; something he'd never grown used to after fourteen years of teaching. That small panic in the pit of his stomach that never went, no matter how many classes he taught over the years.

The first period, every period, not knowing how his students would be; quiet and studious, or toey, on edge, ready to disrupt any lesson he'd planned and prepared. A fine line he walked every day when he walked into a class. Something he tried not to think about, in order to teach, in order to survive.

He struggled down the narrow line of the corridor, squeezing himself through the pack of male bodies; a violent effort in itself just to make the classroom. And the short journey wasn't without event; the occasional elbow in the ribs, a foot shot out to trip him, sometimes told to get fucked. Things he ignored because he was surrounded by a hundred or more students and it was almost impossible to nail a culprit. And if he managed to pinpoint a student, it would be on. He knew. He'd seen it with the other teachers; the mob of students closing around and protesting the culprit's innocence. Blades of din until the teacher couldn't think. And backed off, backed down.

Jim was almost there; twenty metres to go when he saw the seething knot of bodies around Michael Cousins. Michael's shock of blood-red hair just visible above the sea of mouths, open. Jim could see, even from that distance; the hard shapes of the front teeth, the incisors, the shocking, ice-block pink of the gums of the boys. And the manacle click of the bodies, and Michael Cousins, the new Social Science teacher, the new boy among the boys. The boys knew.

As Jim drew near he wondered whether to intervene, to pull away the students, who were jostling Michael Cousins away from the direction he was supposed to go. A difficult line to cross for Jim; likely to make matters worse for Michael in the long run if he needed another teacher to keep the kids at bay for him. Word could, would, spread among the boys, and Michael would be even more vulnerable.

Jim watched the man, drowning, about to go down in the pack. Michael Cousins who hadn't taught for five years; his first appointment after his marriage breakdown, after his nervous breakdown had torn apart his life. Five years living back with his parents; cocooned in their kindness, nursed back into some sort of emotional and physical health. And reinstated by the Department, keen to fill positions at Borderland High, the school at which no one wanted to teach. The Department desperate and prepared to turn a blind eye to the health record of Michael Cousins.

Thomas Maclean broke the deadlock, wading in and wielding the cane about him; laying it about the legs and backs of a dozen boys who scattered like curs on the run.

'Go on yer bastards! Fuck off before I really get stuck inter yer!' growled Maclean, pursuing the pack remnants out of sight.

Thomas Maclean, fifty and close to retirement. And stark raving mad the students thought, the other teachers thought. A gently quiet man, Thomas Maclean, until two years ago when students broke into Maclean's science lab and cut the throats of eight rabbits in cages.

Michael Cousins pulled himself together, straightened his tie pushed by a boy into a hard lynch knot at the fold of his throat. Pale and sweaty like a man caught in a fever, a malaria of past panic tripped back into life by the students who now hounded him every day.

Jim Brothers stepped into his class, watched, from the corner of his eye, Michael Cousins walking away. Jim turned his attention to his students, still restless, some milling about, not sitting down, others talking among themselves, ignoring him.

Jim began the process.

'Right! Be quiet! Craig Coward shift yourself. I told you you're not to sit next to Gary Fear. The rest of you get out your books. Stop talking! Pay attention!'

Grumblings, threats of insurrection from the boys. Every period. Almost. Grudgingly obeying him. Slowly. A go slow; an arrogance that was unstoppable and unpunishable.

The nausea in Jim's stomach as he watched the students belligerently settle themselves. He thought about Michael Cousins and how he was so close to Michael; a fine line between Jim's classes and the pandemonium of Michael's classes — spit balls, abuse, kids jumping out of windows. And the principal at his wit's end with Michael.

Not because of the riotous classes, but because of the effect Michael Cousins was having on the rest of the staff, whose morale was low enough as it was.

Michael Cousins spooked most of the teachers, including Jim. Nearly all of them saw themselves in Michael: a fine line they might lose sight of and wander across to find their students rampaging out of control.

*

Michael Cousins disappeared from the school; disappeared between a Friday and a Monday. No excuses. No explanations from the Principal or the Department.

And the other teachers didn't ask, didn't want to know. Just breathed a little easier not having him in their midst.

THE HILL SCHOOL

Helen Wakefield

Beautiful. Old. Sturdy. Such strength in those earthen bricks. How magnificent! They don't make schools like this anymore, I thought, longing for that proud era. I approached the grand old building, built in the gold rush days, confidently. Three weeks into the *school* year and here I was at my new *school*.

The Principal greeted me warmly, assured me several times over that I could take all the time I needed before deciding what I would teach, whom I would teach and when I might begin. I might not even begin ... As long as I was here that was wonderful. I didn't need to start today, or even tomorrow, he said. There was absolutely no rush. If I stayed for today, that would be a miracle. Should I happen to linger for two days, this would indeed break the record. Record? I was curious by now. It seemed that in ten days he'd had ten teachers come, look, and bolt out the door. The most recent stayed but three hours. No problems said I. A teacher with my vast experience couldn't possibly encounter too many difficulties. I was not daunted or even slightly puzzled. Not yet anyway. It seemed a friendly enough place so far. After all, it was 9.15 am. I had met the Principal, Mr Wade, and a few others by now. They were welcoming and happy to see me.

That afternoon, after spending all day 'settling in' I felt suitably embarrassed by my inactivity. It was time for work. I ventured into the Years 5/6 room, deciding that a game would be the first thing to build a rapport with the kids. A game of rounders out on the oval. So off we went. Or should I say, off *they* went. In all directions. They ran amok. They ran up walls, over cliffs, up trees, hurdled fences and ignored with relish my demands.

'Come children . . . line up in two rows so that we can make two teams.' My whistle went quite unheard. The rounders bat flew skywards. Gravel showered upon one and all. They fought, they eye-gouged, they spat, they hurled stones accurately at their mates. They brandished sticks ripped from the silent sugar gums. They were wild. They were angry. They didn't want to play anything but war. How did I get them back alive into the classroom? I didn't. The bell mercifully rang and they tore out of the grounds, hiding, dodging missiles, weaving their way through enemy territory and ambushes to their respective places of abode. Note that I do not say homes.

The next day I thought that I might try the Preps. Four and five year olds. Dear little things I thought, much less stressful. I decided to take them for Art, as that was my area of expertise. When they entered the art room half of the class vanished into thin air. On searching further, I discovered them hiding in bins of art materials, wool, foil, string and rope, cloth, foam rubber and shredded paper. They refused to come out. Meanwhile the ones unable to fit into the bins were executing high dives from a row of tea chests. I was quite baffled by this strange expression of physical activity. Somehow we managed to survive the hour-long incarceration with each other. Nevertheless, I felt more than slightly exhausted by this unexpected divergence, or was it departure, from my carefully prepared lesson plan. As the Support Specialist Teacher, my position allowed classroom teachers two hours a week each for Planning and Preparation. This meant that I had responsibility for their classes (from Preps to Year 6) twice per week for one hour at a time. The subjects I officially taught were Personal Development, Art and Computer Support. The 'taught' tag could be safely translated as 'attended'. The lessons were largely self-preservation and protection of students from each other. The first and only reaction to any movement or twitch, bump or accidental brush, was to punch. Punch hard. Preferably until the guilty party was unconscious.

Keeping them occupied, or distracted, long enough for us all to survive the sixty minutes was a major challenge. If they learnt anything along the way that was a bonus. My lessons changed. Personal Development now meant lessons with real food. Little Daniel had never seen a sultana. A large plateful was irresistible to him. He consumed vast quantities of the dried fruit. I couldn't bring myself to stop him. I also couldn't bring myself to imagine the turmoil which surely must have erupted within his tiny shrunken stomach some hours later. The sight of his joy in tasting such wonderful things far outweighed any thoughts of after effects. I wonder whether Daniel ever had sultanas again.

I once again took the challenging Years 5/6, the group I'd taken on the first day. This time I took the lesson safely inside their classroom. From the beginning it was difficult. Despite my by now feeble attempts, I was unable to detect which child switched the overhead fans on full blast, just as those who threw scissors at the same throbbing fans seemed not to be amongst the angelic faces sitting cross-legged on the floor. They were the picture of innocence. One young lad meanwhile decided to flee to the fire escape stairs, from where access to the steep, high, second storey slate rooftop was easily gained. Inside a couple of girls insisted on bouncing each other, head first, off the heaters. The corners of the metal heaters that is. I felt sick. It was a nightmare. I was unable to leave the room to help Bobby, who by now was out on the roof, his death wish about to be accomplished. His chubby little body was poised ready for the leap to the asphalt below. My carefully worded suggestions such as 'Bobby do come in ... Bobby you must come and look at this ...' fell on deaf ears. The Principal had fortunately been summoned. Many years later, I asked him how he had encouraged Bobby to come down from the roof, how had he got him to abort his suicide mission?

'I unrolled the fire hose, aimed it at him and said that if he didn't get off I'd bloody well blow him off,' Mr Wade said. There was absolutely no argument from Bobby.

Each day brought new and varied teaching experiences. To say that finding a starting point for a lesson was difficult, was an understatement. The biggest challenge, however, fast became that of actually plucking up enough courage to get out of bed in the mornings, knowing what lay ahead. After acquiring an unbearable itchy rash across my body, soon after I began at The Hill School, a visit to the doctor revealed that it was shingles. Nothing could be done, he said. But he did give me three days off work. Miraculously the rash vanished the moment those words were uttered. A colleague developed heart problems as a result of the stressful situation.

But our lives were bliss compared to those of the children. We could go home to a normal environment, but their problems were just beginning when school was out. Home was a nightmare, in reality, for most of them. We believed that the children were victims of violent families, violent streets and a violent community. We heard things indirectly and from various sources such as the police, news and television reports and the children themselves. However there were subtle indicators too, such as an acceptance of pain and suffering and indifference to the pain of others. One boy calmly sliced the legs off a live lizard he had inside his desk while a lesson was in progress. Behaviour which was appalling to us was everyday and commonplace to many of these children. They seemed desensitised.

Family fights overflowed into the school grounds. The grisly activities at home included hanging other people's pets, starting fires and stealing animals. 'Morning Talk' provided an insight into the background of many of the students. One day a child calmly announced that he'd set the neighbours' back yard alight and as the neighbour clambered back over the fence into her place to extinguish the fire, she fell, breaking her leg. The response from the class was laughter and hilarity. Police were often called to the homes of the warring parties.

'William's father stabbed my dad last night,' one Prep boy told the class. William, also in Prep replied:

'The police took dad away again last night.'

'Dad's in court today because he bashed Andrew's dad with a cricket bat.' It was all recounted in a monotone voice. There was no emotion, just facts.

A distrust of law, order and lack of respect for others was entrenched in some students. If the students are dismantling someone's bike while they are in Prep, and selling the parts, and in Year 4 possess a 'Crocodile Dundee' style knife, whilst holding hostages on the way to school, it is a real challenge for any teacher to change such patterns of behaviour. The tiny lives were being charted on a frightening course. No one really knew what went on at home. Apart from 'Morning Talk', we did learn of other incidents which happened on the way to or from school. The Hill shop was often raided by the Preps and Year 1's en route to school. They were well organised, distracting the shopkeeper while the others filled their pockets with a sugar fix, or two, or three. What drives a child to such desperate actions? No breakfast makes even a tiny child creative.

Every day, one boy would stand at the gate, his thin little legs blue from the cold in winter. No socks, just a grubby tee-shirt and shorts. Frost on the ground and a hungry belly. Waiting for mum to turn up with lunch as promised. It didn't ever happen, but the child would wait in hope, every day. These things suggested a fair degree of neglect, but it was difficult to prove. Today, of course, this would all be reported as a form of abuse, but there was no Mandatory Reporting in 1991.

It must be said that things became easier as the staff united. As soldiers must surely bond in war, so we did. Mr Wade was a wonderful leader, supportive and strong. He organised Assertive Discipline Training for the entire school, and this enabled a less threatening atmosphere to be established. Children were taken on camps and excursions, the highlights for them being evident in comments regarding the accommodation. School camp accommodation was seen as palatial by the majority of the children.

Life at the Hill School was so different to anything I'd encountered. I felt helpless, but the Year 5/6 teacher remained calm throughout most of the crises. I asked her how she coped.

'I was an abused child. A teacher helped me to get where I am today. If I can help one child that will make everything else endurable.' I couldn't help but admire her. She knew exactly where these kids were coming from. I came from a loving family and had not a care in the world as a child. I would never understand as this teacher did. I didn't know where to start. Thank goodness for teachers like her. They are our only hope. I remained at the Hill School for one year. It was the longest year of my life.

THE THREE MICROPHONES

Peter Howe

Joey had a fixation on music technology. In the playground he was never without his little ghetto-blaster, surrounded by the team of pupils who were assigned to help him. The kids would happily talk to him while he held the speaker to his ear and looked into the distance.

I was under pressure from Joey because I had the biggest ghetto-blaster of them all. The first time he saw it I was packing up after a music lesson. He stuck his head around the hall door in search of where the music had come from and beheld the school music system. For a few seconds his eyes widened, then he came in for the attack. I walked briskly to him and said as assertively as I could, 'Joey, you are not allowed in this hall without permission. Now go and play.'

He ignored me and headed straight for the machine. I beat him to it and lifted it high in the air. He clawed at me, trying to climb to the magic box. I ran to the staffroom holding the stereo aloft with Joey still grabbing at me.

'Lisa,' I said, attempting to appear relaxed and in control, 'what should I do next?'

Lisa, his teacher, called him off and sent him into the playground with his minders.

'Peter,' she said, fixing me with her young, idealistic brown eyes. 'While we're on the subject of Joey I want to talk with you about putting him in the Education Week Performance with the other kids.'

'But Lisa, he's autistic. How could he handle it? How could we handle it? How could the other kids handle it? It's a beautiful concept but I don't think it's possible.'

She looked at me again and said in a slightly firmer voice, 'Peter, who is this school for? Just normal kids? And what's normal anyway? What are we saying if we don't put the kids in my class on stage? That they don't count? What are we going to say to their parents?'

'Lisa, the others are okay. But Joey's ... well ... how is he going to react in front of two hundred parents?'

'Just leave it to me. I'll put him with my dance group. He'll be okay.' She said this with such confidence and finality that I believed her.

Two days later I walked in on the rehearsal. They were dancing to 'Monster Mash', the 1960s hit about Frankenstein and friends dancing together. From the back of the hall I could see Joey in the front row. He was rocking with the best of them. As I walked up to congratulate Lisa I took a closer look at Joey. In his shaky grip he held the school microphone.

'*Aaaaagh!*' I screamed. 'That's our only microphone!'

'Can Joey use it on the night?' asked Lisa.

'*No!*' I screamed, outraged.

She paused, then said, 'Watch this.' She plucked the microphone from Joey's hand and hid it behind her. As he looked at the cone-shaped void in his fist a change came over him. Deep dismay clouded his face and his body slouched into a lifeless shape. The other children danced on but Joey had lost the desire.

'Lisa,' I said, 'he can't have that mike. It's worth too much money. Why don't you get him a toy microphone?'

'He won't fall for that,' said Lisa flatly.

Life was busy for the next few days and there were no further chances to discuss Joey's role in Education Week. I was heartened though when I saw a large plastic microphone on a shelf in the backstage room. Surely that would satisfy him.

On the night of the performance things went well until it was time for the dance group.

THE THREE MICROPHONES

Joey was not happy. He came on stage and stood dejectedly in his spot at the front of the stage. (Probably where Lisa could get to him if things started to go wrong.) He was looking disdainfully at the green plastic microphone in his hand. 'Monster Mash' rang out and the group started to dance but Joey just stood there in the front row looking sadly at the toy microphone. Not moving at all. Feelings of remorse got the better of me. I was a meanie. I was spoiling a great show. I reached out, unplugged the school microphone and gave it to Joey. His eyes lit up and he began to move like a pop star. He was alive. He was performing. He was gripping the mike reasonably tightly and I was beginning to relax.

In his excitement he began to dribble on the mike. I gulped back my reservations. Then I noticed that because the microphone was being lubricated by dribble it was being squeezed upwards in Joey's wet hand. He rocked on oblivious as it wobbled higher and higher. I crawled across to him, holding my hands out for the catch. I missed. The microphone crunched onto the stage. I passed it back up to him. He rocked on. The next time I caught it. And the next time. The dance group was great. Joey was great. The night was great.

The microphone was stuffed.

I took it to Magpie Music.

'Peter,' said Darren the microphone man, 'this mike is stuffed. There's no way I can fix it.'

'How much to replace?' I asked, mentally crossing off items from next year's music budget.

'Two hundred bucks tax exempt,' he replied. I was silent for quite a while.

'Any other options?' I asked.

'Well, there's three ex-hire mikes we could give you for forty-five bucks.'

'How long would they last?'

'Hard to say. They're pretty tough.'

I bought the three mikes. Four years later they're still going strong. They've been dribbled on, stood on, sat on and fallen on. In spite of all this they continue to emit a clear and vibrant signal. Those three microphones remind me that performing is for all our kids.

I've never met Joey's parents but I bet they remember the night he rocked with the best of them.

OUT OF UNIFORM

Sue Utting

G rey stone walls shored up the world of the privileged. Imposing wrought-iron gates flanked a stately entrance, where a weathered lintels frowned down on green-clad guards. Only those of correct rank and uniform were granted admission to the sweeping lawns within, where raked-gravel paths curved and curled between looping beds of severely pruned hybrid roses. Through the leaf-lined years of the 1960s, niggling rumours persisted, mouthed by the envious no doubt, that this stately pillar of inner urban establishment closely resembled an equally Victorian place of correction. Both institutions, it is claimed, insulate inmates from the morally corrupting influences of society, while purporting to prepare them for life on 'the outside', after an appointed term of incarceration. Both imposed strict codes of conduct designed to quash individuality and initiative. While one institution catered for the economically and socially privileged, its counterpart attracted the poor and culturally disadvantaged. Coiling above the walls of the former, the barbed wire was invisible.

Janine came at the start of Third Form. The rest of us reluctant inmates of an all girls' private school, had been together since Grade 6 or before. Janine's assimilation into the inner sanctum of the daughters of the silvertails proved very difficult. Girls can be such bitches and rich, classy bitches are the worst. It didn't impress anyone that Janine's father had donated enough cash to the school to warrant the new Domestic Science wing being named after him. In fact, it seemed bizarrely appropriate that the owner of a most lucrative cake-manufacturing chain in the southern hemisphere should have his initials emblazoned across rooms brimming with gleaming new stoves and fridges and all the latest kitchen gadgets that nouveau riche millions could provide.

If anything, it separated Janine even more distinctly from the old moneyed families who gave their names and inherited wealth to higher, more prestigious projects, such as libraries and chapels. Only Freya was a companion, a lunchtime half-caste fringe-dweller in the locker bay. Tainted millions acquired in the undertaking business failed to secure fickle girlhood friendships. However, such subtle distinctions in the schoolyard pecking order didn't stop us from accepting Janine's handouts at recess, throwing our mothers' roast beef sandwiches in the bin before listening, open mouths stuffed with sticky cream buns, while Freya revealed the latest tacky secrets of the embalming process.

The Prune had taught our mothers English at least a millennium ago. She was so old that she often called us by our sisters' names and, on stressful Fridays, forgot who we were altogether. Except for Janine. Having been forced to make a special slot in her ancient brain to accommodate a student with no previous pedigree, she loved to ejaculate Janine's name, together with sufficient spittle to completely drench those unfortunate enough to occupy the front row. It took about two weeks into term for The Prune to realise that the new girl couldn't parse.

The daily diet of a private school education demanded huge dollops of grammar, mixed with declension of nouns and verbs in a multitude of tenses. The more radical, modern-thinking public school system had already thrown out such antiquated teaching strategies, together with any staff old enough to remember them. Its other recent failing, as bemoaned by many, was an addiction to trashy modern literature, at the expense of Shakespeare and the classics. How could the literacy standards of Victoria's only reputable university be maintained if the private school system failed to churn out graduates familiar with gerunds and past participles no longer in common usage?

The Prune's persecution of Janine culminated in the Despicable Spondee Affair of Term Two. The entire upper middle school was studying *Julius Caesar*. In our class, this involved reading the various parts around the room while The Prune made annoying interruptions to show off her knowledge of the Bard's syntactical skills. We took bets on the unlikely but hugely popular event of The Prune slipping off the dais and partially strangling herself in her academic gown, before being fatally concussed on her own desk corner.

Freya and Janine were sitting in the back row, exchanging cryptic whispers relating to last weekend's sexual conquests. The room hushed as The Prune peered over rimless glass moons at unsuspecting prey. She spat at Freya first, referring to her by her older sisters' names, before passing sentence of a 1000 word analytical appraisal of the patriotic sentiments expressed in Antony's famous burial speech. For Janine, she determined a suitably daunting punishment. Fifty examples of the use of spondees in the last two acts of *Julius Caesar* were to be listed and on her desk by tomorrow.

Freya turned as wax-pale as one of her father's corpses while Janine just stared off across the loops of manicured playing fields to where the first and second elevens were thrashing the Geelong visitors at vigoro. What in the name of John Lennon was a spondee and how could she possibly find that many in less than twenty-four hours?

At home that evening, most of us scurried to dictionaries to ponder the absurdity of 'metrical feet'. Was it a bizarre oxymoronic joke? But The Prune lacked any glint of a sense of humour. No one objected when Freya and Janine worked together on Antony's speech. After all, 'Friends, Romans, countrymen' fairly spewed out spondees. In all subsequent

English lessons, in neat uniform rows, we mutely united against a common enemy. The Spondee Affair permanently cemented III B's antipathy towards ridiculous, poetically inspired punishments and stirred group sympathy for Janine.

From that time on, Freya and Janine always sat together, close enough to the blackboard and the front row 'brains' to avoid the beak-nosed scrutiny of black-gowned sadists as they prowled the back rows, seizing on unruly scribbled notebooks for public ridicule. In spelling tests, the pair miraculously made the same one or two mistakes but The Prune never thought to delve. When Janine's turn came to read to the class – a passage from 'The Flight of the Heron', for example – Freya whispered the more difficult polysyllabics behind a slender white hand. The Prune surreptitiously adjusted her hearing aid before commanding 'that geel' to speak up.

In Geography, the roles were reversed. On two test maps, Janine would quickly scribble in the names of capital cities as demographically diverse as Reykjavik and Bogota. It was easy to recall places visited on trips overseas with a much-loved father. Consequently, neither he, nor those who wrote and signed, knew how inaccurate the term report was: 'Janine possesses a solid grasp of literary skills but must avoid the distracting behaviour of others'. Beneath the grey forbidding walls of the gym, we nervously giggled as Freya read out loud this pompous assessment of her friend's academic potential. The delicious irony of a system fooled did not escape the more courageous among us. Rather, it spurred us on to prise open our own envelopes marked 'Confidential to Parents'. Such rebellious behaviour was worth the acrid taste of brown envelope glue. While we read about our various educational iniquities, Janine laughed and the wind swept her hat under the lurching undercarriage of an oncoming tram. 'Poetic justice!' she wryly observed, as she stuck the sodden pile of crumpled felt into her bag. 'This school is so backward that even last century's transport system can crush it beneath ancient wheels. It stands in the path of all progress!'

The year lumbered on. Time to audition for parts in an interschool Gilbert and Sullivan production, an opportunity not to be missed. What schoolgirl joy it was to be squished, like adolescent salmon, on teetering wooden rows of a temporary stage platform, between 122 boys from a neighbouring boys' college. Naturally, our choir was involved but its number was swelled by 'extras' – singers and orchestra recruits especially selected for this annual performance. Unwritten schoolgirl laws, regarding non-involvement in extracurricular activities generally pursued by 'brains' and 'squares', were obviated in this instance. The chance to press up against the captain of the Combined Public School athletics team was worth the indignity of auditioning with the head of the music school, who never deigned to acknowledge the existence of girls who had failed to complete at least eighth grade piano by the end of lower middle school.

Other music held a great fascination too. Huddled around the strip heater on a raw July Friday, we munched into yesterday's Boston buns from one of Janine's father's cake shops while she described the scene at Festival Hall during the Beatles tour. The rest of us spent that exciting visit locked in bedrooms by fretting parents, convinced that a long-haired group of Liverpool louts, from an open stage no less, could steal their daughters' virginity. Four B's form room served as a graveyard for an ancient piano, moved out of the music school during maintenance at least a decade ago. Yet the sagging wires sang as Janine pounded through the opening bars of 'She's a Woman', taking Paul McCartney's jagging chords to a stunned lunchtime audience. Janine didn't need to know how to read – music or Shakespeare. The appropriate keys magically slotted under sensitive, tapering fingers. Later, during auditions, the Head of Music couldn't believe Janine had never completed a scale in her entire, uncultivated life. Miraculously, she landed the role of assistant pianist for the performance.

During rehearsals over the coming weeks, Janine and Freya managed to capture the hearts of most of the delectable members of our brother college. The back row of the staggered platform constantly rollicked with mirth over Freya's jokes while the orchestra pit resonated with uninhibited joy in Janine's latest 'battered hat' escapade. The respective heads of the two music schools commented on the exceptional repartee of this year's group and secretly congratulated themselves on their adroit leadership skills and perceptive assessment of group dynamics. This smug self-aggrandisement ended abruptly on opening night.

Janine had not yet encountered the boredom and traditional stuffiness surrounding an extra-curricular dress code. It was expected that girls would wear their mother's white formal dresses, the style of which last century's decorum dictated that hemlines extended at least three inches below the knee. Nobody had thought to warn Janine. When she arrived on opening night, a shimmering vision in plunging white chiffon, the male orchestra members went berserk. The strapless bodice lasciviously enclosed two perfect breasts while the mid-calf split revealed exquisitely stockinged legs. The base notes drifted apathetically to the gilded dress circle as the news seeped round that Janine had been sent home in disgrace.

The senior school assembly hall accommodated at least three hundred girls for daily prayers and addresses from the Principal. He and his entourage always entered by the western door in a flurry of academic gowns and self-importance. The whole school rose to acknowledge their procession to the central dais, where a huge Bible resided on an imposing turned-wood podium. Those girls chosen to read the lesson for the day huddled in the wings, behind immense swathes of blue velvet curtains. Only the most outstanding members of the school community ever trod the polished boards near the Principal's throne on centre stage. Only the academically brilliant or musically gifted were selected to turn the gilded pages of the Old Testament, to read in clear, piping voices how Jezebel was eaten by dogs near the wall of Jezreal for her betrayal of Naboth and her Lord.

One dreadful morning this ritual was interrupted. The Principal called for the girl, who had dared to travel on the Sandringham line last Tuesday evening without a hat to come forward immediately. The entire student body would have to witness her shame but several of us knew her identity already. There would be after-school detention for all travellers on that particular rail route, if the guilty party failed to step forward. Six hundred pairs of eyes watched Janine rise from her seat near the eastern door and begin the long, humiliating journey down the central aisle of the hushed hall. Several members of staff bent scrawny necks to twitter about how they always knew this new girl would never fit in.

The outer world had noted a weak point in the wall, a breach of uniformity. This was an even graver sin than the actual lapse itself. Together with other members of III B, I squirmed uncomfortably in my seat and thanked those compassionate martyrs, petrified in red and blue stained glass in the school chapel windows, for protecting those of less moral fibre from such public ruin.

The following Monday, before form assembly, Janine relayed the more salient details of a Saturday detention. The worst part was having to travel to school by train on the weekend in full school uniform. She had attempted to repair the latest damage to her hat by placing the brim under a complete set of Encyclopaedia Britannica. Red bindings leached dye into wet felt and a subsequent stint in pink-tinctured bathwater had done little to restore a rigid shape. At least the guys on their way to Combined Public School cricket matches, resplendent in creams under Eton-style blazers, empathised with her shame.

Ironically, it was the scruffy primary school kids going to the footy who gave her the worst abuse.

Her first task was to clean the Principal's office. She tiptoed round his desk, flicking a feather duster over hardback school magazines dating back one hundred years. She wondered if other miscreants had wielded similar cleaning items down the decades. The Principal sneezed and immediately launched into a litany of homilies relating to public and personal hygiene and tidiness. The outer self reflected and also defined the inner. A correctly attired physique clothed an ordered mind and unburdened soul. Janine straightened her tie and rearranged her future plans. She could never grow accustomed to the cloying suffocation of this establishment's restrictions on personal dreams and wondered if she could bear it till the end of the year. But she owed her father that much.

The final straw fluttered earthwards when The Prune accused Freya of cheating in English. We often joked that she never seemed able to tell the two friends apart, constantly calling them by each other's name. It soon became a class joke we all conspired in, relishing the duplicity and secretly gloating how simple a fool was The Prune. We never dreamed it would backfire so terribly. Our final essay for the year was a 2000 word analysis of the use of setting and characterisation in *Lorna Doone*. The topic was even more boring than the novel, possibly written for ignorant virgins in a previous century. Janine didn't make it past the second chapter. When The Prune discovered two identical papers, she immediately blamed Freya. After all, hadn't the new 'geel' improved dramatically under her tuition? Besides, the undertaking business was an even more odious livelihood than devising assembly lines to produce tasteless white bread. No respectable living woman painted her face. Yet Freya's father rouged and lipsticked the dead. The Prune, no doubt, took great glee in writing a nought in the column next to Freya's name. It would guarantee the upstart's exclusion from the honours list. A more than satisfactory result in English was a prerequisite for consideration for a school prize, so Freya was sure to miss out on a hardback copy of an out of print novel as deadly dull as *Tom Brown's Schooldays*.

Characteristically, Freya shrugged it off as a joke but those of us who considered ourselves her friends knew better. The ridicule of 'brains' and other swats generally fell away towards Speech Night, when dewy-eyed parents leaned forward in plush seats, in the hope of catching a daughter's name among the rollcall to the stage to receive an honour. In vain, Janine tried to convince The Prune that she was to blame. The withered jaws twitched with annoyance as a shrunken claw tore the hearing aid away and reduced the world to unobtrusive silence.

On the last day of term before the Christmas break, the final assembly was traditionally two periods long – a full-scale pomp-and-circumstance affair. The President of the School Council delivered a boring report of the year's achievements. A well-known geriatric clerical identity followed, dribbling yuletide warnings against excessive culinary indulgences and pleas to recall the true meaning of the season.

As the black-gowned staff snail-trailed dutifully behind the shuffling pack of special guests, the organ flooded the hall with the dirgent strains of Chopin's 'Funeral March' in B flat minor. This year's geriatric bishop slapped full-bellied into the Principal, propped dead in the central aisle to the right of the orchestra pit. All heads twisted upwards to the minstrel gallery, where Janine sat boldly erect, blonde head and slender hands held high over the multilevel organ keyboard. The panelled roof rang with her contempt for the conceited and morally blind. We relished the delicious irony that the withered remains of college academic staff would inevitably repose, stripped of all their pretentious worldly trappings, on cold stone slabs in Freya's father's place of business.

The first hesitant titters erupted in the upper middle ranks before a sway of rippling laughter engulfed the standing student mass and caused the more timid members of staff to slump into the nearest vacant seats. The whole of III B began to chant Janine's name. By the time the Principal reached the podium and vainly attempted to glare the entire school into silence, the hall erupted into tumultuous cheering and wolf whistles. It was the best Christmas present ever.

Janine dropped like a stone from our schoolgirl lives. Few of us were privileged ever to see her again. Two decades later, on George Street in Brisbane heat, through a dizzying waft of expensive perfume, she stepped from the past and invited me to lunch. We reminisced about The Prune, the infamous spondee episode and that final assembly. She laughed at her younger self, who knew nothing of the secret codes of exclusive private girls' schools and even less about esoteric rules of grammar and archaic parts of speech.

When her father died, Janine took over his affairs and successfully conducted a multimillion dollar international business. Of course, she had secretaries to deal with all written correspondence and computer whiz kids who researched the latest market trends and condensed them into script she could comprehend.

After Janine's father withdrew his financial support from the school, those of us who understood enjoyed immensely the final revenge: Freya's family name was emblazoned across the refurbished Domestic Science wing.

Today, the same grey walls still confine the hopes and dreams of those who fear prim-lipped guards in drab green uniforms. For the young and brave, invisible barbed wire will always fail to snare vibrant minds.

THE KEY

Bev McGregor

The old-fashioned key lay heavily in my hand.

'You'll find it under the doormat,' they'd said.

'Ridiculous,' I thought, noting the open window to my left.

'It's a Departmental rule that all school buildings are to be kept locked when there's no one on the premises. Security, you know.' They'd been quite insistent.

But so many keys had been lost that it was easier to just leave it under the mat. I sighed, wondering how many other absurdities I was going to find. This was my first teaching appointment, and judging by what I'd seen so far there was a lot of work ahead. It had already required a lot of work just to get here. The letter of appointment had arrived among a pile of Christmas mail at my parents' suburban home.

Eurumberie Provisional Mission School, it informed me, had need of my services. It had been a shock to realise I'd not be teaching in one of the large suburban schools for which I'd mentally prepared myself, but the Department did not enter into correspondence on matters such as this.

Fortunately a letter arrived within the week from a resident of Eurumberie, giving general directions to the nearest big town and specific directions from there to Eurumberie. The letter had a 'pre-loved' appearance and contained some highly creative spelling. The writer had not bothered to express any form of welcome. He just provided basic information such as directions and the availability of accommodation.

There was something about Eurumberie that was beginning

to make me nervous but I'd just passed with honours from one of the state's foremost teacher training facilities. I knew how to teach – I had a piece of paper that said so. It was presented to me at a very impressive ceremony where the Chancellor of the college had stressed the significance of the work I was about to undertake. The key to the nation's future lay in my hands and I did not intend to let my nation down.

Unfortunately my car had not been advised of the national importance of our mission. It overheated less than 100 kilometres from our destination. The February heat combined with the burden of my enormous supply of teaching aids was too much for the tiny engine that had coped so well in the crowded streets of Sydney. Thus my ailing vehicle and I arrived in Werrigan, the nearest town to my destination, under cover of darkness. In truth, this is the best time to see Werrigan. Daylight is not kind to the clutter of buildings, generally regarded as the 'big smoke' by the residents of Eurumberie. The curving main street wanders dispiritedly along the river's edge. Huge river gums tower over its muddied water, casting their shade where it is of little use and leaving the street sunburnt and blistering. Paint peels from fading signs and shops stare mournfully at the passer-by, pleading their attractions.

I ignored it all. I was here on a great educational mission and neither bright lights nor dull ones would distract me from my purpose. I settled happily enough into Mrs Campbell's boarding house – only slightly disconcerted by her welcome.

My landlady's maternally rotund figure wobbled sympathetically as she patted me on the arm.

'The last teacher had this room but we won't talk about him. It's all a bit depressing isn't it? Anyway, I'm sure you'll be just fine.'

I nodded without conviction and tried not to think about why the last teacher hadn't been just fine.

Driving to school the next morning I considered my new

title of 'Teacher-In-Charge of Eurumberie Provisional Mission School'. The grandeur of it all momentarily overcame the tension I'd begun to feel the previous evening. I held my head high with pride as I drove towards this new responsibility in the soft glow of the early morning light.

The directions I followed proved to be surprisingly accurate and I had no trouble finding the way. Eventually I came to a large swing gate with a badly painted sign that read RUMBERIE. The EU had been demolished by culprits unknown. A clearly defined dirt track wound its way carelessly across the paddock, disappearing into the early morning heat haze.

Four gates and four paddocks later the collection of buildings that composed Eurumberie could finally be seen. With a sigh of relief I realised there were no more gates – I had only to negotiate a dilapidated cattle grid to reach my goal.

At first there appeared to be no sign of activity among the clutter of buildings, but as the wheels of the car hit the cattle grid the settlement came to life. The vibration of the grid set sheets of corrugated iron rattling with thunderous percussion, alerting every dog within earshot to rise and form an honour guard to greet the unwary arrival.

Immediately I was surrounded by canines of elephantine proportions. Each of them intent on committing suicide beneath my vehicle's wheels or determined to test my potential as dog food. Their heads lolled in through the open car windows dripping saliva on the upholstery while their teeth loomed threateningly in my direction. In desperation I closed the nearest window, almost snaring a battle-scarred snout in my haste. With a foot pressed heavily on the accelerator I escaped these hounds of hell, most of them having transferred their interest to the corpse of one of their own, which had apparently succeeded in fulfilling its death wish. The canine pack had learnt by experience that I would offer them further sport when I made my return trip.

My sense of relief at escaping the pack quickly dissipated with the realisation that I had inadvertently killed one of their number. I was far too frightened of the dogs to risk looking for the owner. I stayed in the car and prayed I hadn't permanently damaged any chance of a good relationship with the community.

At the far end of the settlement I found the school. Of traditional grey weatherboard, with high-pitched corrugated-iron roof and wide shady verandahs, it appeared to be the sturdiest building in view.

And so, here I was. The key to my future lying in my hand, waiting for me to take up the challenge. For just one moment I hesitated. Faint doubts whispering in the darkened corners of my mind. But the memory of the Chancellor's assuring words strengthened me in this moment of weakness. With renewed confidence I stepped forward and resolutely inserted the key into the lock.

It grated painfully, its innards protesting at being expected to function. The door to the classroom finally swung wide to reveal a thick layer of dust over everything, probably the result of the open windows. I wondered again at the security procedures.

For the next hour I attempted to clean the room and prepare for the day's lessons. The occasional sound of muffled laughter and running feet on the hard-packed earth assured me the pupils knew of my arrival. At precisely 9.30 I walked out onto the verandah and found the students waiting in a ragged group under the shade of a nearby peppercorn tree. I smiled reassuringly and using what I hoped would be recognised as a friendly voice, called for them to come into the classroom.

No one moved. They glanced at one another in obvious discomfort, their eyes avoiding mine as they giggled awkwardly and drew patterns in the dust with their naked toes. I called a second time.

More giggling, but still no one moved. My consideration of the correct procedure for handling a mutiny was interrupted as a figure reluctantly sidled forward. She was darker than the other children, her clothes bedraggled and ill-fitting but she was beautiful. Her dark brown eyes were raised no higher than the hem of my carefully ironed skirt as she explained.

'Pleaz Miz. We ain't allowed inside til after ya dun the specshun.' The situation was no clearer. I thought carefully.

'Perhaps you'd like to show me, er . . .'

'Gayle,' she responded quickly, rewarding me with a glorious smile. Gayle darted past me into the room and returned with a bright yellow tray indicating I should follow her to the peppercorn tree. She produced two plastic sticks – actually they were a pair of chopsticks still bearing the name of Lee Wong's Palace of Fine Food. After placing them firmly in my hands she gave the orders.

'Ya gotta check for doolums, Miz.' When I failed to move, Gayle took a second pair of chopsticks and began to lift sections of each child's hair in demonstration of how to search for the elusive 'doolum'. I had no idea what a 'doolum' looked like nor what I should do about it, if by chance I came across one, but, if rifling through the hair of each child with chopsticks, in order to get them into the classroom was required, then that was what I would do.

Doolum check now complete the children rushed for the classroom, but instead of moving to their seats they attacked a cupboard at the back of the room. Bowls, spoons and packets of cereal were soon spread out along the shelf.

'Breakfas,' explained Gayle. 'Ya got the milk?' I suddenly recalled the two litre carton of milk Mrs Campbell had generously provided with my lunch and pointed dumbly to where it stood by my desk. Gayle gave it to the other children, who helped themselves liberally.

'You gotta get Tony now.'

'Tony?'

'Yeah. He don' come to school unless the teacha gits 'im.' Gayle pointed out Tony's place of residence and explained that Tony lived with his grandmother.

The old woman could be seen comfortably resting on a bench outside the lean-to, as I approached. She nodded in a friendly fashion and hooked a thumb in the direction behind her.

''E's in there. Grumpy as all 'ell I can tell ya.'

The interior was dark, dusty but orderly. In one corner was a bed – not quite a double bed, but larger than a single – the only sleeping accommodation for the old woman and the boy. A brown arm dangled carelessly to the floor from beneath the mound of tangled bedclothes. I touched the arm gingerly, while calling the boy's name. The words were barely out of my mouth when the covers flew in the air and a whirlwind of anger snapped and snarled before me. Fists were clenched and raised before the eyes were open or the mind had registered the cause of the touch.

'Get ya hands off me ya . . .' The string of colourful language faded as his eyes came into focus. Being a lad of some discernment Tony could tell it was the new teacher he'd just sworn at. Apologising was not one of Tony's acquired skills but self-preservation was.

'Thought ya was me Gran. Jus' stan' at tha door an yell when youse wants me.' He struggled to free himself from the tangle of bedding. 'I'm cummin.'

The boy stormed out of the house ahead of me, still wearing the clothes in which he'd slept. Gran nodded at me, looking relieved to see Tony heading away from her. It was a feeling that I would come to appreciate.

By the time I re-entered the classroom all but Tony had finished their breakfast and one of the smaller children was washing the dishes.

This appeared to be a favoured job as it gave the worker an opportunity to avoid lessons and to play with the soap bubbles formed by the overenthusiastic application of detergent. I again prepared to begin the morning's lessons but Gayle shook her head.

From the same tray that had produced the chopsticks she now handed out toothbrushes. Each child had their name carefully inscribed on their own brush in a futile attempt to prevent the cross-infection of dental caries. A pointless exercise considering all brushes were thrust into a communal holder when not in use.

As time went by I learnt to admire the creative uses to which the children put those brushes. Along with cleaning teeth, each brush was useful during painting classes, for removing dirt from the fingernails, for cleaning gunge from the drainhole, for removing acid build-up from a car battery and provided an excellent weapon for firing spit balls.

Armed with a toothbrush each child filed past my table while I loaded their ration of toothpaste. Then it was out to the metal trough that ran along the outside of the building. Here a number of taps were fed from a rainwater tank. Using a maximum of water they brushed their teeth, the trough and each other, eventually returning to the classroom. I looked at Gayle hopefully. She nodded.

In the fifteen minutes left before recess I talked to my students about my hopes for their educational progress and the standards of dress, neatness and punctuality that I would require from them. They listened without comment. At least I hoped they listened. It was difficult to tell with every eye fixed firmly on the floor. Only Gayle rewarded me with the occasional timid smile.

By the end of the fifteen minutes, I'd begun to recognise the children by the tops of their heads. In time I hoped I would be able to associate faces as well. Calling the roll taught me that

Priscilla was the tall girl with the crooked parting, Mona was the tangled mop. Jonathon was the straight black hair with hidden eyes, Damien was the brown hair slicked back, Carrie was the long hair chewed at the ends and Garry was the shaved head.

Shaving the head and applying liberal quantities of insect spray was Eurumberie's approved method of eradicating doolums. It certainly worked, although the insect spray had no part in the success of the plan. It was simply a matter of no hair, no doolums!

At eleven o'clock I released my charges into the sunshine. They immediately became a mass of movement and noise totally different from the personalities they'd shown in the classroom.

But as soon as they returned to the room after recess they resumed the contemplation of their inner beings. They were neither rude nor disobedient, yet their body language conveyed what words could not. I and the Department might demand their physical presence but their minds and souls were their own to command. I would gain access to their inner selves when the children were ready and not a moment before.

The planned lessons lay before us untouched – Spelling, Maths, Reading, Drama, Written Expression, Singing and Local History. I tackled the list with an air of determination. Eleven heads presented themselves attentively as eleven pairs of eyes studied the floor. The first written activity required another trip to the wash trough. Gayle produced pieces of soap from the yellow tray and the class came to life as they squiggled their hands through pulpy soap and running water. Gayle's tray provided a hand towel so filthy that it only served to smear the recently cleaned hands with a fresh layer of dirt which then clung affectionately to their books.

At 12.30 the class disappeared in the direction of their homes for the midday meal. I sighed with frustration. Only two lessons had been completed and neither of those would meet the pristine standards I'd been taught to expect at the college.

I was grateful that I wouldn't need to do playground duty. There appeared to be no playground and there were certainly no children to observe. In fact, the whole of Eurumberie appeared to be in a state of suspended animation – only the loud thrumming of the cicadas indicated the possibility of life.

At 1.30 when my students should have reappeared in the classroom, the stillness continued. I stood on the verandah letting my eyes travel over the dusty, sun-bright settlement, searching beneath shaded verandahs and towering eucalypt shadows for signs of movement.

A small figure emerged from the shadow of a building and moved unhurriedly in my direction. A flash of smile preceded Gayle's explanation.

'Good m'day movie t'day, Miz. Kids'll be back when it's ova.'

Having performed her duty she wandered back to the building, presumably to return to the movie before the commercial break ended. The forest of television antennae sprouting from every building taunted me through the waves of midday heat.

The teacher training facility had not prepared me for this. The ache that had been a dull throb in the back of my head shifted to a harsh staccato in my temples. This would not do. I strode to the end of the verandah where a Departmental issue school bell hung neglected from the railing. A handy piece of metal piping provided the necessary implement to set it ringing – unsympathetically disturbing a nest of red-back spiders that had domiciled in its shady chamber. As the raucous noise continued insistently, children began to appear from all corners of the settlement. Thrust protestingly from their homes by parents irritated at having their daily viewing interrupted, their sullen faces indicated their displeasure.

I smiled with satisfaction. I had won this point. Tomorrow

and all the following days I would ring the bell loud and long till each child turned up on time.

The children took their seats and without seeking Gayle's permission I charged into my planned lesson. Barely two sentences later the cicadas were silenced by the screaming wail of a wounded bunyip. Ten heads in the classroom lifted to look at the one empty chair. The screeching stopped.

'Tony!' came the mutter of agreement, and for the first time all eyes were watching me. The bunyip must have paused to refill its lungs with air, for that one moment of silence was followed by screaming at an increased decibel level. Ten pairs of eyes watched wordlessly as I hurried to the verandah, and ten eager bodies crowded after me as I hurried to the source of the screams.

On the riverbank, in the shade of an ancient red gum, Tony's foot had found a rusted cod hook. Tony had endeavoured to remove the offending piece of hardware, but as the cod is an enormous fish requiring a large and strong hook specially designed to tangle itself in fishy flesh, Tony's struggles had only succeeded in embedding the hook deeper.

A steady flow of blood was forming a blackened puddle, which was proving most attractive to the children and an increasing number of flies. Despite the uncomfortable lurch in my stomach I examined the wound and sent Gayle to find something with which to staunch the flow of blood. She returned with the well-used hand towel, applied it enthusiastically to Tony's foot and managed to embed the hook still further. Tony's enraged howl and colourful expletives added to the general air of festivity.

Even though the midday movie was not yet over the live entertainment on the riverbank was too good to resist. The bulk of Eurumberie's population gathered to watch and listen. A general discussion decided that it would be best if Tony's foot were attended to by a doctor, all present being well aware of Tony's ability to wreck havoc on any of them who might cause him distress by attempting to remove it themselves.

Then there was a discussion about how Tony's foot was to be transported to the doctor. As all functioning vehicles on the settlement had been used to transport the men to work as fruit pickers at a distant property, I was unanimously elected as chauffeur and medical assistant. The children generously agreed to forgo the remainder of the day's lessons in the name of humanity.

Tony was dumped unceremoniously into the front passenger seat of my car while Grandma climbed in the back. The remainder of the settlement stayed on the riverbank to watch the flies crawl through the blood puddle and discuss the best method of removing cod hooks.

As I turned the car in the direction of the cattle grid I had temporarily forgotten the pack of canines waiting in ambush for me. At the sound of the car's engine they had assumed attack positions and as the vehicle approached they charged joyously, their fangs bared as they menaced us from all directions. Saliva ran in ghastly dribbles down the windscreen and claw marks scrawled angrily into the paintwork.

The movement of the car had increased Tony's discomfort and decreased his patience in equal proportions. As the dogs surged around the car he wound down the window and let forth with the full force of his colourful vocabulary. Shocked at their quarry's unexpected response, the pack fell back and slunk sullenly into the shadows. I considered the possibility of paying Tony to ride to the first gate every day.

After his brief discourse with the dogs Tony lapsed into suffering silence. Grandma hummed happily to herself and seemed in no need of passing the time with polite small talk. After assuring herself that the window winders, light, and ashtrays were all operative, she settled back and enjoyed the comfort of her transport.

Arriving in Werrigan, Grandma indicated the way to the doctor's surgery. Upon arrival she steadfastly refused to leave the vehicle. She folded her arms across her ample bosom and fixed her eyes on the floor.

'I wait here.'

Once inside I had no trouble in persuading the doctor to see Tony ahead of his other patients. The bloodsoaked towel sweating its contents on his clean floor provided sufficient impetus. After inspecting the damage the doctor applied a local anaesthetic to the area and asked me to step outside with him. Tony was left in the care of the nurse, who was attempting to clean blood and dirt from his injured foot. Going to the boot of his car and gathering an assortment of tools, the doctor explained.

'I'll have to push the hook through his foot, cut off the barb with these tinsnips and then draw it back out the way it came in. I'll need you to hold him steady.' I tried to look confident but suspected that it had been a long time since Tony had been held against his will by anyone. I wasn't sure if I would be able to achieve this seemingly simple task.

With pliers and tinsnips in hand we re-entered the surgery. Tony took one look at the tools and let forth with the vocabulary that'd been so effective on the dogs at the mission. He made a valiant attempt to reach the door but with united intention doctor, nurse and teacher pinned him to the bed. I wished fervently that Tony would transfer to his bunyip impressions as the language flowed around us. The medical team seemed unimpressed but worked smartly to remove the hook while I sweated with the effort of holding Tony still.

I wondered what the Chancellor of my college would say. Nothing in my four years of training had prepared me for this moment. While the child squirmed beneath me I began to suspect that the lecturers and writers of educational philosophy knew little of the real world. And as Tony continued to educate us all in the niceties of a drover's vocabulary, I perceived that my own education was just beginning.

The foot was at last encased in a sterile dressing. It hung limply as Tony sat on the bed filling his mouth with jelly beans offered to him by the nurse. Making the most of Tony's filled mouth, the doctor quickly gave the boy a tetanus injection.

It had been a false hope. Half-chewed jelly beans sprayed across the room as the bunyip wail burst forth. Tony's bunched fist narrowly missed the doctor's left ear then dropped, knocking the jelly bean jar from the nurse's hands. Jelly beans slithered over the lino and disappeared under cupboards and trolleys.

Unrepentant, Tony stepped down from the bed and walked out through the doorway, courageously refusing to favour his injured foot and deliberately stepping on as many of the fallen jelly beans as he was able.

I sighed in frustration and was about to apologise when the doctor began to laugh.

'Don't worry about Tony. He and I understand each other. He'll not thank me for forcing him to show pain in front of a woman but if I'm not mistaken a good feed of fish will come my way in the next day or two.' He spoke softly, watching my reaction.

'A man has his pride, you know – even if he is only eight years old.' I felt confused.

Back in the car Tony remained silent and Grandma continued her soft humming as we drove back to Eurumberie. At each of the four gates Tony got out of the car and walked firmly on the bandaged foot. The dogs once again received a verbal assault as we crossed the cattle grid.

I stopped the car outside their house while Tony and Grandma left the vehicle without thanks or comment. Their return having been marked by the noise of the dogs, the entire settlement now arrived to enjoy the gory details.

Grandma, who had not been present for the main act was not one to let the truth stand in the way of a good story. With enviable dramatic flair and a vivid imagination she enacted the entire story in a way that would preserve it permanently in the annals of tribal history.

Eventually the bandage was removed from Tony's foot and the doctor's handiwork inspected. Approval and admiration having been expressed by the whole assembly the foot was rewrapped in the now heavily soiled bandage. So much for the sterile dressing I thought as I returned to the classroom.

On my first day at Eurumberie I had succeeded in teaching just two lessons. Only one child actually spoke to me, if you didn't count Tony's swearing. To make matters worse I would now have to fill out an accident report and explain why I had closed the school for the afternoon.

My head ached from heat fatigue and stress. If days like this were to be the key to the nation's future I began to hold genuine concern for the nation. And I began to entertain doubts about my ability to survive as a teacher. Too exhausted to plan the next day's work I tidied away a few papers and prepared to go home.

It was late now, the sun hanging low on the horizon burned red, sending long-fingered shadows across the earth. The heavy key in my hand felt warm after lying in a beam of sunlight on the desk. I closed the door, turned the key in the lock and then placed it under the doormat thinking dismally about keys and the future.

Turning towards the car I almost tripped on a pile of garbage lying on the top step. Half wrapped in a soiled sheet of newspaper were three of the largest fish I had ever seen, their gills flaring in a desperate attempt to hold onto life. I noted the beauty of the dying creatures, confusion and pain seeming to shine from their eyes.

I thought about Tony, and his life of pain and confusion as

he struggled to find his place in a hostile world. It wouldn't be easy, but with care, maybe . . .

I collected the parcel, fatigue beginning to fade as future thoughts became more optimistic. Perhaps the key lay not in myself but in the children. Tomorrow I would try again.

WHY DO I KEEP TEACHING?

Gordon Holder

Friday, 8.50 am
First up 10M, and Penny has the gym. Better give 'em soccer again – they like that and there's no hassles. Off to the oval. As usual, most of the girls bring notes and opt out. The enlightened guru who invented mixed PE classes after Year 7 should be made to take them for a year. Hope the rain keeps off, three classes in the gym is the pits. Bell rings. One down, five to go.

Period two, and three classes are running wild outside the gym. Penny takes hers. I organise the emergency again, who hasn't a clue. I give him a volley ball and point east-north-east, in the direction of the canteen. There's a net outside permanently, so off he goes. They give him hell. Period two finishes without drama so off to the staffroom.

'Can I have a ball, sir?'

'Yes, Michael, we have big balls, small balls, black balls, blue balls, white balls, netballs, soccer balls, footy balls, tennis balls, cricket balls, basketballs, lacrosse balls, soft balls, hard balls, lost balls and found balls. Which is it?'

Laughs. 'A footy, sir.'

I retrace my steps back to the gym and hand out a footy, two table tennis bats, one soccer ball and a skipping rope. Missed my cuppa.

Bell rings, so up to 302 on the top floor for 8K Maths. On the way up, John from 10M reminds me about the tennis semi-final at lunchtime. Damn, I'd forgotten – no lunchbreak again. Two kids fighting outside 302, sort it out and into classroom. Class settles down.

'I don't understand that.'

'Well, listen in future. I'm a Maths teacher, not a magician.'

Everyone laughs. I interrupt a note which reads, 'Do you like sir? – yes or no?' I score a consensus. Eat your heart out Bob Hawke, the 'no' column is full. Do they really mean it?

'Yes, Anne, I know your parents are coming to parent-teacher evening, I want to see them too.'

'Someone at the door, sir. Miss Smith forgot her key.'

'Okay, take mine. No, I don't fancy Miss Smith. Yes, I'll open the window.'

'Bet you don't know where the Irish Sea is, sir?'

'Okay Scott, where is the Irish Sea?'

'Between Irish B and Irish D.'

Great laughter.

'It is the wrong key, sir.'

'Tell her I don't have the right one. Okay Mary, you can go. No Raelene, you can't go. Very well then, when Mary comes back. If she's gone for a smoke, I don't want to know.'

'All right, Rita, I know Mr Jones was better than me.'

'What is a nervous breakdown, sir?'

'Ask Mr Jones.'

'The sun's in your eyes? Pull the blinds down.'

'Only teachers are allowed to adjust the blinds.'

'Then shift.'

'You can't see the board now?'

Bell rings, a free – great. I'll get something from the canteen. Hell, a bloody extra and it's the notorious 8D with Elsie and Ruth. As usual, no work left, so I dash to the staffroom, grab my standby lessons and off down the corridor.

I reach the art room and the doors and windows are still intact. 8D start performing.

'Where's Miss Kasatis?'

'She's sick and we have to live together for forty-three minutes and thirty-five seconds. Inside please.'

Katie insists on painting a scene with me and accidentally puts yellow paint on the top of my red tracksuit pants.

'Sorry, sir. I'll wash it off.'

I now have yellow paint on both my top and my bottom.

'Yes, I like the picture.'

'No, I don't want to take it home.'

'I *do* like it.'

Bell rings, room clears in thirty seconds. Pick up three chairs and lock door. Back to the gym, collect nets, racquets and balls then off to the tennis courts. Game finishes five minutes before lunchtime ends. Race back to gym and replace equipment then off to the staffroom. Latest gazette is there, a quick look at the in-services. It must be my turn for the Maths conference and yes, it is on a Tuesday when I have six on. See VSTA news, read Cossar, then dash to the Home Eco room for 10L Maths. Hand back yesterday's tests.

'Now Ronny, for my last two tests you made 9 per cent and 12 per cent. Well this time you haven't been quite so successful.' Thunderous applause. Ronny acknowledges and stands on desk hands held high like Rambo, smiling broadly. He finds Maths a mystery. Still, he gets his kicks.

Bell rings, off to Portable Two, no carpets, heating off, next to woodwork room and noise amplification factor of one million. I go off the planet. How can you teach twenty-six budding terrorists in here? From now on, this period is for tests or glue sniffing.

Bell rings and I fall out of Portable Two, still warm and vertical and navigate to the gym on sound. It's last period on Friday. It's raining, the wind's howling and the kids are demented. Mario is doing his kung fu act on Arthur who has a glazed look in his eyes, probably thinking about the weekend. So am I. Some Year 9 kids are running at the crash mat and bouncing off it. The skill level is high. My three years at uni haven't been wasted. I suggest they try the gym wall, but there are no takers. The mat has magical properties. I ask the class if Mario has been fed today. Great laugher. Mario grins. He has got his strokes. The class runs for five minutes over time and then suddenly they have gone. The silence is deafening. I fix the ropes, pick up a green Exacto windcheater, size 12 with 'I'm living with Tommy' splashed across the front, a blue comb, a bunch of keys and a grey school bag full of books left on the stage. I check the store. We are now short of a footy, two table tennis bats, one soccer ball and a skipping rope.

Off to the photocopier to copy Maths exercise 3M from the textbook, page 76, but the machine has more flashing lights than a Chernobyl power station. If the VW is known as Hitler's revenge, then school photocopiers are definitely Tojo's. If ever I go into business, I'll make 'Out of Order' signs for photocopiers. I'll make a fortune.

Only five years to long service leave and two weeks to the end of term. There's really only seven working days as next Friday's a correction day. There is a disco on Wednesday afternoon and we finish at 2.30 on the last Friday. I walk through the school gates, head down with the wind blowing rain in my face. Exhausted. It is then that I hear the voice with all its urgency.

'Have a good weekend, sir. Have a good weekend.'

It is young Wayne from 8K shouting and waving like mad as he peddles off furiously down the road on his BMX. It is only then that it hits me, how fortunate teachers really are.

We are surrounded by laughter and tears, plus all the impetuosity, curiosity and vagrancy of the young. How very lucky we are. My step quickens. At least I'll get a cuppa at home.

WALLS AND BRIDGES

Susan Lane

Every class has at least one student who is an outsider, and in my English class José was it. He just didn't fit in. The other students ignored him or made fun of him, they didn't include him in class tasks nor did he make any effort to join with them. It was as if there was a wall around him, a fortress that kept the other students at a distance.

When I asked the class to split into small groups to work, everyone tried to avoid having José assigned to their group. And when José was told to do group work, he wouldn't join in.

'Let Betty and Trang help you, José,' I said. 'And you help them with their work.'

'Okay, Miss,' he would say, completely ignoring any group interaction and concentrating on his own work.

But it was a different story with his teachers. José sat at the front of the class and constantly demanded my attention. He would repeat things I said and always checked whether he was performing the simplest of tasks the right way.

'Miss, is this how you spell Sydney?' he said, just after I had checked that piece of work and reassured him he was right.

'Miss, is this how you spell Sydney?' he asked again a few minutes later.

'Yes José, that's right, that's how you spell Sydney.'

On and on like this.

Compared to his classmates he was gauche and unsophisticated, even though he was already in his late teens. He didn't own a baseball cap, never mind wearing it turned around, nor did he wear a pair of running shoes or bring music tapes to class and play them at a deafening pitch. The other boys in his group tended towards leanness and hyperactivity, but José was solid and broad and deliberate and serious.

When the rest of the class went on excursions José wouldn't join us. We didn't know why. All he said was that his father wouldn't allow him to go. It was more usual for the girls not to be allowed on excursions. José was the only boy we had known who couldn't gain permission from his parents.

Teachers at his old school hinted he was mildly developmentally delayed but his new teachers weren't so sure. He picked up spoken English as quickly as the others in the class, although he did have some problems with his written English. But it was his obsessive need for approval and affirmation and his isolation that most concerned us. The school counsellor said he could be suffering from anxiety or depression. No one was sure. She suggested we try to find out more about his background.

The difficulty with trying to figure out what was going on for José was compounded by the fact that English was his second language. The school counsellor called in an interpreter so she could conduct the interview with José in Spanish, but as he still wasn't very forthcoming, we were none the wiser.

After a meeting with the counsellor and mindful of the subtleties of language and culture, we decided to enlist the services of Esperanza, a Spanish-speaking community health worker. We explained our concerns about José, and our confusion over what his behaviour meant. She said she would assess José and make contact with his family if they were agreeable.

Meanwhile, José was becoming more and more isolated in class; the other students stopped taunting him and now completely ignored him. He developed a nervous tic and would constantly pick at his clothing. He wore the same T-shirt several days in a row and quite frankly smelt less than hygienic.

Once, in a lesson based on life back in the students' countries of origin, the class was asked to draw their memories of home. Except for José's, the pictures were fairly idealised and nostalgic representations of 'home': birds chirping, sun shining, friends and family and so on. José drew a picture of a house with a large brick fence around it, not one bird or tree in sight. There was no sunshine or people either. 'It's my home,' was all he said, compulsively picking at the same grimy off-white T-shirt he'd now worn for the last two weeks.

Esperanza left a message for me telling me that she had completed her interviews with José and his family, and we arranged to meet.

'As you know, José is not very forthcoming about himself, but what I found to be more revealing was my interview with José's father,' she said. 'He was on the wrong side of the political fence in Chile, a very dangerous situation to be in, I'm sure you know. When José was three he was kidnapped as some kind of warning to his father. He went missing for two months. No one knows what happened to him in that time.

'Eventually, and by a series of strange coincidences that his father sees as small miracles, he was found abandoned, starving and filthy. He was reunited with his family, but was completely mute and remained so for a year. He was nervous and suspicious of everybody, including his own family; a completely different three year old from the one his family had known before. It took many months for him to regain the most basic level of attachment to them. I feel this disruption of his early attachments has led to his current behaviour, coupled with the fact that two years later his mother, a high school principal who refused to inform on dissident students "disappeared" for good. Attachments are difficult for José, his sense of self is shaky. No wonder he needs continual affirmation that he is doing okay.'

Esperanza agreed to see José for counselling and support. She liaised with the school counsellor so that he might find a suitable course at TAFE or a job. My contact with him ceased shortly afterwards. The last I heard, José was working as a labourer for a horticulture firm specialising in Japanese gardens, planting trees, carrying rocks and building bridges over ponds filled with koi carp.

REUNION AT THE STAR HOTEL

Susie Armillei

I wondered for the one hundredth time why I was going. A school reunion. A time for reminiscing, meeting old friends, catching up on gossip and generally having a good time. So why then was I feeling like I should be turning the car around and heading for the nearest ... well anything, as long as it wasn't a reunion? I had even contemplated going to visit the in-laws for the weekend rather than joining the auspicious crowd bound to be in attendance at the Star Hotel. The location was a hint of impending disaster too. The old haunt was a dark smelly bar where many a night was spent trying to plan daring ways of going in for a drink without being told to leave by Lloyd the barman, who knew perfectly well we were under age because he played golf with my dad. I was sure it was not possible to have an inspirational or enjoyable event at the Star Hotel, especially if it was the reunion of the Class of '78.

It had been twenty years. I was heading back to my past. No! I don't think I can do it! Time to go somewhere else. Even going home to do housework sounded better than a night with all those school buddies from long ago. I guess I had not realised that I would be so nervous about attending. 'Okay,' I thought. 'Time for some self-analysis. Why do I desperately not want to attend?' I pondered this as an old Meatloaf song came on the radio, 'Paradise by the Dashboard Light'. Oh God! Even the radio is against me. The song we played constantly in our last year of high school fantasising about boys and someone taking you parking and ... now I was getting distracted.

Okay. Start again. Why did I not want to go? My life had not been a failure. I had made it through uni. I had my Bachelor of Science and had passed my teacher training year. I have a cute husband, which I'm sure no one thought I would ever have. Okay I don't have any children, but that's no big deal. So what is my problem? Then suddenly I knew. It was my job. People were going to ask me about work. Wasn't that what it was all about? Find out all the information and then see how everyone compares.

'Where are you living now?'

'Are you married?'

'Do you have kids?'

'Where do you work?'

'Do you like your job?'

'Are you happy with how things worked out?'

'Hey! Great to see you again. Yeah, things are great. I am a teacher now and my life is fantastic.' Could I be plausible and have a straight face when saying that? I tried a couple of times in the car as I drove. I could hear the frown in my voice. It was no good. I'd have to turn round and go home. Instead I continued the self-analysis. A most dangerous move!

'How is my life going so far? Well, basically, if you want the truth I'm stressed. I'm working in a "challenging" high school and trying to teach Maths and Science to some delightful Grade 7, 8, 9 and 10 students. The kids are usually really horrible to each other ... well to just about everyone really. I manage to teach and prepare for most of my classes during school hours and then do all my marking at home. I spend hours trying to work out fun ways to teach algebra or trigonometry only to find that the students aren't really interested anyway. I organise interesting science experiments for classes who only really want to see their pens melt into the Bunsen burner. That's if they are organised enough to actually arrive with their pens. And just last week when we were investigating acids and bases, one of the girls came up to me holding her bottom, jumping from one foot to the other like she was dying to go to the toilet. Someone had left acid on the chair and she had sat on it. (Actually that was not so bad because she was usually a real pain in class.) I had to spend ages dealing with that so it had been quite annoying. I am definitely not breeding mice again. Poor things. The students tried to tell me it was 'a kind of a science experiment' to throw a mouse across the room! To see what happened. Frankly, apart from feeling that it was really much easier not to ever do any practical work again, I was also wondering whether I was there to teach or to just discipline constantly.

Why couldn't my students be like we were at school? We worked hard. We did our homework. I spent hours on my homework. And we were polite to our teachers. The more I thought about it, the greater the injustice seemed. But then this was not a new line of thought.

But tonight perhaps a chord had been struck inside me. All this self-analysis had finally induced a decision. After tonight my life would change. It was time to find a new career. No more vile students. I could have a lunch hour for a change. No more boring meetings after school. No more working at night and on weekends. My life was about to improve, even if my holidays would decrease. At least I wouldn't spend the first week or two of my holidays either recovering from the latest virus spreading through the school or sleeping to recover enough to do anything that required energy during the break. Nor would I spend the last week preparing to go back to work.

Planning my fantastic new future, I continued the drive. There was almost a sense of relief as I ran the different possibilities through my head.

I arrived about fifteen minutes late.

My resolve was wavering as I thought about getting out of the car. Was I dressed appropriately? Did I look ten years older than everyone else? (Because I sure felt like it.) Would I recognise everyone, anyone?

But I shouldn't have worried. My friend Emma arrived and parked behind me and we went in together. From then on it was a sea of faces and stories. There had been 110 students in our Grade 10 year and most of them were there. Actually, most of them had never really left our small country town. Only about fifteen of us, 'the smart ones', had left for greener pastures while the rest languished in their small farming community, either working on the farm, in the local shops or just getting married and having children.

The Star Hotel had received a bit of a facelift since I last saw it. The addition of a new window, some paint and decent food had assisted with the revitalisation. So the night held more promise than I'd previously thought.

I met most of my closer friends after about an hour. I had a few drinks and was beginning to feel quite mellow. We recalled all the great things about school: the school production, the camps (where Sara had sneaked out of the tent to meet Dave without the teachers knowing) and some of the fun things we did in class. I was almost glad that I'd come.

I did a quick survey of the room. It was then that I spotted them. 'The girls.' At school they had been naughty, did no work, wore make-up and uniforms that were far too short, and they always had all the cute guys hanging around. God how we envied them and wished that we could have belonged to their group. This was all mere fantasy because there was no way I could have coped with being in trouble all the time, and if you think I could have got out of the house with a short uniform and make-up then you are not living in the same world as my mother. It took me several years to convince her that I did not have to wear the matching green underpants that they sold in the uniform shop.

I wandered over to say Hi, and to thank them for organising

the night. Apparently they had learned to organise things since leaving school.

I stood by listening to their chatter. On the periphery again. They were gossiping about all their conquests and deeds from back then. Nothing changes. Mindy turned and saw me.

'Hey, Susan, great to see you. We were just talking about that Speech and Drama class we had. Do you remember?'

Of course I remembered. It was the class I did for 'enjoyment' — as all my other classes were level 3 subjects like Advanced Maths and French. The 'fun' subject where all the good parts in the plays went to the prettiest or the slimmest girls in the class. But I deviate . . .

'Yeah, sure I do. What in particular?'

'Do you remember when Jessica decided not to talk to the teacher and she made us ignore her too?'

I had actually forgotten about that. I'd felt really bad because Miss Simms was a new teacher and she was really nice. But these girls always gave her a hard time. We were all scared of Jessica, so when she told us not to speak that's what we did. So Miss Simms came in and for the whole lesson she tried to get us to talk or participate but no one would. I felt the shame of it start creeping onto my face.

'I remember,' laughed Kate. 'She left the room crying, didn't she?'

'Yes,' answered Mindy. 'I guess it was a bit mean really but it was still funny.' Everyone laughed. Joanna pitched in with her story.

'Do you remember the day when we were all smoking up the back of the science block and Jimmy wanted to come too? So we told him the only way we would let him stay was if he took his shirt, trousers, socks and shoes off. And he did! We just laughed and laughed because he had really hairy legs. Remember when the bell went we took his stuff and threw it in the hedge. He was so late for class. Was it you, Mindy, who stole his shoes?'

'No, that was Jess. And she didn't give them back to him so when he arrived in Maths he had no shoes on. You should have seen him trying to explain that!'

Everyone was laughing hysterically at this stage so no one noticed that I wasn't. I remembered that Maths lesson as well.

I then recalled a couple of guys, who I had noticed were not at the reunion. They were unfortunate enough to wear white socks and trousers to school one day. Everyone knows that if you do that you must be a 'poof', so from then on they were branded and their lives were made a misery. I remembered now who the main perpetrators of this persecution were. Then I felt bad myself because I thought that the guys were quite nice, especially Greg. But I never actually worked up the courage to say anything more than a passing 'Hello' because I was too scared that I would be next on the list for associating with them.

My school memories were not so rosy now. Suddenly I had heard enough. I mumbled something about getting another drink and took off. I found myself outside, taking big, deep breaths as memories of my childhood threatened to embarrass me by bringing on hysterical weeping. Realisation dawned on me. If I thought teaching was bad now and that the behaviour and attitude of the students were 'challenging', then I can't imagine what our teachers must have thought. Did they think about us in the same way I think about my students? Probably worse. Does this mean that the students have always been the same and it is our perceptions that have changed? Maybe it was all my own fault. Maybe teaching had always been like this and I had just fantasised that you really taught kids and that they really wanted to learn.

These thoughts were too difficult to come to terms with in the car park of the Star Hotel. I would think about it tomorrow. I got into the car and started the long drive home.

A Winter's Tale

Robby Wright

It was the scarlet boxer shorts that really alerted me to the fact that something was wrong. A fifteen-year-old boy does not voluntarily appear publicly, at seven o'clock on a winter's morning, in underwear. Nor does he tell aged couples from Inverell that he had been robbed in the night. My hand was still attached to the motel room doorknob when I took in such a scene.

As I hastily pulled on the clothes I had draped across the foot of the bed the night before, I rubbed the back of my hand across my sleep-clogged eyes before I charged out the door. A weak sun silhouetted Matt and Alan who were still explaining to the old couple from Inverell, busy packing their car, how someone had come into their room in the night and taken their clothes, watches, money and backpacks.

At this point I interrupted. 'What did you say, Alan?'

'Oh, hi Mrs Wright. I was just telling these people that we've been robbed.'

'Robbed!' I squeaked. 'How? Are you both all right?'

'Well . . . Alan reckons we didn't lock the door after you and the girls left last night,' Matt admitted. 'But I'm sure we did, Miss.'

'Must've just walked right in,' Alan said.

Remembering the boys were in their underwear I shepherded them into their room. 'We'd better call the police and try and make you two a bit more respectable. Andrea, have you got any spare track pants with you?' I called into the next room.

'Think so, I'll look. Why?' came the reply.

'Now, what about the police.' I was terrified they would consider me an unfit person to be in charge of young people.

Alan explained the police had already been. They had called them last night.

'Why the hell didn't you wake me up?' I demanded.

'Look Miss, we didn't want to worry you and you know how Chloe's been. Anyway what could you have done other than phone the cops and we did that anyway,' Alan replied.

The old couple from Inverell were backing away from the front of their room. 'Hope things go well, boys. Funny, May and I didn't hear a thing,' the man called out the window. 'Oh, and good luck with the debate.'

'Oh God, the debate!' Matt groaned. 'We can't debate, we've got no clothes and those bastards ... Oh jeez, sorry Miss, but they've got my Road Runner tie.'

Shit. We were in the finals of the Regional Debating Competition. That's all I need, I thought. 'Look, let's survey the damage. Andrea, have you found those track pants yet?' I yelled. 'Oh, thanks. How's Chloe?'

Andrea was standing in the door, pants in hand. 'Not too good really. When she heard Matt talking to those people she rushed off to the bathroom and was really, really sick. She's back in bed, shivering and saying we shouldn't have come.'

'Andrea, can you see if Chloe has any track pants in her pack?'

I still couldn't believe they hadn't locked their door last night. My fault probably.

Inside their room Alan and Matt were sitting on the beds, the television was on and they were gloomily staring at the flickerings of *Good Morning Australia*. I sat down in the chair near the long laminex counter that served as both table and dressing table.

'Well, what did the police say?'

Alan filled in the details. It seemed there were a number of similar incidents last night around the Coffs motels and it took the police about an hour to get there. They had a quick look around, checked that the boys were all right and explained they would send an officer around this morning for a statement. When I repeated that I couldn't believe they hadn't locked their door they told me they had been watching television and discussing the Sean Connery film *The Rock* until after midnight. Matt had turned the light off but had obviously forgotten about the door. Next thing Matt remembered was being woken from a sound sleep by someone kneeling over him on the bed. What had been really creepy was that the man had one hand under the bed covers. He was touching his thigh and that caused Matt to leap up onto his knees calling to Alan.

'That's what woke me, Miss. Matt was saying, "Is that you Alan?" I can't believe he'd think I'd want to touch him up, Miss! Anyway I saw this shadow run out, sort of crouching if you know what I mean, and, well I chased him. I saw him bend and snatch something up as he rounded the corner to the back of the motel. He threw a bundle over the fence and shinnied over after it. It was dark and I had no shoes so I came back to see how Matt was . . . and that's it, Miss.'

I was having nightmares about being involved in a sexual abuse case and the fact that Matt was so silent only added to my fear. He was picking at the blue chenille bedspread. He seemed to be in shock. I gathered all the tea and sugar sachets I could find, sent Andrea next door to check on Chloe and bring back all the milk from the fridge, and boiled the jug. A sweet, hot drink was probably what Matt needed now and I sure as hell could do with one. Andrea returned with the milk and a pair of navy track pants for Alan.

'She's okay, Miss, but says she still feels sick. She wanted to know if we were going home. What do you reckon, Miss? I mean the boys have no clothes and Matt doesn't look too keen.'

'No way are we going home,' yelled Alan. 'We came to debate and that's what we're gonna do.'

'We can't do anything until the police have been,' I reminded him as I handed milky tea to Matt. 'Then we'll see.'

Renewed visions of those scarlet boxer shorts made me think about the difference between this morning and yesterday morning when we set out on our journey. My Statesman had bumped over the railway crossing and come to a smooth standstill beside Alan and his mother waiting in front of the post office, where Chloe's mother's small grey car was parked. Andrea's arrival had caused a fight over the front passenger seat. She had reminded me not to forget to stop at the turnoff to pick up Matt, the fourth member of the team. He complained about us being late.

To travel 250 kilometres with four voluble teenagers is not something many adults would appreciate but for a teacher, especially for a debating coach, it is part and parcel of the job. When we stopped for coffee Chloe, who had been silent, quietly mentioned she felt sick. Travel sickness, four would-be medicos diagnosed. As we stuffed ourselves with coffee and toast and basked in the young sun through the plate glass window of the Ampol roadhouse Chloe, nibbling on a Vegemite cracker, strolled about in the still brisk air.

After having successfully persuaded Andrea to relinquish the front seat to a still sick Chloe, the Statesman cruised back onto the highway. Never did the conversation flag for one instant: Mabo was dealt with, Pauline Hanson was decried and criticised mercilessly, the outskirts of Grafton were viewed with both pity and sorrow, although the highway Maccas was greeted with a cheer, and the schoolchildren waiting by the side of the road were inspected and sympathised with. 'I Spy' was tried but Matt cheated, and their singing was considered a failure because poor sick Chloe couldn't concentrate on her part in the round.

As we drew closer to Coffs Harbour the students had caught glimpses of the sea, home territory for them. Even Chloe, who had begun to slump further into the bucket seat, began to revive. Our destination was the senior high school cum university. A quick left at a motel had us moving in the right direction. By then it was 9.30 and we were almost thirty minutes late.

Alan had indicated our destination ahead on a small hill and observed that universities and schools are always located either on top of a hill or in a hole. Stiff bodies uncoiled and stretched. In the car park board shorts had been exchanged for long pants and the girls brushed and tied their hair up. Matt had knotted his Road Runner tie, borrowed for the occasion from a very fierce girl in Year 11. Grey school blazers were proudly put on.

As we had the greatest distance to travel, the finals organisers had scheduled a bye for us in the first round. We were to be part of the audience for the first three debates, an opportunity, we thought, to observe the opposition. After a lunch purchased from a student coffee shop on the campus we were to participate in Round Two. Chloe, still feeling sick, had begged to be team adviser. Reluctantly the other three had agreed despite the fact she was a very reliable and solid first speaker. Our opponents were the team Matt had watched win, an all-girls team dressed in crisp white shirts, navy blazers and polished shoes. In comparison our team appeared disgracefully louche despite the formality of Matt's red Road Runner tie. The team was locked away, with a dictionary, for the hour's preparation.

Matt had returned complaining that the prep room had been devoid of any inspiration whatsoever. He was an ideas man who took notice of his surroundings, and had achieved a degree of fame by introducing a red fire extinguisher he had observed in a previous preparation room into a debate we had won against a local high school. The debating venue, Matt despairingly observed, was also uninspiring. However, it had been inspiring enough to give us a narrow victory and a shot at the finals that were on today.

I was jolted out of my reminiscence by a knock on the door. Andrea opened it and a young constable came in. She took a black notebook from her jacket pocket and began to question the boys. She asked about the time of the robbery and Alan told her when he got back to the room after chasing the bloke the bedside clock said about 2.30.

'You chased him?'

'Yeah, sort've just responded. Bit of a surprise really.'

'Did you get a look at him?'

'Not really. All I saw was a dark shadow rushing out the door and then over the back fence. Matt must've, but, because the man was kneeling on the bed over him.'

The constable asked Matt if he could describe the person he saw.

'Well, I didn't take much notice really, I was kind'a shocked. I think he was a big bloke – bulky – or that's how he seemed. He may have been wearing a jacket of some kind. I know he had a beard ... anyway I think so.'

She seemed to have someone in mind. Obviously concerned about the touching incident, she remarked, 'He's never been known to do that before. Are you absolutely certain it was not an accidental brushing against your leg, Matt?'

'No, I'm positive!'

Alan interrupted. 'Anyway what was he doing leaning over Matt's bed? That's real weird stuff. Surely if he was just a thief he'd have wanted to grab a few things and run.'

She explained that the police would drive around the streets close by checking to see if some of their stuff had been dumped. 'I'll just get your home phone numbers in case anything comes up. And remember, boys, about doors ... after this little experience I hope you'll be more careful.' She glanced at me, folded her notebook, put it in her shirt pocket and left.

Alan dismally noted that he didn't think they'd ever see any of their stuff again but I pointed out that thieves wouldn't want folders or worn adolescent clothing. They might have quickly gone through it looking for money and then dumped it as the police said.

Andrea piped up, 'What are we going to do, Miss? Are we going home or what?'

Alan was adamant about wanting to debate. He pointed out that they had track pants they could wear and the blazers were still in the boot of my car and that surely the organisers would understand. 'Come on, Matt. What do you say? Andrea, what do you want to do?'

'I want to debate . . . but I wasn't robbed. So, Miss, what do you think?'

'Well, it's poor Matt who's most affected. He's had a real shock. It's up to him really and it's not as if we can let him be silent what with Chloe being sick and everything. Let's all pack up and get out of here. What we really need is some breakfast inside us and perhaps then we can make some kind of decision that is okay with everyone.' This wasn't what I really thought at all: I wished like crazy I was home getting ready for a normal school day.

I thought I should check the car. I was feeling as jumpy as poor Matt. As I was opening the car door I noticed one of the other debating coaches packing her car. I called across, 'Did you hear anything in the night by any chance? My boys had their room broken into and all their stuff taken.'

'You're joking! Are they all right?'

'Not too bad, considering. Although Matt's a bit shaken – the bloke was kneeling on his bed touching his leg.'

'Good God, the poor kid! That would come as a real shock . . . Actually now I think about it I do remember someone running past our room and I thought I heard the doorhandle being turned. That really woke me up and I glanced at the clock ... it was just before two-thirty. Anyway there was no more noise and I thought someone must have made a mistake with their room number. But, really, it could have been your thief, couldn't it?'

'Yep, that tallies with the boys' time. Lucky your door was locked, that's how come my kids were robbed ... they hadn't locked their door.'

'What are you plans now? Surely your kids won't want to debate.'

'We're going to get some breakfast and make up our minds. Oh, hang on! There's the police pulling in, I'd better see what they want.'

Two policemen were taking bags out of the back of a paddy wagon. They said an old lady had called the station early and told them there was clothing and a couple of bags in her front garden. I called to the boys and they both erupted out of their rooms and charged across the forecourt. They ripped their bags open and searched through their stuff, holding things up and whooping.

'Yeah, that's our stuff!' yelled Matt. 'Look Miss, I've got my Road Runner tie back.'

We thanked the police and lugged the whole mess back to the boys' room.

'That's it, Miss! We're going to debate. We've got our stuff back. Right, Matt?'

'Yeah, I suppose so.'

'Okay, okay,' I reluctantly agreed. 'You'd better get dressed and I'll see if I can catch that teacher before she and her team leave. If she tells the organisers what happened I'm certain they won't mind delaying. That'll give us a chance to eat and settle down a bit.'

Andrea and Chloe, fully dressed, were carrying their bags outside. I gave them the keys so they could pack the car while I quickly tidied myself and cleared the room. I could hear Alan next door prodding Matt along and telling him that the police would catch the bastards, that they'd probably taken fingerprints from their bags.

Whether it was shock, hunger or what, I don't know, but we all downed two breakfast burgers each, with orange juice. I am constantly amazed at the salutary effect food has on adolescents because almost immediately we began to feel as if life wasn't so bad after all, although Chloe deflated everyone by remarking that we should all go home, now. She was shouted down, called a wimp. Even Matt joined in.

The Statesman flew the last few kilometres and we arrived in the quadrangle a mere thirty minutes late. The girls' team had informed everyone about the great robbery and the heroic deeds of the boys who had chased the thief for more than a kilometre, without shoes. People were coming up, patting them on the back, commiserating with me and saying they hoped we'd win.

We were led towards the foyer of the auditorium where the opposing team was waiting. The organiser strode across the red carpet with two sheets of paper in his hand. As coaches were not allowed to participate in the topic selection, I stood back and observed my four debaters. I was happy to see they automatically went into business-as-usual mode. Chloe was holding the paper and pointing to one of the topics, Alan was gesticulating with his arms and Andrea was nodding her head in agreement. Then Matt calmly took the sheet from Chloe, ran his eyes over it, gave it back and made a statement. Respectfully the other three listened, looked at each other and nodded.

Chloe took her biro and quickly numbered the topics one to three. Coincidentally, both teams had agreed. The topic of the final debate was 'That Walt Disney was the William Shakespeare of the Twentieth Century'. A toss of the coin determined we would be the negative. I wished the kids good luck, found the cafeteria, a good soft chair, a cup of coffee and collapsed.

The hour flew. When we entered the auditorium it was full. I patted my kids on the back, whispered encouragement to Matt and sat in the end seat about ten rows from the front.

The debate began. The first speaker of the affirmative, a short, mousy girl, began to lay out her team's argument that both Disney and Shakespeare, in their day, were populist and appealed to a mass audience.

Andrea, our first speaker, began nervously. She argued that William Shakespeare was a more significant figure because he dealt with universal themes that were more important than flying elephants and dwarfs. Her rebuttal, although not telling, was adequate and she was able to sit down knowing she had done a reasonable job.

Speaker two, from the opposition, assumed the stance of a great rhetorician, looked around at our team and began to read, in a haughty and unpleasant voice, about the importance of Walt Disney as an innovator. I felt the audience was finding the speech a little too patronising and that this would give us a boost.

Matt, I noticed, was sitting quietly with his eyes closed. I hoped he was just relaxing, not cutting himself off from the present to brood on the events of last night. Chloe was watching him carefully and every now and then she spoke softly to him. I was relieved to find he nodded every time.

I crossed all my fingers as Alan rose to his feet, walked to the centre of the platform, looked the opposition in the eyes, turned back to the audience and grinned. As usual his timing was impeccable. What a load of rubbish we have heard today was his accusation. He repeated himself for good measure. Alan never needed notes. He would jot down three or four words on the palm of his hand and they would be the fuel for ten minutes or so of well-organised, logical argument. He was at his superb best today; it was as if the sleepless night and the shock had stripped away any childishness. He was an adult, battling misunderstanding and ignorance. The girls in front of me were riveted on his tall form as he strode along the very edge of the platform. Alan worked the audience; he confided in them, he asked them questions, he informed them but he never preached. At the end the applause was deafening, some cheered and he acknowledged their appreciation with a little bow.

The last speaker for the affirmative rose to her feet. I was shocked to see that the kids' nickname for her, Pinocchio, was most appropriate for she had the most extraordinary nose I'd ever seen on a young girl. Although she read her speech, what she was presenting to the audience was compelling. It was during her rebuttal of a point that Andrea had raised that the vitriol appeared. She sneered at Andrea for introducing something personal into the debate; Andrea had mentioned that she had performed in our school production of *Macbeth* and that it had drawn huge crowds. This girl, Sally, supposed that Andrea had played one of the witches and that she had not needed much make-up either. The audience gasped, and when she went on to suggest that the audience was probably made up of senile grannies and snotty-nosed little brothers and sisters I felt she had lost their respect. There was very little applause, only murmurs of disapproval.

Matt couldn't get to the front of the platform quickly enough. He began to address the audience as if they were friends. He only briefly touched on the unsuitability of personal abuse in a debate. Such was the prerogative of politicians, he explained, and the audience laughed knowledgeably. He summarised the team's arguments using examples to add authority to the central premise that Shakespeare shows mankind's faults and aspirations in a timeless fashion and that he was as relevant today as he had been over the past four hundred years. He adjusted his lucky tie and humorously remarked that if Walt Disney had been responsible for the creation of the Road Runner then he would have unreservedly judged him a great man. But as he hadn't, Shakespeare's place as the greatest commentator on humanity was unassailable. He sat to thunderous applause. Against the odds the team had somehow overcome. I thought this almost Shakespearean.

Although I had been reassured by many in the audience that my team were the undoubted winners, I was still uncertain. The final result was our victory, ultimately by a considerable margin and selection in the Regional Debating team for both Alan and Matt.

The Statesman, as it roared out of Coffs Harbour, reverberated to 'We Are the Champions' and Chloe's solemn announcement that she wasn't feeling sick any more interrupted my nightmare vision of scarlet boxer shorts on a winter's morning.

THE POLE

James Johnson

The Inspector of Schools, the District Inspector, the 'DI'. He was the controller of chalkies, young and old, raw and experienced, green and grey, those chasing promotion or those biding their time for a more suitable school.

The man to be feared, revered, and wondered at. The checker of work programs, attendance rolls, corporal punishment registers, test results, official school accounts, minutes of school committee meetings. The appellant for all matters scholastic and educational within his sphere of influence, his district. The source of information, the inspiration for the insipid, the fulfiller of the fawning, the urn of wondrous knowledge for the empty vessels in one-teacher deserts. The orb around which the educational earth rotated. The magician, who with a stroke of his pen could make hopes disappear, and with a wave of his magic tongue could produce frustration and a deep sense of despair. The DI demanded undying loyalty and devotion to Queen and country from every poor little bugger both sides of the stump.

Johnson had met his first DI under unusual circumstances, and in circumstances that were to hinder the incubation of undying friendship, let alone the hatching of undying loyalty and devotion. Having introduced himself, and asserted his right to be respectfully greeted in future, Frank (not that Johnson ever addressed him that way to his face) Pointer asked Johnson why he was a week late to take up his appointment. He listened with a low level of fascination to the reply, said he would return to 'officially inspect' Johnson within a few weeks, and headed for the door.

'Oh, by the way,' DI Pointer said by way of parting gesture, and in place of a warm handshake, 'I didn't notice the flag flying from the pole as I arrived. Did you conduct your Monday morning ceremony?'

For those who might not know, it was customary, essential, vital, and the right thing to do in schools at that time, to raise the flag up the school pole every Monday morning. This was done at the full school assembly, whether the school consisted of several hundred pupils and many teachers, or a dozen or so pupils and one teacher, as was the case at Ainnec, Johnson's school. The children, on command, would salute the flag, then, with hands on hearts would recite the Oath of Allegiance.

The oath went something like, 'I will honour the flag, my Queen and my country, and will respectfully obey my parents, teachers and the law.' The exact words remained vague to Johnson despite participation in hundreds of such ceremonies over the years. Actually it was more like 'I will honour the flag, serve my Queen, and cheerfully obey etc. etc.' The oath was followed by the sung national anthem: 'God Save the Queen'.

Anyhow, had Johnson conducted the Monday morning ceremony? Well, no, he hadn't.

'I suppose you were a bit busy on your first day? Please make sure you always conduct the ceremony in the future.' No. That wasn't it. When Johnson went to the cupboard to find the Australian flag, the only flag he could find was a Union Jack, and that was not the flag of Australia. 'I will get an Australian flag, and then we will conduct the ceremony,' said Johnson.

From Johnson's perspective that was a perfectly reasonable course of action. If twelve youngsters ranging in age from four to fourteen, and their nineteen-year-old teacher, must stand in front of and salute a flag a million miles from anywhere, in the middle of the Victorian mallee, at least it should be an

Australian flag to which they pay homage. That seemed like a reasoned argument, and Johnson felt quite proud of himself for expressing it so simply and directly to his master.

He could have said what he really felt: 'This isn't bloody England. These kids aren't little Poms many thousands of miles from their homeland.'

He should have said it immediately, because Frank's response to his more polite explanation made him blurt it out hotly, and without, as he was to learn, due regard and respect. Let's just say Johnson was left with a 'lawful instruction' that he would fly the Union Jack from the pole each Monday, and carry out the prescribed ceremony, by the book. Frank did promise to approach the local Member of Parliament and have an Australian flag presented to the school in the future, but in the meantime . . .

Pointer would return in the near future and give Johnson a proper inspection, paying due attention to account books, attendance rolls, time books, corporal punishment registers work program, timetable, standards of attainment, matters of general cleanliness and flag flying.

Johnson said he was looking forward to that, and to the additional progressive ideas the DI would provide him as his educational superior and leader. Further inspiration and wholehearted support were undoubtedly forthcoming.

Johnson and the kids got on with their first day together, got to know each other a little, and in an unspoken way decided that they could enjoy their time together. After all, all good things – Christmas, birthdays, New Year, grand finals and inspectors – usually come only once a year.

The DI had gone, but something else kept nagging at Johnson for the remainder of the day. Pointer had said the flag must fly from the pole every Monday. He had made the flag a constant in the equation, and Monday was obviously another constant. But what about the pole, standing as it was out the front of the ragged little hall, naked, dejected, unwanted and unused?

There was Johnson's variable. The flag must fly from the pole, Pointer had said. Flags can't fly from poles that are lying on the ground.

'Glen, have you got an axe at home?' Glen lived close to the school, just a few hundred yards away.

'Cliff. You whiz off with Glen after school and borrow the axe.'

After school the boys were back in a trice, happy to please their new teacher, and the variable quickly bit the dust.

The DI did return a couple of months later, and after testing the kids, and writing out Johnson's first school report, inquired as anticipated about Johnson's adherence to ceremonies of loyalty, respect and cheerfulness. Johnson told him of the enormous dust storm that had hit the area, and the damage it had done. Johnson told him the flagpole no longer stood, and quickly came to believe Frank connected the two events. Johnson explained that since his last visit they had conducted their ceremonies indoors, and always recited the oath on Mondays.

'You could salute the picture of the Queen,' said Pointer turning to the mantelpiece over the fireplace, where such things always resided.

The picture of the Queen. Now that's another story.

As part of Johnson's reaching out program for these country kids, he had conducted a 'Sporting Favourite of the Year' competition. Whether due to Johnson's influence or not, Jack Clarke, that great Essendon, Victorian and all-Australian footballer had won. In fact, had the 'bubs' realised a vote was being taken, the decision would have been unanimous.

As part of their writing program the youngsters had written to the Essendon Football Club to inform them of the honour they had bestowed on one of their members. The Essendon

Football Club had responded with a lovely letter from the great man himself, autographs of the entire team, and a large photo of their 'Sporting Favourite 1958'. There was a great need to frame it appropriately and immediately. When Johnson and the students had looked around the tiny schoolroom they found only one frame in the entire place. The Queen had to give over.

An Australian flag arrived in the mail within a fortnight and a couple of the local farmers, with whom Johnson had shared the joke, replanted the flagpole with no trouble and many laughs. Outdoor saluting and oathing became once more a regular part of school life.

During the four years that followed this incident, tons of beautiful, rich-red mallee soil was deposited in Bendigo, and beyond, as that part of the Mallee suffered at the hands of numerous ferocious dust storms. Throughout them all the variable stood unmoved.

WRITE FOR LIFE

Christine Melican

One day after school I was having afternoon tea with a Year 10 student of mine, Dianne. We were doing some follow-up work to an English assignment, a folio of her original writing. This may sound academic, but in reality, it was a matter of the heart – her heart in particular. On this spring day in a coffee shop in Canberra, Dianne talked about a book she had read and how it related to the death of her mother when she was a tiny girl in Year 2. We sipped our drinks over a table covered with photos in frames, photo albums, copies of Dianne's work and a Florentine design covered exercise book, a journal ready for future writing.

While this has been a remarkable and deepening journey for Dianne, it has also been part of a teaching journey for me. I have discovered, through many students, that the work we do in secondary school English can offer them a unique, safe and nurturing opportunity to reflect on and write about significant issues and events in their lives. Given time, a positive environment and encouragement, adolescents produce powerful writing.

This story really begins with Dianne's older sister, Karen, whom I taught several years ago when she was in Year 9. Karen was frequently in trouble for poor behaviour, lack of focus and effort, and incomplete work. She was sent to my office one day because I was also the Student Welfare Coordinator. As we talked I sensed this girl's utter unhappiness.

After chatting about the immediate situation I paused and

asked, 'Karen, what really is the problem?' Her reply was gulped out between sobs.

'I just miss Mum.' After putting my arm around her and feeling emotional myself, I invited her to bring in some family photos. On a couple of occasions we sat and talked about her mother, who'd only been in her early thirties when she died of cancer, two years earlier, leaving five children aged three to thirteen. Karen was the eldest.

Soon after my talk with Karen, the Year 9 English classes began a Writers' Workshop unit. This culminated in a Writers' Cafe, where we'd set up a room with tables decorated with tablecloths, flowers, drinks and nibbles and where several students from each class would read their work. Karen had written about her mother's death, simply and movingly, and our class wanted her to do a reading. When it was her turn to read, she found that she just couldn't, so I read it for her. At the end there was a gentle silence, and then one of her friends began to clap and the whole year level joined in. Some got out of their seats to hug her. The session allowed a small amount of healing for Karen as her friends expressed their love, support and had an increased understanding of her grief.

This experience was followed the next year with another student, Alicia, who came to the school during the year and joined my Year 8 English class. We were in the middle of a Year 8 Writers' Workshop unit. I explained to Alicia what we did, how there was a choice of writing topics and that the final piece would be redrafted and edited. We talked about some ideas, mostly light-hearted ones like the other students' and about her interests. But Alicia was hesitant and seemed unable to get started. I came back to her at the beginning of the next lesson and said that perhaps she could think about the funniest, happiest, most significant or saddest thing that had happened to her and use that as a starting point. Within minutes her pen was busy. When I returned she told me about the death of her brother and said she was working on a poem about it. The poem, framed, became a gift to her parents who later commented that it was the first time Alicia had opened up about their family tragedy.

The next year saw me journeying again, not only with Dianne but also with two Year 9 students, Emma and Gavin. As part of a Poetry unit in an English elective, Emma had enjoyed studying various poets but was having difficulty writing a poem of her own. Her mind seemed to drift from one topic to another, all somehow lacking the right substance to engage her efforts. I knew, from conversations we'd had, that her mind was often on her mother, who died on Christmas Day, at the end of Emma's Year 4. I knew she felt abandoned by her father, and that she worried about the health of her beautiful grandmother who looked after her. During one lesson Emma was frustrated. I moved her desk to a corner where she wouldn't be distracted and said to her that she should just write down what was on her mind, anything at all, but to make sure that the pen kept moving – words, phrases, even if it seemed like a list, down the page. As I moved around the class I glanced back and the pen was moving. She could easily have been writing about something humorous or topical, but the timing was right for her to reflect on the greatest tragedy in her life. The result was a powerful stream of consciousness poem. Her writing needed little redrafting because Emma felt it said what she wanted to express. A more important result was Emma realising that writing was more than something you do in English, that writing is for life. This is her poem:

DEATH IS
Unknown
Pain
Heartache
Less one in life

Loss Separation
Depression
A deep void that can never be filled
Where's the sun?
Tears burning
Grieving process???? CRAP!
WHY????
Missed opportunities
Things undone and unsaid
Relief for the pain in sickness
People's ignorance
Feelings
Crazy, insane
Comfort WHERE??
Tell yourself to deal with it
Tell yourself to cope
CAN'T ... CRACK
Calm, calm, calm
Be still Mummy will keep you safe ...
NO NO NO
Not any more
Don't want pain, don't want it!!
Death is unexpected even when it is foretold
Sickness may come to an end in health, but,
Can end in a way so cold
Their hands feel so cold to touch
She was just asleep. Pain gone, no more for she ...
Eyes closed
Priest? What? No!
Bye ... I think she's dead ...
Home? What home? I don't want to leave!
Look up ... What a brilliant star!
Look it's for her, everything, the night so crisp and calm ...

> Where is she now ... I want her back
> Feel her, hear her and see her in the FLESH
> People say they know and understand and make other
>   stupid comments that contradict each other
> Pain NEVER GOES AWAY!!
> You live with it as part of your life
> Every day, any time, any place
> Can't remember much about the funeral
> Tears ... so many people just too late to see her
> Nice 'friends' they were
> People just don't understand
> I couldn't see the coffin carrying her beautiful
>   self being put into the ground
> Was it wrong? If people would just let me be and cry all on
>   my own then it would be better
> No one else should be upset?
> No. One life lost is a tragedy for more than
>   myself ... especially hers.

Gavin's story is somewhat different. When he was four and a half years old, his three-year-old sister ran in front of a car and was killed. Gavin witnessed it. Then, in late 1996 he faced another trauma, finding the body of a favourite uncle whom he'd gone to visit. Just recently, as part of a folio of original writing he began to explore his feelings about these two deaths. He wasn't very happy with his poem and wanted to do more work on it. However, some of the lines clearly show the power of his reflections:

> I did recover eventually
> If only by pushing those memories to the dark recesses of my
>   head.
> Every so often it hits me
> Like an arrow from an unseen foe.

> When I was thirteen it seemed that I would taste again of death.
> Like a submarine, it lay hidden
> Treacherously resurfacing to inflict more hurt.
> That day is forever engraved in my memory –
> That blue corpse, now subject to rigormortis
> With a look of excruciating pain
> Forever fashioned upon his face
> My Uncle, as dear to me as a brother . . .

English isn't Dianne's strongest subject, but she works hard and achieves well. For her Year 10 folio of work she chose, from a given list of themes, one called *Ordinary and Extraordinary Lives*. Dianne saw that, in many ways, her mother's death was ordinary (the death of a loved one happens in all families at some time or other), but that it was also extraordinary in its impact on her and her sisters, brother and father.

For her main reading task Dianne chose a book called *Motherless Daughters* by Hope Edelman. She wrote a journal entry on it, responding personally and commenting at the end that this was the first time she'd really let herself think about 'what happened to me eight years ago, when I was seven'. She later wrote an essay on the topic 'Good books and films stir readers and viewers to consider some aspects of life in more depth and from a different point of view'. It was a topic that had to be relevant to a wide range of reading levels within the class, but that explored the notion of what constitutes a 'good' text.

Dianne managed to construct a formal essay that was also very moving. She quoted Edelman: 'A daughter who loses a mother does pass through stages of denial, anger, confusion, and re-orientation, but these responses repeat and circle back on themselves as each new developmental task reawakens her need for the parent.' She then discussed the main themes of the book, relating them carefully to the topic.

Dianne then presented more original work in her poems, which reflected her personal journey and the desire to craft her language to express her heart:

REMEMBER
R   is for **r**emembering, which I cannot do
E   is for **e**ternity, which I wish I could have with you
M   is for **m**emories, which are lessening to a few
E   is for **e**ver, which is the love I have for you
M   is for **M**other, whom I miss greatly
B   is for what you gave me, always the **b**est
E   is for the **e**nd, the end of your life
R   is for **r**est, the peaceful rest I wish for you.

MUM
I loved you when you were here,
I love you now even though you're not.
I wish that I could see you,
but I know that I cannot.
I want to tell you I love you
I want to tell you face to face.
I want to have a mother
And not an empty space.

I WISH
I wish that I could remember
your laugh
your cry
Your sweet hello and
sad goodbye.

> I wish I could remember
> your whispers
> your screams
> Your loving 'Good morning' and
> your wish for sweet dreams.
>
> I wish I could remember
> your hopes
> your fears
> Your last good-bye kiss and
> Last painful tears.
>
> I wish I could remember
> your last words
> while you were in pain,
> but I'm waiting for that one sweet day
> when I'll see you again.

Dianne's and my conversation that afternoon over coffee and cheesecake was about the power of writing, the strength it can bring and the way it can help make sense of life. She will continue writing, sometimes in a journal, sometimes visiting this ground again for further English writing. She doesn't always spell correctly, scores poorly on standardised tests, and probably won't become a published poet. But she is a reflective, empowered and literate person.

I would hate anyone to think that the atmosphere in my classroom is always serious. Mostly it isn't, because I believe passionately that 'When it's fun you learn'. But I would add that 'When it's meaningful you also learn' – learn to craft language, to look for images to express what you want, to read and understand, to push the boundaries of literacy far beyond the standardised tests that seem, to me, to distract politicians, journalists and sometimes parents, from the wealth of competency that students can demonstrate. Sometimes I wish that the critics of young people and teachers would visit my classroom and the thousands of other classrooms where similar 'work' is done, and see what is really being achieved. There will probably be some spelling errors, but dictionaries are close at hand, and there is always more to learn about written expression. However, students like Karen, Alicia, Emma, Gavin and Dianne, and their stories, are the best outcomes that any course would want to achieve.

HER MASTER'S VOICE

Michael Small

A paper dart dived over his shoulder, struck the whiteboard and self-destructed at his feet. In a surprise swivel, Slater caught Jarod leaning out of the window to suspend Lenka's bag, Lachlan throwing a crumpled note across to Dirty Harriet and Robbie spitballing at the ceiling. Even Lincoln was dribbling a globule of spittle on to the end of his ruler ready to answer the hail of staples launched by Travis Moriarty in a frenzy of glee. The gum-chewing wags of the back row were still rocking their chairs against the wall, the soles of their Doc Martens sticking up like skittles on the desk-tops.

'Take your hooves off the desk,' he would've snapped, had his voice not carked it, creaky as a rusty hawser. Twenty years ago he would've fired off, 'This is not a knobbly knees contest,' but his splats of humour had withered in the trenches. Instead, Slater clenched his jaw, shook his head and wagged a finger. The barricade of boots came down with the scrape of slow, sullen deliberation.

So many lines of babble twanged the air waves: school rules were unreal, dets unfair, heaps of homework, dads throwing wobblies about marijuana parties, mums doing bag checks for grog, boring English books oh so dumb. 'Why can't we read Stephen King?'

Due to a partial hearing loss, not wholly attributable to 9G, Slater darted his neck of pinched nerves in different directions to pick up signals for help from the few pensuckers, head-scratchers and bemused observers. From among whom peered Rhys Parris with the resigned air of a faithful bloodhound that might at any moment sniff with contempt. For whom, exactly, Slater dared not consider.

'Sir, I think you've lost control of your class,' the boy said with satisfaction, ensconced in the corner of the front row, half-turned to gawp at the accelerated socialisation program fast becoming Circus Oz. 'Aren't we supposed to be doing Writers' Workshop?

'Thanks, Rhys, for your reminder,' Slater croaked, a warm flush beading his forehead. 'Finish off your story!'

To dislodge the irritation at the back of his throat that inhibited the deep breathing required for his jousts with 9G, Slater hawked at the apparently immovable stringy knot of catarrh, only to wheeze into a gale of spluttering that rained over Rhys' curly cornered sheet of A4 inscribed simply with a heading of possibilities: 'A Venndetta baised on a storey by Ghie der Mo . . .'

Slater thumped his rattly chest, out of sympathy for himself, but also to impress on the heathens closing in that he was mortally wounded, like Richard III being stuck like a boar – yes, I am a bore – by one hundred pikes, too sick to bring them to order. Helen Salvaris wondered if this strange tattoo was how Henry V or II, it wasn't Henry VIII, had whipped himself . . . flagel . . . flagel . . . flagellation over that disgusting murder of . . .

This is the pits, he thought. Thirty years on chalk-and-talk man. Now the talk had dried up, it was time to hang up the chalk. He glimmered his final hour, falling in the line of duty before a victory parade of leering fourteen year olds, Macbeth's head on a pike, stretchered out to the sick bay cum morgue by two Year 9 pall-bearers. Appalling.

Principal: Whom have we here?

Travis Moriarty: 679,435, Slater, sir. Bachelor of Arts, 3rd class. Gassed something shocking by the enemy – too many baked beans and cokes.

Lachlan Mackenzie: Battle of 45. Room 45. Nerves shot through. Chappie couldn't hold the line when the going got heavy.

Principal: Life's a bastard. Carry on, chaps!

Perhaps he should bequeath his spleen to the reliquary in the school museum. He remembered how Gough Burbridge, even with a hearing aid, had wangled workers comp, pleading acute deafness. When the boys frisked by in the quad and said, 'G'day, fuckwit,' he'd reply, 'G'day, boys,' in that singsong voice that lulled them to sleep in History of Revolutions.

He remembered Jack Allinson, good old Jock, always kept a snort of whisky in his filing cabinet before bashing the Bard. The guy could scarcely see through his pebbled lenses, his eyes bugged out like skewered jellied eels, the back row stroking their flies and thighs with an abandon far from gay as he shuffled between rows, blind to their provocation.

Thank God he still had his sense of smell.

Two boys leapt sideways out of their chairs, fingers covering their noses, faces bursting with maniacal laughter then feigned disgust.

'Moriarty's farted!'

'Kick him out, sir!'

'Give him an hour's det!'

'Open all the windows, sir!'

It was that wet-weather, stale body odour that added to the nausea of impotence. What could he do but open a window and frown? And throw himself out? He used to say, 'I trust that you were not expressing a personal opinion, lad,' and draw off the embarrassment that way. Nowadays boys were shameless; more shameless.

He wondered how Mireille coped, splashing her wrist with Knowing, snorting lungfuls of green air from her sleeve before slicing through classroom fug. What made her a survivor, apart from that olfactory defence mechanism? And chocolate binges during exam marking, when she'd put on half a kilo.

Moon-faced Georgie was drawing up a list in her Record Book opposite class telephone numbers underneath SKOOL SUX:

my class
people i don't like	I want to kill my friends
Helen Salvaris	and befriend my enemies
Lachlan Mackenzie	and blow them up too
Jarod	
Sundhip	
me	

'What are you writing, Georgie?'

'Charlie!' she exclaimed through tight lips and eyes that drilled holes in the back of your head. 'Why can't you remember my name?'

Disgraceful, and he'd bitten his tongue at once. But his memory was fogging up in the currents of ripe air. He'd recommended *Jane Eyre* to Helen Salvaris, but was mortified that he couldn't haul in the name of the Bronte sister. Of course, it was Charlotte, Georgie's name, rather Charlie's name. And he'd called Helen Garner, Alan. Or vice versa.

'Sorry, Charlie. Can you climb back into your story?' he whispered. 'You have a special way with words.'

'No, I don't. Do you like my poem?'

> **The Charlie Song**
> being fat is fun
> that's why i weigh a ton
> always bouncing
> always fowl
> lose some weight
> you ugly cow

'Well, it's ... er ... got a strong rhythm.'

'It's grunge.'

'Finish your version of "A Vendetta" before the bell.'

'It's boring vegie stuff and I've read the original story anyhow.'

'Hand it in at the end of the period, please.'

'Get real!'

'Do we have oral work tomorrow, sir?' Toby yelled from the darkest corner.

'You do,' he nodded. 'Thursdays.'

'One-minute talks, no hesitation, no repetition, no relevance?'

'Irrelevance,' he rasped.

'Orals suck, sir.'

Charlie was singing, passing notes (Travis M is spunky with his dunny-brush haircut), doodling (Sherbet yum ... being rude is cool, it's a great way to be cruel).

'How are you going, Helen?'

'I miss your voice,' replied a straight-backed girl with an urgency bordering on desperation, her olive complexion underlining large, black-olive eyes.

'Not half as much as I do,' he cracked.

'It was so ... reassuring, like when you acted out "The Necklace". I'll never forget that moment when Mathilde gets home from the ball in that dingy horse-cab and she doesn't want to take off her gown. Then when she looks at herself in the mirror and sees the necklace missing ... It took my breath away when you acted that bit when she touches her neck, not believing. Then she really flipped.'

At least someone danced on my grave, he smiled.

She tugged his sleeve. 'What does your doctor say?'

'Some bronchial complication.' He coaxed a little flurry of coughs to prove the diagnosis, but his throat, Mireille had said, was really about his fear of hanging loose – a split between his inner and outer world – that he was a choker.

Which he tried not to be right now, although there was a tightening in his throat, partly brought about by Helen's tut-tutting and shaking of her straight, black hair and matronly smile.

I should have taken monastic vows – he had moved into contemplative mode – listening to the winds of silence rather than constipated bowels, worming over illuminated manuscripts instead of illiterate sludge, leading a chaste life instead of witnessing hormones jumping out of every eyeball, gathering sheaves of herbal medicines from the water meadows ... catmint ... marigold and evening primrose ...

Thud! Lenka's bag bombed from the windowledge onto the concourse outside, bursting into brays of laughter.

'Would you like to try a warhead?' Jarod sucked up. 'Sour cherry.'

'Go on, sir! It'll only burn your throat for thirty seconds.'

'Hey, sir!' wailed Charlie. 'Shall I stay at my mum's place tonight, or my dad's? Or Felix the Cat's?'

'Charlie's a whore,' muttered Travis, as if bending low over a fuse.

'No, I'm not, gay boy. Just you wait!'

'Sir, can I show you my story now?' Helen was waving her paper under his nose: ' "A Vendetta, based on a story by Guy de Maupassant," I can take criticism.'

'Of course, I'm looking forward to reading it.' Already he was turning with curiosity to the closing lines:

> Then Frisky leapt up at Nicolas Ravolati, knocked him to the ground and began tearing at his throat. 'Help, help!' he cried. 'Mercy!'
>
> The widow Saverini had a softer side in her nature and felt sorry to have let Frisky off the leash. She cried, 'Heel, Frisky!'

Immediately the mangy dog, even though it was starving hungry, obeyed the old woman.

The widow Saverini also had a guilty conscience. So she stayed at Ravolati's house on Longosardo to dress his hurt. Every day she bathed his scarred throat, straining low over his body to hear his voice once again. And every day she mixed up a magical potion of marigold and evening primrose to make him better.

How Yellow Changed to Gold

Joy Price

'Aw Miss, do we hafta do this?' complained Phillip, leaning back in his desk with a sidelong look towards Jono for approval.

I sighed, the day was sweltering, and the class was restless. Writing was the last thing they wanted to do. A paper dart sailed across the room. I was beginning to wish I hadn't taken them on.

'Yes, Phillip, just five minutes to finish, then I'll read you *The Runaway Truck*. This was a story I'd found in the *Reader's Digest*, a cliff-hanger about a truck driver whose brakes had failed at the beginning of a five kilometre descent. A good story for a hot afternoon.

I thought about the week before the Christmas holidays when Mr Irwin, the English master, had called me into his office.

'Joy, we've got a special group of kids coming in next year, a remedial group from the local primary school. Shouldn't be too much of a problem, only about sixteen of them altogether.' I was a little apprehensive, but agreed to take them, and do what I could. 'They'll be known as 7 Yellow,' he went on. It was the practice of the school to label the Year 7 classes with colours to disguise the fact that classes were being streamed, although it didn't take long before the students realised this.

On the first day of school, 7 Yellow had trooped into the classroom, arranged themselves in their seats, faces still expressing awe at their first day of high school. There were fifteen of them: five girls and ten boys. They were clean, tidy and cooperative, anxious to find out about high school, and somewhat relieved that the older students were not around on that first day.

Oh, that it could have stayed that way. Within a week, the class had found its place in the pecking order of the school, and began to behave accordingly. By the second week 7 Yellow had acquired a reputation of roughness, rudeness and unteachability. Their Maths teacher threw up his hands in horror at the mere mention of their names, the Science teacher banned them from using equipment, and the library staff could not keep them in their seats. The boys had discovered the magical qualities of the new library carpet. They found they could pass on electric shocks to each other by rubbing their feet on the carpet and then touching an unsuspecting victim, usually one of the girls, who had become absorbed in her book. The ringleaders were Phillip, Frank and Jono.

The rest of the class really wasn't too bad. There was Glenn, a good-natured English lad with a North Country accent. His size saved him from being bullied by the others, but his loudness was his main problem. There was Goran, with his attractive chip-toothed smile, who did his best but had a temper that was easily roused. Dark-eyed Abdul kept to himself. Bradley, with the cheeky grin, had an appealing personality, but also was prone to temper tantrums. The girls were more quiet and restrained. Erin had the personality, always ready to give advice with a sunny smile; shy Katie never said a word; and Janette was stolid and defensive. Alison and Margaret ignored the others and sat together talking secretively, occasionally rising to the surface.

As a class, however, they were becoming a real problem. They had an attention span of only a few minutes, and teaching them anything was a challenge. Yet, when I thought about it, there were just a few really naughty students in the class, and it seemed sad that the others should be deprived of a comfortable classroom environment and made to wear the reputation bestowed on the class as a whole. Other students looked down on them as slow learners, teachers punished them for their behaviour, and their self-esteem was trodden into the ground.

What to do? Their behaviour in English hadn't been too bad, and they enjoyed talking about themselves and their interests. It was when the reading and writing was required that the atmosphere changed and the restlessness, teasing and arguments began. I could see the potential for anarchy and I had to think of a way of managing 7 Yellow before they became worse. Survival came in the form of a parent–teacher night at the local primary school, where a visiting speaker was talking to parents about the problems she was encountering in her remedial reading centre, and how the staff were dealing with them.

The problem, she said, lay in low self-esteem, and the only way in which any of these children had gained recognition was by their bad behaviour. They learned early that good, quiet children were often ignored, and that a child embarrassed by a learning problem could easily 'disappear' in a classroom. While they had nothing to offer in the way of clever answers, good writing and fluent reading, they found they could earn the recognition of their peers by playing up in the classroom and tormenting the teacher. The way to turn the tables on this kind of behaviour was to reinforce *any* good behaviour, no matter how small. For instance, if Johnny could cross the classroom without hitting Kelly, he would be rewarded.

Rewards were in the form of a point-scoring system, which was added up at the end of the week. Winners were given a toy or a book.

'A form of bribery?' one parent asked.

'In a way,' replied the reading teacher, 'but really it is a form of recognition for good behaviour. It can be built upon, and it *does* work.'

Well now, I thought on my way home, how do I adapt this method to my own class? Determined to begin right away and give it a try, I covered an exercise book in bright paper and wrote the students' names down one side of the first page. The next day 7 Yellow entered class in their usual manner, with the boys hurling their bags against their desks. They sat down with their usual attitudes: Phillip sprawled across the desk, Jono leaning back with his elbows on the back of his seat, Frank with his head down on the desk, and Alison and Margaret arranging their bottles of nailpolish. Only Erin, Katy and a couple of the boys took their books out, ready for work, pencil cases neatly beside them, pens and rulers at the ready.

I slowly walked round the class and observed each one. Fifteen pairs of eyes gazed at me wondering what I was up to. I stopped at Erin's desk and said 'Hmmm' in an impressed way. All eyes followed me as I pulled the gaudy book from under my arm, and with a show of exaggerated concentration I moved my pen down the list and placed a tick against her name before moving on to the others.

'Hey, wotcher doin', Miss?' called out Phillip, suspicion and interest doing battle on his face. Even Alison and Margaret were distracted from painting their nails. I knew I had the class attention, and made the most of it.

'It's an idea I have that you might like to try. Let's talk about it.' By the end of the lesson we had worked out the point system, with the check-up day on Friday, in second last period in the afternoon. We discussed points and prizes for the top six point-earners every week.

We ran through the system that lesson and the class co-operated with writing, listening and taking turns to speak. The nailpolish was discreetly packed away. Ticks appeared against every name. When the bell rang and they packed up to go, I gave a special tick to those who had actually put their chairs back under their desks, and to those who put their rubbish in the bin.

The point system worked beautifully that week. On Thursday afternoon I went shopping and bought a number of small items: novelty pens, pencils, sharpeners, little notebooks, rulers – nothing expensive.

They loved the idea, and over the weeks we kept it going and points were awarded for all kinds of activities. The usually naughty ones were given points for trying, and I found it wasn't hard to spot good behaviour. Encouragement was the watchword. Everybody had a go at being in the top six.

I decided it was time to test the method elsewhere. The class had been virtually banned from the library because of their behaviour. A talk to the librarian about 'the system' and she agreed to give it a try. Together we selected a box of high interest readers, specials from the Ashtons Book Club, and last period Tuesday was designated for the trial. I prepared the class on Monday by telling them they would be doing some sustained silent reading in the library the next day.

'What does that mean, Miss?' asked Glenn.

'It means that you'll be reading a book of your choice quietly in the library, for as long as you possibly can,' and I gave them cardboard, scissors, coloured pencils, old magazines and glue to make some attractive bookmarks.

'Put your name on the bookmarks, so you'll know which is your book for next time.' If there is a next time, I thought to myself.

Into the library we marched on Tuesday. Books were selected and the students sat at a special group of tables. For every five minutes of quiet reading each student was given one point. I moved around them with a quiet word of praise and encouragement, and the time passed quietly. At the end of the half-hour they had all achieved their five ticks. Bookmarks were then placed carefully in the books, and 7 Yellow's book box was established. They were welcomed to the library every Tuesday afternoon, and began to appreciate the peaceful and quiet atmosphere.

I was amazed at the cooperation of the class. Only one boy, Jono, was cynical about the process, but luckily his mates weren't giving him any support. One day the precious point book disappeared from my desk, and was missing for two days. I kept my cool and transferred the ticks onto paper. Two days later the book turned up, and I suspect that some pressure had been put upon Jono to return it.

A subtle change was occurring in this group over the term. They still wanted the points and their little rewards, but there was really no need for it any more. We kept it going, however, on the weekly basis, but arranged for the points to be added up at the end of the year to see who was the winner. Abdul, who sat at the back of the classroom, was forging ahead, with Erin not far behind. I was wondering how long the magic would last, and whether the students would tire of it eventually. But it was surprising how many other rewards were accumulating from the system and their improved behaviour.

Mr Webster, the Principal, had a word with Mr Irwin. He had been contacted by the Department, which was sending two people over to see how this remedial group was coming along. They asked if they could sit in on a lesson and observe the students at work. Perhaps an English lesson could be arranged? I gave the students a letter-writing exercise, with a difference. They were to compose a letter to the Principal from a parent giving a reason for their child's absence from school. The reason, however, was to be left to the creative imagination of each student. It worked.

The august couple were ushered into the classroom and introduced to the students and myself by Mr Irwin. 7 Yellow was sitting up straight, books and pens at the ready, and the point book sat conspicuously on top of the register. They loved the idea of making up the letter, and excuses were discussed, each becoming more absurd by the minute.

'Wot about a bank hold-up?' suggested Glenn.

'And being taken hostage,' added Phillip, 'and then getting shot.'

'Yeah, but yer couldn't die, or yer wouldn't need an absence letter,' put in Bradley.

'Nah,' objected Frank, 'bein' dead's a good excuse. Anyway, what about getting trampled by a herd of elephants escaping from Ashton's Circus?' And so it went on. The people from the Department were delighted, and when, with much chewing of pens and scuffling of feet, the class settled to their task, they folded up their notes and with nods and smiles tiptoed from the classroom.

The Principal called me to his office that afternoon, and told me how pleased the visitors had been with the class. I explained to him what we had been doing, and asked him if he would be interested in reading the students' creations.

'Certainly,' he said. 'Send a couple of the students up to me when the letters are ready.'

Next day, the class were polishing their letters to be read to the Principal. Flourishing signatures were practised, artistic stamps drawn in the corner of the envelopes, and the Principal's name and school address centred nicely. Erin and Phillip were selected to deliver the letters, which were gravely received by Mr Webster in the recesses of his highly polished mahogany furnitured office. He shook their hands, thanking them for their trouble and assured them he would read them straight away. And he did. The bank robberies, elephants, bus crashes, falling rocks, earthquakes, fire and floods tickled his sense of humour. He loved them.

For a Year 7 class, a visit from the Principal is an awesome thing, but on the following day there was Mr Webster telling 7 Yellow how much he had enjoyed their letters, and that he had laughed so much he had had to wipe the tears away.

'Now, I'm going to ask a favour of you,' he said speaking seriously. 'I would like to keep these letters in my drawer, and when I'm feeling tired and cross I'll read them again to cheer myself up.'

Nothing could have had a more profound effect upon the class. This display of recognition and approval by the school Principal made them beam with pride, and I was eternally grateful to him.

The class went on to bigger and better things. In term Three, inspired by the James Bond movies and music, I took the opportunity to encourage them to make up their own James Bond drama. Phillip was James Bond, Erin Miss Moneypenny, and parts were quickly thought up and allocated to every member of the class. Except Glenn. He had volunteered to be the musical technician for the group and was in charge of the record player and choice of music for each scene. That term, English stopped being just 'English'. It became music, script writing, program writing, artwork, costume design and stage management, all revolving around the subject 'James Bond – special agent'.

The play grew over the weeks. Katy brought in a length of leopard skin towelling print, and immediately the idea of a desert island scene materialised. Janette, Katy, Alison and Margaret worked out a hula dance. Imaginations ran wild, with cannibalistic creatures and a particularly nasty chieftain, played by Jono. The first scenes were based in London, where James was given his assignment, then in the plane which crashed onto the desert island. There was plenty of blood and gore, but James Bond came through every time, to the stunning conclusion, all beautifully orchestrated with the James Bond themes played so skilfully by Glenn, seated at the record player, working the microphone, and looking the part with headphones clamped over his ears.

Mr Webster was contacted by the special education coordinator in the Department to arrange another visit to the class. I had told him about the James Bond production, and we organised a special morning to present the play to the coordinator, Mr Webster and interested parents and teachers. The class put on a delightful performance, and the Department official was instantly won over by their enthusiasm, humour and practicality.

The class never looked back. The point system was abandoned after Year 7 – 'kid stuff', they'd said – and they were squarely on their own two feet for the rest of their school life.

The following year the girls were included in a series of special typing classes run by a motherly TAFE teacher, who became very fond of them. The Department Special Education official had organised for half-a-dozen second-hand typewriters to be purchased for the class. In Year 9 all the students were placed in paid work experience for one or two days a week, and as coordinating teacher I worked with the Commonwealth Employment Service to find them special places. They worked in various department stores, garages and workshops, nurseries and plant hire firms, butcher's shops, bakeries, and spare parts distributors, and this work continued until most of them left at the end of Year 10 – three of them to go on to secondary college, the rest of them into the workforce.

I was their English teacher throughout high school, and by Year 10 I had seen them mature into responsible young people. Lessons were a joy, and they were appreciating some of the texts that were allocated for the School Certificate, a memorable one being *My Family and Other Animals* by Gerald Durrell. Glenn, Frank and Jono decided to go on to college and tackle the ACT Year 12 certificate.

From time to time over the years I had wondered about this class, and what had become of them. Like Mr Chipps, most high school teachers always remember their past students as being forever sixteen. But one day, something special happened.

I was in Sydney on business, and as I walked down the main shopping centre of Burwood I heard a cry.

'Mrs Price!' It was Erin. 'Oh, Mrs Price, how lovely to see you! You haven't changed a bit, I knew you straight away!'

In five minutes, we caught up as much as we could on twenty years.

'We're having a Year 10 reunion in two weeks' time,' she said excitedly. 'Would you be able to come?'

So, in October 1997, I went to the reunion of the Class of 1977 and was delighted to meet some of my students. As with many reunions, it's not possible for everyone to make it, but as soon as I set foot in the reception room, I heard the voices.

'Mrs Price, it's Mrs Price!' And there was Erin, who quickly took me to her table. Bradley, with his cheeky grin, was there, introducing me to Betty, his wife. He's now running a landscape gardening service, after fourteen years as a greenkeeper. Janette was there with her husband, and she showed me the photographs of her two children and talked about her job in the public service. Erin had just sold her takeaway business, and was looking forward to moving north with her husband. Goran, who had grown into a giant outside his chipped-tooth smile, told me he was managing the spare parts shop where he'd been placed in Year 9. They filled me in with news of the others: Glenn was a telephone technician, Phillip was running his own butcher's shop, and, sadly, Abdul had been killed in a car accident. We talked about school.

'You know, I never liked the colour yellow,' remarked Janette.

'No, neither did I,' agreed Erin. 'Why didn't they give us a better colour?'

'I know,' said Bradley. 'It should have been gold.'

'Yes, Bradley.' I nodded thoughtfully. 'Yes. It should.'

I met many other ex-students at that reunion night whom I'd taught in other classes during those years, but the highlight of the night was meeting my Year 7 Yellows again, and finding that the bond was still there. No teacher could ask for more than that.

THE GREAT GREASY PIG CHASE OF 1967

Russell James

His message was succinct but his manner conveyed just a hint of sadistic pleasure.

'My boy,' he pronounced, 'you've got the hillbillies of 4G for intermediate geography. You won't get much work out of them, so just make sure that they stay in their desks, leave their chewing gum outside and that you keep your class rolls neat and up to date.'

These few words from the Vice-Principal only added to my nervous anticipation of what lay ahead for me in my first year out as a young and enthusiastic secondary school teacher. And what did lie ahead, for me and the boys of 4G, still remains the most evocative memory I have in more than three memory-filled decades of teaching.

The 'hillbillies', all boys, were from the Ridge and the Hill – local vernacular for the then sleepy rural hollows of Main Ridge and Red Hill on Victoria's Mornington Peninsula. They were twenty farm boys collected together and labelled 4G, so as to emphasise their remoteness from the so-called more academically capable students of 4A, B and C. The burden of such politically incorrect labelling was, however, not one that weighed heavily on the boys of 4G. Instead they wore it with pride, as some form of collective badge of honour. What a collective of down-to-earth, ruddy-faced and uncomplicated characters they were. And their names – not a Brad or a Jason or a Scott among them, but a Phil, two Norms, a Joe, a Frank and no less than three Freds. Most of them were destined to leave school at the end of that year – to take up an assortment of apprenticeships offered by local tradesmen, or to help out on their parents' farm, or Uncle Jack's orchard, or both. Consequently, their approach to learning the essential elements of climatology, vulcanicity, meteorology and all the other 'ologys' and 'icitys' that the prescribed syllabus of study insisted upon was, to put it kindly, less than enthusiastic. They presented a challenge for any teacher and one that saw me try a wide variety of classroom techniques in an effort to stimulate their interest in things geographical.

But it was to no avail. The boys were always, or nearly always, what the Principal called the 'three praiseworthy P's' – polite, punctual and patient – yet I felt a failure. But with the words of my Methods of Teaching lecturer ringing in my ears I continued to search for that 'elusive light of inquisitiveness' that he assured us was 'at the end of everyone's tunnel of learning'.

It was more out of desperation than inspiration that I decided, at the start of Term Two, to take 4G out of the classroom and into their natural habitat, the great outdoors. My desperation, cunningly disguised as youthful exuberance, managed to persuade a hesitant Vice-Principal to allow me to supervise 4G's own agri-business, a 1990s term for what in effect was to be a small vegie patch with a few chooks and rabbits on the side.

One of his many conditions was that the vegetable patch and animal hutches were to be located in the far back corner of the grounds well away from the main school building. The results of this 'hands on' approach to Geography were quick to emerge. Almost overnight the boys displayed, not just an interest, but a fascination bordering on obsession with such diverse topics as trace elements, animal husbandry and the macro-economics of government price intervention in the demand and supply forces of the competitive egg market. Daily work rosters were meticulously drawn up, cash crops chosen and the requisite agrarian tools begged, borrowed and I suspect in some instances, stolen from assorted parents and Uncle Jacks.

The intention was for the class to grow and then sell their farm produce to other students. The retail price was to be set according to the individual buyer concerned: trade discounts being offered to the Form 3 and 4 commercial-stream girls with the highest price to be paid by anyone from the professional stream. The two rabbits were to be fattened up prior to their sale to the Home Economics teacher who was widely respected for the excellence of her braised rabbit casserole cooked in port.

This final aspect of the business plan was, however, doomed from the outset. The two rabbits quickly became class mascots and in a moving ceremony, under a large pine tree that shielded the vegie patch, they were duly anointed with the names of Arthur and Martha; two lovely old-fashioned names that blended in well with those of their keepers and which, coincidentally, matched those of the school's Principal and senior mistress. My self-esteem received a much needed boost and thoughts of an imminent career change began to subside. Even the Principal started to recognise me whenever our paths crossed, which made a welcome change.

It was a decision made by the Student Teacher Council that brought my improving status to a screaming halt – or, more appropriately, a squealing halt. In their combined wisdom the members of the STC decided to run an end of term mega fair, another 1990s term for what 4G described at the time as 'a bloody big carnival, mate'. Then, as now, such fundraisers required groups of students to set up, stock and run a stall or organise some sort of game or activity for the big day. The boys were adamant. There would be no craft stalls or spinning wheels for them. No, they would use their emerging entrepreneurial spirit to do something bigger and better, but above all, completely different. With what I suspected at the time was undue haste, they unanimously opted for a greasy pig chase, just like the one Norm and Spider had seen recently at the Dromana drive-in theatre, in that 'grouse Yankee picture with John Wayne'.

All ideas for the fair had to be vetted by the Vice-Principal and I had serious reservations about the acceptability of a greasy pig chase. As expected, he was very dubious about it, but eventually said yes. I would like to think that his decision was influenced by the success of 4G's agri-business, but I suspect that it was most strongly affected by his forthcoming long service leave, and the knowledge that he would be miles away, fishing on the Murray, during the end of term festivities.

The boys quickly put their evolving time and resource management skills into action. Phil's dad, a tractor repairer of considerable local repute, had plenty of grease to donate to the cause. Norm could, as he so aptly put it, 'lay his hands on some chook wire' for the pig run and Frank assured us he could rustle up (which, on recollection, I fear is exactly what he did) the most important item of all – the pig. With only two weeks left before the fair, all aspects of the agri-business suffered severe neglect as the boys diverted their energies to the construction of a 30 yard run and two pig holding pens, one at each end of the chicken wire enclosed run.

Almost before we realised it, fair day arrived. The fact that it was a Friday the 13th should've, but didn't, register with any of us, such was the build-up of excitement and anticipation surrounding 4G's latest venture.

The morning preparations had been well organised and went all too smoothly. Freddo Frog, so named because of his distinctive hopping gait and to distinguish him from 4G's other two Freds, co-opted his brother to chauffeur the pig to school in the back of his ute. A rather large and unappealing sow, it was secured by rope to a stake dug into the ground and in close proximity to the gleaming new pig run. The sow's new home was also right alongside the rabbit hutch and vegetable patch. As planned, several of the boys applied a more than liberal coating of grease to the pig during morning recess. Frank Gadsby (or the 'Great Gadsby' as he was referred to by his long-suffering English teacher) volunteered to be the pig's head keeper, and absented himself from the two periods after recess in order to keep the star attraction company and attend to any last-minute preparations.

Of course rabbits are always hungry, but after two weeks of neglect and reduced rations, Arthur and Martha were more than just hungry. The sight of two ripe lettuces in the vegie patch on that fateful morning had them salivating at the prospect of lunching on their succulent, fresh leaves. For the first time in their, until recently, pampered captivity, the rabbits plotted their escape.

Their frantic burrowing out of Stalag Hutch 17 soon aroused the curiosity of the nearby sow, who by now was also in a state of some agitation. She was quite used to being covered in mud, but being greased from head to toe was another matter entirely. Her faithful keeper was nearby and busily engaged in erecting a large sign. The sign, hand-painted on one of his mum's best double sheets, invited one and all to 'The Ultimate Chase – Get a Grip on the Greasy Pig and Win a Bonzer Prize'. Frank's attention, easily diverted at the best of times, was well and truly focused on this important task, so it was understandable that he failed to notice the sow wrench her tethering stake out of the ground at almost the same moment as the rabbits emerged from their escape tunnel. But before Arthur and Martha could, if you will excuse the expression, 'pig out' on the lettuce, they were startled by the sight and sound of the sow rushing to join them. Their appetite suddenly gone and in fear of their lives, they bolted. In a blind panic they headed due south towards the main school building. The pig, under the mistaken illusion that the rabbits knew the best way out of their predicament, naturally followed them.

By now, Master Francis Gadsby, Official Keeper of the Swine, was well aware of the mass escape and its portent for disaster – or worse! Abandoning his mum's sheet to flap deliriously in the strengthening sea breeze, the Great Gadsby took off in hot pursuit of the errant pig and the two fleeing rabbits.

Arthur, Martha and the sow were now rapidly approaching the North Wing, the doors of which were invitingly wide open. The three steps leading up to the door were hurdled with ease by both rabbits – they seemed to fly over the freshly polished linoleum of the corridor like two small furry hovercraft hell-bent for the coast. Not so the pig. Her much greater bulk and greased trotters did not prevent her from successfully negotiating the entrance steps, but the polished linoleum produced a long and dramatic slide – one that Joe Di Maggio would have been proud of. In fact, her slide to first base was only terminated by her crashing into a bank of metal lockers. By the time the nearest teachers and some of their students had come out into the corridor to investigate the cause of the crash, this 'Greasy Joe' had regained her equilibrium and was off again after the rabbits.

The Great Gadsby, meanwhile, more used to being pursued than a pursuer, had done well to keep the three escapees in his sight. Racing past the astonished teachers and students, he could see, up ahead, that Arthur and Martha were almost at the T-intersection at the end of the corridor. Here the two rabbits decided to confuse the determined posse behind them by splitting up. Perhaps they too had seen John Wayne employ this tactic successfully at the Dromana drive-in. Martha turned right, while Arthur veered left towards the school's office and administration section. A split-second decision was also needed by the pig – right or left?

Instinctively, and perhaps because it was preordained, the sow turned left and raced after Arthur into what the late race caller Bill Collins would have accurately described as porcine immortality. Frank, several lengths behind, had no such choice – after all, his main quarry was the fugitive pig.

As Arthur neared the administration offices, he could see a group of students further along the corridor blocking his preferred escape route. Reaching the small foyer in front of the offices, he espied an alternative, a door that was slightly ajar. Arthur probably did not see the sign on this door which read 'The Principal, Knock Before Entering', but even if he did, he was in no state to observe such formalities. Through the gap in the door he darted, and under the largest piece of furniture in the room – a regulation Departmental desk of sizeable proportions. Motionless for the first time since absconding from the hutch, and his heart pounding, Arthur prayed that his temporary haven would at least give him some brief respite from the rigours of the chase.

The pursuing pig had observed Arthur's forced detour and sensing that the end of her valiant quest was near, started squealing even more loudly. She also failed to knock as requested prior to her own dramatic entry into the office. Instead, she allowed her considerable momentum to be abruptly halted by the bulk of the desk. The desk was no match for the well-fed corpulence of the pig and was jerked viciously back towards the rear wall, upturning the chair behind it in the process. This rearrangement of the office furniture exposed a distressed and convulsively twitching Arthur. The sow, now completely exhausted and dripping torrents of sweat and grease, summoned one last supreme effort. Panting heavily, she spread-eagled her lathered bulk onto the twitching Arthur. It was at this point that Frank, with a small delegation of teachers, curious students and a school secretary close behind him, entered the Principal's office.

To this day, more than thirty years later, Frank has no

recollection of Arthur making good his escape from the chaos of that room. Much more vivid in Frank's memory is the sight that befell him on bursting into that office: a greased and profusely sweating pig, flopped prostrate in exhaustion beside an upturned chair and thereby effectively pinning into whimpering submission the school's other Arthur – the Principal! A signed statement prepared later that day (for the Principal's hastily arranged inquiry into what he called simply 'The Incident') confirmed what several had witnessed. Arthur the rabbit, choosing the precise moment well, and taking advantage of Frank's sudden entrance into the room, darted right through the boy's permanently bowed legs into the foyer and to the freedom that lay beyond.

THE LESSON

Sheila Duke

Whack!
 Whack!
  Whack!
The sound was no worse than the pain, yet no one flinched. Not even the new girl. Finally Sister Cyril stopped. Maybe she was worn out. Her arm mysteriously drooped by her side. The gleam had vanished from her eyes. No one spoke.

'Go back to your seats and I hope that will be a lesson to you. And take that smirk off your face, Sarah Byrne, or you'll get some more.' Sister Cyril still had the energy to scream.

But what was the lesson? How to hit people with a strap? How to line up the girls and belt the living daylights out of them in front of the boys? How to exercise your arm?

And why? A lesson in punctuality? A lesson for watching the Sun Bike Tour?

Anna, the new girl, looked confused. Obviously she didn't know what the lesson was either. Maybe there'll be a test tomorrow to see if we've remembered it. I certainly won't forget the belting but I'm still not sure what part of the curriculum the lesson came under. Silently we went back to our seats.

'Get out your writing books and write one hundred times, "I must not be late for school",' said Sister C.

This was pretty easy once you knew how many pages made up 100 lines. Then you could write all the words vertically. That saved time.

I glanced over at Anna and caught her looking at me.

'Get your book out and write, "I must not be late for school",' I whispered.

She sat holding her pencil and looking at her book. I mouthed the words again. Slowly. Still she sat.

'Sister, why isn't Anna writing?' This was from the class dobber, goody-goody, teacher's pet. Every class had one. They were the ones who brought flowers to Sister every Monday and volunteered to empty the bins. Yuk.

Sister Cyril stormed over, her face looking like thunder.

'Start writing at once and why aren't you looking at me when I'm talking to you?' Anna's lip trembled.

Why doesn't she write? I thought. I even prayed which I only did in an extreme emergency.

'Please write, Anna,' I begged St Theresa, my favourite saint of the week. I tried to show her my writing when Sister C wasn't looking. Maybe Anna was deaf. Then I grabbed her book and quickly wrote, 'I must not be late for school'. With many hand movements I tried to get her to copy the words. But she just sat with her head in her hands looking at her book. Sister C didn't seem to notice any more.

Finally the bell rang and we could escape. We walked out and got on our bikes.

'Anna, we don't always get a belting. And you were very brave not crying, especially on your second day. Anyway it was great seeing the cyclists, wasn't it? We were only ten minutes late. Wait till I tell my mum and dad. About the belting, I mean. They saw the cyclists too. In fact, everyone in town must have been there. I don't normally tell them about beltings but I think my mum will notice the marks on my legs, this time.

'Anna, why are you crying?'

Anna turned her face away, but I could see. Tears glistening on her cheeks. I looked the other way and nearly ran into a post.

'Anna, let's pretend we're in the Sun Tour. I'll race you to the corner.'

I sped down the dirt road, plaits flying and school bag flapping against my hip. I loved pedalling as fast as I could, dodging the potholes. There weren't many cars to worry about.

'I won,' I yelled. To no one.

I looked round. Anna was still slowly cycling along, head bent.

Oh, well, when she learns how to speak English I guess she'll be able to race me, I thought. Funny thing was, I hadn't realised until now that she probably hadn't understood a word I'd said. Anyone had said. Bet she understood the belting, though. A belting's the same in any language. But I still don't know why she was crying.

Then I remembered what my dad said last night. We were having our tea: lamb chops, mashed potato, peas and carrots. Followed by ice-cream and tinned peaches. And washing up. Dad talked pretty slowly as if he had all the time in the world. He often told us great stories. But he looked sort of sad, so I knew this story was for real.

'That new family are living out the Bogie road. Hear they come from Poland. Been in Bonegilla for a while. Must be glad to be here after what they've been through. Poor buggers.'

Anna didn't seem too glad to be here.

Fatemah arrived late again. She had been at school for a few days. Her hair was tousled, her eyes red-rimmed. And no, she did not have a note. Or even an excuse to say why she was late. Fatemah knew I never asked any more. What was the point when no one at her home spoke English? And when would they have had time to write a note? Fatemah had to get her sister up and ready for school, as well as herself, and make something – if she could find it – for lunch. And walk to school. No extra money for buses in that family.

Having both parents on shift work at the local factory can't be all that easy. At least she was here. Just as well as today was the day we were visiting Parliament House and having a tour of Canberra.

'Why do you wear a veil, Fatemah? asked Yuso.

'Yes,' Fatemah answered. Some of the children smiled. A few giggled.

'Don't raugh. Lemember when we were new.' Yumiko always brought the class into line. She even took over from me if I was out of the room for a few minutes.

'Why you write from back of book, Ali?'

'Why you not go swimming, Faezah?'

'Why you not look at teacher, Trang?'

'Why not you talk to Miss Byrne, Ling?'

'Why you eat with chopsticks, Kusaki?'

'Why you get under desk when siren goes for playtime, Mohammad?'

Why? Why? Why?

'I think Fatemah has just a few words of English and one of them is, "Yes", but she doesn't yet understand any questions,' I said.

Yumiko took Fatemah by the hand and got in line for the bus.

The trip didn't take long. We filed in through the security check. Gasps of amazement came from the children. None had been to Parliament House.

'Prime Minister live here?'

'Why it called House?'

'Wow.'

'Too big.'

'*Shit!*'

A group of elderly tourists looked around in amazement. Eddison's expletive described most things, good or bad. I was happy that he was talking at all.

'Where are all these children from, dear?' asked one lady with a blue rinse. They gathered round, marble pillars and possible sightings of politicians forgotten, cameras directed at this unique group of children.

'Everywhere. Great, isn't it?' I answered.

'Miss Byrne, why that lady have blue hair?'

'Why, indeed, Joses.'

A Place for the Living

Wendy Ratawa

Some aspects of remembering are like stings of a scorpion: sharp, hurting, and so sudden that palpitations start and the body sweats. As the stings subside, the memory is pushed back into darkness.

Other memories are less violent. A large spotted cowrie shell, when tucked up to an ear, can suggest the muffled rush of water, the purr of the ocean, and nothing is more beautiful than Fiji's coral reefs.

I remember Davuilevu Methodist compound as a life-affirming environment, a place for the living. Then, I remember something dreadful happened there.

I was going through photos kept from the time I taught in Fiji, at two schools particularly – Dudley High School, the prestigious girls' boarding school in Suva, and Lelean Memorial School, the co-ed school at Davuilevu set in lush pastoral land near the Rewa River. My view of the world was then refracted through rose-tinted glasses, seeing only good will and laughter, as I embraced the Pacific people with lightness and affection and loved teaching the Fijian and Indian children there.

I was an adventurer, attached like a limpet to some of the indigenous families, spending weekends and holidays with them, mesmerised in an exploration of the local cultures. 'Here comes Waltzing Matilda,' some would say. In the villages and farms of students, I practised a childish version of the local languages, was at ease in simple clothes and ate exotic food. I'd left Bendigo High School when I was twenty-three. It was the years of folk music, the Global Village concept, where unwashed Western youth travelled freely in search of ethnic adventures. I fitted into those criteria.

I met many expatriates in Fiji – the Swiss tart who slept with Indian men, the New Zealand doctor who lived in a slum full of books, the two English maidens who taught lessons on a badly tuned piano, the American girl who married a Fijian chief three times her age. I was an artist/art teacher constrained by religion and obligation, yet freed by imagination, transient as a gypsy.

I had wanted to change the world, shake the waters, leap into the Boeing jet at Melbourne to teach black-eyed adolescents and send them on their way alert and courageous. In hindsight, I was opinionated, colonial, and imposed a Christian framework.

'The jolly lady!' an Indian family called me.

'Always full of ideas for the youth group.' An urban church.

'A good art teacher!' students said. 'And gives away her paintings.'

I accepted the Methodist Mission rules, and they were part of the compromise.

I remember Davuilevu with its sign near the bus-stop, highly decorated with a logo of a conch shell. I used to stroll up the track, sandals slapping the mud, feeling the heat wrap my body, and look in amazement at the intensity of the colour of the palms and mango trees, and then see the imposing stone Baker Memorial Church on the highest hill where Years 7 and 8 were taught. Despite the moist, enveloping atmosphere I was energetic, teaching forty to a class, in the cement-block buildings. I lived in a large wooden bungalow called Veitalacagi – Place of the Winds – with three missionary women; and we looked after the Fijian girls boarding nearby. At Davuilevu I made friends with theological students, visited other teachers in wooden houses tucked into hillsides, painted landscapes at weekends, played the organ in a church, became an aunt to girls in an orphanage.

The students were earnest for an education, and at that time barely questioned the political system of colonialism and hierarchical social structures. Fiji was still a British colony and paternalism from expatriate teachers was the norm.

Davuilevu had the status of a life-affirming place with high ideals. Despite the moral rectitude of the Methodist environment, Davuilevu was also a place of laughter, joking and teasing in the interplay of Hindi, Fijian and English languages. Morning and night the boarders cleaned the hillsides of weeds and long grass, slashing with their cane-knives, and they would often sing in harmony.

It was here that an unthinkable thing happened to Phyllis, the Principal of Lelean Memorial School.

I knew Phyllis over nine years, first as Principal of Dudley High School before she became Principal of Lelean Memorial School; a prestigious girls' boarding school in Suva, different from Davuilevu because it was at the end of an untidy street of shabby, crowded bungalows, unpainted, cement-block houses and *kava* saloons. The inner suburb of Toorak had seen better days. There was a sensuousness about the suburb with the call to prayer at the mosque, choir practices in the hall opposite, the smell of coconut oil, spices and curry, the majesty of flame trees, bougainvillea creepers, and the physical beauty of the people.

Dudley High School had about 600 students from Year 7 to Year 12 then, the school named after an Australian, Hannah Dudley, who had worked in Fiji at the turn of the century.

Phyllis had left her home in Queensland aged about twenty-one, though she never talked to me about her life in Australia before becoming a missionary/teacher. She was Principal of Dudley for ten years, a task thrust upon her at the age of twenty-eight.

When I first taught there as an art teacher, it was a women's world, with hundreds of Indian and Fijian boarders, four

Australians and two Indian women and we shared hostel duties. I had a tiny curtained-off room beside a sitting room shared with Phyllis. My bedroom space was about seven feet by seven feet, even smaller than my childhood cubby, barely big enough for a bed with mosquito net, a cupboard and my radio. Phyllis had a similar bedroom cubicle nearby at the end of the dormitory wing. The other residential teachers lived in a wooden bungalow built on an escarpment with steep steps down to a winding road. Meals for the staff were cooked by an elderly Indian man, often roti and curry or rice and lentils. We supervised the boarders' meals, dormitories, prep and chapel each night, Sunday afternoon strolls to get exercise, and vetted visitors very carefully. Girls could go out on Saturday afternoons with relatives. The boarders cleaned the compound with caneknives, helped cook meals, and on Saturday mornings a teacher and six girls would walk down to the Suva market to buy enough vegetables for the week, returning by taxi. There was a puritanism and order there which defied the 1960s and '70s elsewhere.

Phyllis was a thin, angular woman with a triangular face, and her black hair, cut short in the back, fell in heavy waves in front. Her eyes were dark brown and her black eyebrows almost met. She wore modest sleeveless shifts or white shirts and calf-length skirts, and sturdy sandals. No one wore stockings or pantihose there because of the heat. She would move about quickly, often with her head down, walking as if on a relentless errand. The responsibilities dominated her life – as Principal of the school, including the boarders.

Her voice was deep and pleasant, and she spoke in a middle-class manner. She would not gossip or engage in small talk, and never raised her voice, but students cowered when confronted over an error of judgement. Teachers too felt the distance because of her status and her high standards.

Perhaps, underneath the persona, she was a vulnerable person who had to overcome her reticence. Her close friends were other female missionaries experienced in leadership and education, motivated with the same idealism not just to convert people to the foreign religion, but to provide education for girls in Fiji where female roles were usually prescribed and women were subservient to the patriarchy.

Dudley School had an excellent reputation and many students went on to further study. Many of leading Fiji women today – in politics, women's welfare, hospitals, schools, commerce – were educated at Dudley. We didn't talk about feminism in those days, but the school aim was to facilitate opportunities for young women to access careers. Also, in an all-female environment, there wasn't the bother of girls or female staff deferring to men.

Phyllis actively encouraged innovations in education, expecting the staff to use modern teaching methods. She inspired me to be an adaptable teacher in Art, Music and History and she said she valued my particular expertise because specialist teachers were rare in Fiji at the time.

Because of her high moral standards based on Methodist church criteria at the time, and the expectations of parents to keep their daughters 'safe', Phyllis could be severe. Friendships with young men were tabu and Phyllis felt her duty was to keep these girls pure, away from predatory men. A pretty young Indian girl was expelled for receiving amorous letters from a boy. Then an explicitly sexual photo found in a classroom desk led to a phone call and another expulsion. But there was also compassion when Phyllis dealt with homesickness among the boarders, or illness, or first menstrual periods of the younger girls.

Phyllis was enthusiastic about sport and I remember a Learn to Swim campaign at the school because most Indian girls could not swim. Phyllis and I walked them down to Suva Sea Baths once a week for two months. Despite the shrill screams and awkwardness, they eventually gained a life skill needed in the islands. And there was hockey, tennis and netball on Saturdays.

Phyllis and I consulted on teaching world music – from Indonesia, China, Pakistan, France – opening the listening ears of the students to a celebration of difference, always aware of the Indian cultural background of most of the students. I remember teaching a song loved by Gandhi:

> *Raghupati raghava Raja Ram*
> *Pati ta paban Seeta Ram*
> *Eeswara Allah tere nam*
> *Sab ko san moti de bhagwan*

Though English was the medium of education, Phyllis wanted the girls to be fluent in their 'home' languages of Hindustani and Fijian. Also, traditional dances were rehearsed and performed at special school events, held outside under the mango and banyan trees. Hundreds of students in their purple and white uniforms watched graceful Indian dancing or Fijian *meke*.

Phyllis did not share her feelings and intimate thoughts readily but she was sensitive to the staff. One lunchtime when I received news of the death of a friend, and had walked like a zombie into my needlework class, Phyllis came in and took over. 'I've just heard. You take the afternoon off and go and visit the relatives.' While I waltzed through weekends and holidays visiting Sikh dairy farms, helped with weddings and rites of passage, stayed in Fijian villages and sugarcane farms, Phyllis was too busy to do these easygoing things, too absorbed with funding, planning, committees, building programs, fee structures.

The Methodist church officials and the parents respected Miss Furnivall. Her assigned role meant that Phyllis spent most of her waking hours in administration, or preparing and marking work. Yes, she did take classes – prep, Bible studies – and not just sit in an office. On Sundays she walked the boarders down

Amy Street to the Dudley Methodist Church, the girls white-bright in their frocks and veils. As Phyllis cared for others, who cared for Phyllis? The church committees praised hardworking women like her but forgot their pastoral responsibilities for their burnt-out workers. The only reprieve for Phyllis was a rare holiday walking in the rainforest, climbing over misting hilltops, with two or three friends. In quiet moments at the weekends, she used to sit in a cane chair, legs stretched out, her eyes closed, immersed in Beethoven records.

My closest friend at Dudley was Margaret, a missionary from Perth. She was soft and feminine, and though a serious teacher, she could also laugh and confide, 'Phyllis knows, I bet she knows, about the hanky-panky between you and your boyfriend! But go ahead. Get yourself out of this place!' Telephone calls were on a shared line, so colleagues in the hostel overheard the breathless chatter between lovers.

The last time I spoke with Phyllis was when I was preparing to leave Dudley. I was sitting on a log sucking on a mango, resting after the walk up Amy Street to the school compound. I was dressed in a cheesecloth top and tie-dyed wraparound skirt, a happy lark those days.

Phyllis came up to me and said, 'Are you really leaving us to be married?'

That was the only time she remarked on my choice to leave the school. She made me feel I had let the side down by choosing intimacy with the man I loved rather than continue as a single full-time teacher.

Four years later the Methodist Church conference appointed Phyllis to Lelean Memorial School at Davuilevu. She had made Dudley into the finest school in Suva, but a church conference rule decreed that a principal must move on after nine years.

On the last day of the next school year Phyllis was murdered in the night.

On that day most of the boarders would have packed their

bags, bundled their bedding together inside pandanus mats and walked to the road to catch buses to Suva to go to relatives or home to their farms, villages and islands. A few theological students and couples would still be staying in their quarters, some teachers in their bungalows, two or three ministers or lecturers in their hilltop houses. The compound would have been emptying quickly as hundreds of its inhabitants left Davuilevu to the quietude of the summer holidays. Most people would have wanted to get home for Christmas, catch inter-island trading ketches. Some would have been leaving for the last time, such as Year 12 students or teachers on transfer, and at least one expatriate would have been going overseas.

Was it a theft gone wrong? This was unlikely, as missionaries had little money or possessions. An intentional act based on hatred and revenge? A sexual attack by youths and a cover-up?

I cannot forget that news bulletin. 'The Lelean School Principal, Miss Phyllis Furnivall, has been murdered in her own flat. The attacker as yet unknown.' Next day the *Fiji Times* splashed details on the front pages. Three pages of the mutilating knife wounds on her breasts, a knife taken from her kitchen in the flat where she had lived alone.

At Davuilevu, a safe mission compound. That place for living, for hopes and idealism.

Once before a missionary had been killed on duty. Rev Thomas Baker had been trekking into the interior of Viti Levu amid hostile tribes and was clubbed because of a cultural misunderstanding and political manoeuvring between chiefs. A hundred years ago, though. The Baker Memorial Church was built on a hill within view of Phyllis's flat. The Fijians composed songs of remembrance about Baker. Would they do the same for Phyllis?

In the days that followed there were rumours and speculation that she had enemies – not women, but men who were demeaned in the school situation by her demands and discipline, uneasy over having a woman as Principal over male teachers. Was there also a small shift in attitude to the colonial imprint on Fiji as local people asserted themselves against paternalism? Fiji had become independent from Britain in October that year, though without excessive display.

A Lelean teacher, waiting at Nadi airport to board a flight to New Zealand, was stopped by the police. He looked different as he had shaven off his beard. The police questioned him for four days. He was one of the last to be seen near her house. He and Phyllis had argued several times during the year, they said, over his personal habits and drinking with senior students.

An Australian expatriate was interviewed, whose wife had died in peculiar circumstances. Older students were interrogated, particularly the last ones to leave on that fatal day, the final day of term. Was the murderer a local person or a foreigner? Was there more than one person involved?

Shanti, a young female Indian teacher, had stayed with Phyllis during the last week of term but had left that afternoon. Was she involved? No, the police said, that was unthinkable because of the medical evidence. A woman could not have done this, they said.

The largest Protestant church in Suva was overflowing with more than three thousand people – students, former students, church leaders, civil servants, members of the Dudley church, and teachers such as me. (At that time I was teaching Year 10 English part-time, was married, had two toddlers, and lived in the small sugarcane district of Rakiraki, 50 kilometres from Suva.)

The funeral was not the kind we want to remember. We were still in shock. I found it difficult to talk to her brother who had come over from Australia, and felt awkward with Phyllis's intimate friends. We felt ashamed, somehow implicated, in a society where horrible things happened.

The Furnivall Park was named in memory of Phyllis: a large sportsground shared by three schools. Scars remained after the failure in the system, the lack of protection for a female member of staff. Up to that time I had naively believed that God protected those who were called to serve, that there was a mantle of safety.

Police inquiries over the years involving investigations overseas were fruitless. A young Fijian man, in prison for several offences, confessed to her murder, but he was never charged. He had resided on and off at St Giles Psychiatric Hospital, so his confession was not taken seriously.

I still do not know why it happened.

That place, Davuilevu, was for living, but I remember what happened there and when my pink-tinged glasses fell off.

The death was like a cusp leading to a changed viewpoint, not yet to cynicism, but to a dismay about our social world. The military coups in Fiji did the same thing to other people several years later.

There was a shift in perception, like a tremor from an earthquake, when things were felt to be askew. A trusting reciprocal relationship between strangers shifted to caution, and distancing. Now there was an awareness of undercurrents of violence in Fiji, a place I had once considered a paradise.

Acting Up

Lyndall Hough

Would you like to be Acting Deputy?
When do you want to know?
Yesterday.

I believe women should take opportunities presented, be good role models, go for the extra money, etc., but do I fancy getting up at 6.00 am? Copping all the whingeing from fifty-five staff and 800 kids? Do I want this? All my friends say I should when I ring around and ask them that night, so the next day I say yes. Anyway, I should do it I reason, without any real reason for doing so.

I do it for three months, dragging myself out of bed at 5.30 am. I arrive at school, the currawongs carolling, the kookaburras cackling, the water glistening in the distance. Then I take the messages from the answer phone. Mainly they are from staff too sick to come to work. Then I start dialling number after number at 7.30 am.

Good morning, Celia Faite, Acting Deputy from Fabbo High School here. Are you available for casual work today?

A child, obviously employed for this purpose by its mother, and inept at lying, says, I'm sorry, she's not in today, sorry she's sick today, sorry she's got another job for six years, sorry she just left, sorry she can't get a babysitter at such short notice. I often hear the voice in the background instructing the younger voice. Or they are simply unavailable, already employed by an earlier more efficient Deputy.

Dial dial dial your phone. At last. Sure, I'll come, but I live at Outer Black Stump South and I travel by public transport and I can't get there until after first period is that okay? It's fine I reply, relieved to make contact with a living breathing body that will stand in front of a class at short notice. I make a mental note to check phone digits and suburbs and ring up people close to the school.

I have a large sheet on which to enter each individual casual teacher's name above the absent one, fill in their teaching duties for the day plus rollcall plus playground duties, make copies in triplicate for the administration head and the secretaries to type up and distribute on the absentee sheets which will be delivered by hand to fifty-five staff before 9.30 am.

The staff begin to arrive.

Hello, sorry to disturb you. I was just wondering if you'd enter these twenty Higher School Certificate Assessment music tasks onto the planner board in your office? Hello, sorry to disturb you, but would you enter the Rubella Vaccination, Red Cross Calling, and Scoliosis checks in your diary under these dates and put them in the green sheet for tomorrow's notices and put them on the planner board? Hello, I've got a specialist's appointment at lunchtime but I don't think it will finish in time and I've got a class after lunch and I was wondering if you . . .

One of the staff comes in and stares unblinking at what I'm doing for about five minutes. Who is away, he wants to know. Why are they away he wants to know even more. He doesn't get a response from me, keeps staring, unblinking, and finally says, oh well, see you, and walks out. It unnerved me at first, but now I ignore it.

Children of both sexes appear. Seventy-two of them line up outside my office. Miss, the bus was late and we need late bus passes. Okay line up, say your name and take the ticket. I write out seventy-two passes.

After they go, the really late ones turn up all bleary-eyed. Miss, my dog, my grandmother, my car died yesterday, last night, on the way to school. Miss, my sister keeps turning off the alarm clock, I slept at my mother's house last night, my father's house last night, I had to go for my driver's licence, the orthodontist, the osteopath, my little sister's throat . . .

Miss, could I have a uniform pass because the dog chewed my shoes, my mother washed my shirt, it rained yesterday and I haven't got a uniform thing to wear except these $200 Reeboks, Levis and stunning shirt topped off with a $90 haircut and this superb make-up job.

Hello, I'm just ringing to say my son daughter, won't be in today because she he's got a sore throat, asthma, acute scabies, Ebola virus and she he's been under the doctor for a week and doesn't feel well enough to come to school. I just thought I'd call and let you know.

Miss, can I go to sick bay because I've got a headache (ie Maths is on now), I've got a stomach-ache (ie PE is on now) and a bee stung me and I'm really allergic to them and last time it was really serious.

What happened when the bee stung you last time?

It swolled up and I had to get a tetanus shot.

Uh huh. I ask the woman in charge of the boys' clinic to deal with the tetanus-bearing beesting.

Okay, you sick boys, just line up, sign in here, and go and lie down there.

I find the administration head teacher lying down on the boys' sick bay bed (without a boy, thank God). I almost join him but you'd have to see him to understand he's not my type.

Hello is that the Deputy? I'm inquiring about the Science Computing Cooking Typing Ant Farm expert you advertised for in the *Herald*.

Yes, quite so. Could you just give us your details and send in your resumé made up by someone you don't know, about things you never did and skills you could never possibly achieve and for which you paid a great deal of money? Good, post it to the school, then if you get an interview, the Principal will choose the woman with blonde hair who most resembles his wife and the staff will gossip endlessly about it.

You're a male? Good heavens, don't let that put you off applying. Perhaps if you take some oestrogen for the week leading up to the interview?

Hello, is that the Deputy? Look it's Grant from Science here. I'm not feeling well, the alcohol and drugs and sex I had last night are taking their toll. I've told the kids I feel crook and they said they'd just pitch in and get on with the work quietly and not disturb anyone or swing from the fans, or spit on the board all afternoon so I'll just go home if that's okay.

Sure, Grant. He won't see the complaints in quadruplicate from the cleaner who has to deal with the trashed room.

Excuse me, Acting Deputy, I was wondering if you could just interview this boy and get some statements from him and the witnesses. Yes, apparently he beat up a girl on the bus yesterday afternoon. The police have been called, and it's none of our business and we can't do anything about it because it wasn't on school premises but we need to know what happened and the girl's mother has complained.

Doesn't she know what an underprivileged, difficult childhood he's had? That kid's had to live with a yuppie barrister mother and a herbalist father in a three-level waterfront home in one of the trendiest suburbs in Sydney. Where is that mother's compassion? Doesn't she see the years of therapy he's in for?

Hello? Wayne the Principal here. Look I want you to get up completely calmly in three minutes' time and talk to 800 students, maintaining your credibility in front of the rest of the staff, and explain how unbelievably attractive the school uniform is if you wear it every day, the value of staying home and studying Saturday nights, and how much better they'd feel if they all studied in groups at lunchtime, while also discussing homework and other soul-improving ideas. And have you finished the assembly roster, the playground duty roster, the bus roster and the prawns al la Costa?

And would you like to be Acting *Principal* tomorrow? Let me know yesterday, okay?

Well I believe women should take opportunities presented, be good role models, go for the extra money, etc., so without bothering to consult with my friends I say yes. I dress in my upwardly mobile white linen suit with Boeing 747 shoulder pads and I sit at the desk where no other woman has sat in thirty-five years and I answer the phone. Head Teacher English, Acting Deputy, Acting Principal here. Yes we have trouble with late buses, late grandparents, late periods, unwanted pregnancies. I'll ring the bus company and complain. Thank you for calling.

Umm excuse me, chief secretary no.1 but why is that ambulance out there? Oh. Could you get an accident report in triplicate for me with witnesses' signatures? Thanks. Yes, come in. Look I can't actually do anything about that right now, I'm the Acting Principal, Acting Deputy actually, and I'm doing a pretty good job of acting sympathetically don't you think? Would you like a tissue? Yes, I know he said he won't enrol your son. It's because he thinks he's psychotic and will kill some of our less aggressive students. You do understand, don't you? I knew you would. Umm excuse me a minute.

Why hasn't that ambulance left yet? It's the second one? Did what? My god. Get another set of triplicates, you know what to do. Yes, goodbye. Thanks for calling in and begging. No, you keep the tissues. Yes, good morning, sorry who did you say . . . did you have an appointment? Oh, no . . . he went in the ambulance. Local hospital I think. I can't imagine why they asked you to come here. Yes there's been a communication breakdown and I'm sorry you had to get out of the pool to come over, but perhaps you'd like to follow the ambulance to the hospital and see how he is. I know it's silly and seems trivial to you but we put the life of the child first and Grandma's swimming second. Yes, I realise it's terribly inconvenient for you. No, I'm afraid you can't see him at the moment, he's not here. You see, I'm the Acting Principal.

The Acting Deputy's job is looking very attractive. And after all, a female bum hasn't been on that seat for thirty-five years, either. So, I'll still be breaking new ground.

IF NO ONE CARES FOR ME

Helen Gordon

... And this the burthen of his song,
forever us'd to be
I care for nobody, no not I,
If no one cares for me

('LOVE IN A VILLAGE') ISAAC BICKERSTAFFE 1735–1812

'Of course I knew them better,' I expostulated over the inevitable toast and marmalade discussion of current practice versus earlier practice. 'There were thirty-five of them, not two hundred. *Of course* I knew each of them better than a Year Adviser can know most of her two hundred.' I felt pretty passionate about this, and his indifferent attitude was rapidly making me itch.

'I saw them twice a day for four years, for heaven's sake. They knew from the first day that I was their special teacher, and that I would take care of them as if I loved them, even if I didn't. It was called Pastoral Care, if that means anything to you, and it meant me, you, every one of us, not somebody with a title and a special allowance. If there had been such things as role statements in those days it would have been listed as a basic duty, and as such attracting no additional money.'

His toast was all gone by now and mine was cold. Irritatingly, he said nothing. He waited for me to wind myself up.

'After a few weeks I *did* love them anyway, and they knew it. When I had playground duty they followed me around like a pop idol, and in class they menaced any individual defecting from the behaviour standard they'd decided to deliver. Every other teacher in their timetable complained bitterly about their behaviour, but I could never see why.'

'The current system works just as well, and with less pain,' said my husband the seconded Departmental Suit. 'They have a Year Adviser with more responsibility and a rollcall teacher with less contact and less responsibility. And your precious first roll-class sounds more like a Godfather's Mafia gang than a fairy godmother's flock.'

He poured himself some more coffee – black, of course – a Departmental Suit needs his drive well-stimulated. 'They probably collected the money for your present from other people's roll-classes by making them an offer they couldn't refuse. I know it's Sunday, but I have to go to the office for a while.'

And laconic as ever he left. He left the discussion (without losing a point), the dishes, and me feeling both angry and nostalgic.

I went to the drinks cabinet and looked at the present in question. After thirty-one years' use it was reduced from six water glasses to two. It had originally been accompanied by a large matching jug, now no doubt enjoying a recycled life as a wine bottle or some other functional object. The two survivors, though not labelled, were now acknowledged as not for use – sacrosanct. They served the same purpose as the not-yet-sacrosanct two-dimensional stone sculpture from Les Baux, the thick china coffee bowl from Mont Saint Michel, the porcelain liqueur service from Budapest: instant, total recall. I sat down, picked up one glass, and let it turn back the clock.

It was towards the end of their first year. They were in the library with me. In the library for which I was allowed a three-period-per-week management allowance. In the small, loved, but unresourced library where one ageing work on Papua New Guinea was considered sufficient until the Whitlam cabinet came to visit several years later. They were listening attentively to me reading selections from Elyne Mitchell's latest, Ivan Southall's latest, H.F. Brinsmead's first, Ethel Turner's classics. They were laughing nicely at my crummy jokes; they were being real people. They rose as one when the District Inspector walked in, uninvited and unexpected.

'Good afternoon, 1Z,' said Mr Jones.

'Good afternoon, sir,' they chorused in the stilted tones of a religious chant, thought appropriate for the occasion.

'I'll just sit over here till you're finished,' he said. 'I don't want to disturb your lesson.'

1Z believed him. They weren't equipped to do anything else. So they sat down and went on laughing at my jokes, borrowed a book each, and went to their next lesson, clattering and jeering at each other like a real pre-TV family.

'Now,' said Mr Jones in his colourless way, 'they seem to like being here, but they behave exceptionally well. Can you explain that?'

I had to take my time. The Suits were different in those days. Always men, they were men to be feared, not trusted. Their suits were baggy, with shiny patches, and they wore hand-knitted sleeveless vests over their starched blue shirts. Their sleeves might be held up with spring-steel bands. Silk club ties were unheard-of. They had no style but they had real power. They wouldn't sack you, because the Department had paid for your training and was determined to get its money's worth, but they could have you moved to Woolgoolga starting next Monday, or to the Correspondence School where, it was said, you wouldn't see another soul for weeks, or to the Riverina where you would teach whatever they had a spot for, regardless of your training. Such were the myths of the time, blended lovingly with the familiar truth that they could refuse you placement on a promotions list until your socks were more darn than fabric, if you would not toe the line. So I did not hurry to say it.

'I like them,' I said at last. 'They know I like them.' It didn't seem enough, but I was frightened to attribute it to good luck, which I believed to be the most likely explanation. My other, more intelligent language classes were often less well-behaved.

His reply was pure Suit. He grunted. 'That must be nice for them,' he said. 'I'll be off now, then.' I heard him walk straight down the corridor to the Principal's office, and when I left for the day they were still closeted together. I never found out what they decided, or what they were deciding about: you didn't have the right to know, and they thought you worked better if you were afraid.

... It is the last day of their first year. We are in the playground together under the tree allocated us for our class picnic. They have brought cakes, soft drinks, lollies, sandwiches; I have brought fruit and stuffed eggs. They have eaten the stuffed eggs, politely, rolling their eyes at the unfamiliar taste and texture, and now John, the real estate agent's son, gets up and comes towards me with the fragile parcel in his careful hands and his planned message playing like an endless tape in his head. The others look at him in expectant silence, knowing what he is going to say on their behalf. But alas! He is only twelve, and the tape has snapped.

'We want you to have this ...' he says, 'because ... because ... and we all put in to buy it.' He looks knowingly at Mark, the barman's son, who, being short of money, had resisted briefly. There are howls of laughter and squeals of rage. He blushes. I give him a gentle cuddle and tell him thank you very quietly. I say I know what he wanted to say. He is relieved and sits down. They jab him in the ribs. I open the parcel in front of them and admire every single item of the water-set separately. I tell them how I will use it for ever and ever, and remember them every time. They look at each other with universal delight at having chosen so successfully.

... It is the end of second term in their second year. We are in the library together. They are in serious trouble with almost everybody. They have been kept in, placed on emu parades, deprived of sport, caned indiscriminately if male, threatened with letters home – the final ignominy – and all to no avail. It seems strange in the 1990s, when talking is the first, not the last, strategy adopted ... but as a result of that year-before closeting in the Principal's office, I have been delegated, as a last resort, to tell them that they must change their ways. It is a task I feel uncomfortable with, since I have never had occasion to criticise any one of them. Nevertheless, I front them squarely and talk in a way I have never talked to them before. I tell them I have been ashamed of them when I have heard from other teachers of the shocking things they have done and the rude way some of them have spoken. I tell them that at first I could not believe it, and that I still do not want to believe it, but that I must. Two of the girls begin to cry. A venomous silence builds among the boys. Mark gets up spontaneously and says, bitterly, 'We bought you a lovely present, from us all.' His remark receives mumbled, shuffling support. They cannot see the justice of my part in this, and on reflection, neither can I.

... It is the second-last evening of their third year. I have been unable to complete all the returns relating to their annual existence, and I am working very late. The infectious diseases return is a fair cow: on the roll throughout the year I have been required to record in red the reason for each absence, and now I must summarise and collate the information regarding those sicknesses notifiable to the Department. Ricky has been a problem – he has been away a great deal, but his doctor is as yet unable to diagnose the nature of his illness, which is nonetheless serious. I risk leaving him out – no one else looks the way he does, thank goodness, so it is probably safe. I total the roll days, down the columns and across the line for each student. Unfortunately they do not match. I begin again. This time I get it right — it is a simple error of addition. Wearily I turn to the transport returns, one for bus, one for train travellers. I am leaving their annual results sheet, with half-yearly and yearly exam marks for each student, till last; it is the biggest job, but it can be handed in in pencil — the new clerk will check it.

... It is the last day of their fourth year. Their trouble has passed, they are young men and women, eager to earn money, yet timid about leaving each other's brotherhood and the safety net school has after all provided, though the term is not yet a buzzword. Still respectful, they are treating me now as an equal. There are no outdoor picnics this year, and they have brought tablecloths to protect the library furniture, on which their last school party is spread. Their talk is rowdy and happy, giving me that dangerous time to look back over the relationship, which, like a fool, I do. In my mind's eye I re-read the parental notes explaining their family calamities, I see the pale skeletal appearance of Ricky, who has been diagnosed this year with a potentially fatal illness. I look at Katie and think of her mother's death, and her father's inability to cope. I think of the sullen, chubby mien at twelve of Peter the plumber's son, now a muscly footballer with a cheerful countenance and a confident personality; a change too wonderful for words. I marvel that his cousin Matthew has somehow found change unnecessary, or perhaps impossible, that he is as controlled and conventionally virtuous, as quiet and gentle as on his first day here. In a lull I tell them how lovely it has been to have them for my school family, how proud I am of the way they have grown up, especially Peter, I say, who has changed and grown so much and is now so beautiful and happy. They cheer and jab him in the ribs. He blushes. Some things never change. They present me with an ephemeral gift, a box of chocolates, and we part.

For a few years I am still in town. I see Katie and Lyn working in the department store, I see Katie's first baby and buy a rattle. I buy my eggs and chickens from Robbie, who is proud of running his own poultry farm. I sit coincidentally near Ricky in the doctor's surgery and wonder whether he will make it, I notice that David has completed his upholstery apprenticeship and get him to re-cover my chair, I remonstrate with Vinny when he makes a terrible faux pas with a nice girl and I get to hear about it. But after a while I lose touch with their lives. I move to another school, in another town, and mark another roll. I turn over a new leaf, too. Experience and the changing system teach me to be a different sort of teacher, with a crab's shell.

Nevertheless, I feel sick at heart when a colleague from the first town rings and tells me, with some satisfaction, that one of my special class has been charged with murder. See, he appears to be saying triumphantly, you were wrong, we were right, they were a terrible class. He is at work, he cannot remember the name, but he will mail me the newspaper clipping, he says. His wife, also a colleague, has pointed it out to him.

When the clipping arrives, clearly from *another* newspaper than the one I take, I read with disbelief that it is Matthew who has killed. I have not come to the details, but already I am disintegrating with grief and failure. I am telling myself what folly it was to think I knew them, to feel sure that they would have ordinary, safe lives, to have loved them. My shell has cracked. But I read on.

Matthew, it emerges, has fallen deeply in love with a divorced girl. She has a tiny child whom Matthew adores. For a short time they live happily ever after according to the rule of the fairytale. And then the ex-husband appears and demands access to the child – it is uncertain whether or not he has this right, and it is not sensational enough for the rag to mention. What is certain is that the man beats up mother and child, and will not go away, even when the police tell him to. Matthew, with his certainty of right and wrong, shoots him, and is sentenced to a long time in prison.

I suddenly feel a degree of admiration for his rigid standards, and I stop crying. I decide he has still not changed. I know him quite well after all.

After I had put the glass back on the shelf I could see my husband's point of view, as if the curved surface, like a sort of fractal prism, had revealed a new convoluted dimension of teaching. The Suits, in dividing the labour, had surely been thinking of the teacher's welfare at last, not just yielding to union pressure. It did no harm to think so, though cynicism made it difficult to believe. What possible good could it do for one person to know kids so well, to care till it hurt? Indeed, if I'd given John that comforting cuddle this year, 1997, I'd probably be taken to court for it. I needed to abandon comparisons and evaluate the status quo independently. Maybe I should smash the remaining two glasses.

The kids were all grown up, for god's sake, years ago.

FERAL LINE FIVE

Roseanne Wildman

> ... *as a teacher I possess tremendous power to make a child's life miserable or joyous. I can be a tool of torture or an instrument of inspiration. I can humiliate, humour, hurt or heal.*
>
> GINOTT, 1972

Line 5, Year 12 Applied English on a sunny Monday in Term One. This is the English they don't need for university entrance. I knew I was in for fun and games when I saw the class list; three young women and seventeen young men. After fifteen years of teaching, I suspected these students would not be interested in dead or alive poets and playwrights. In fact, they were not interested in secondary college at all except for the odd exercise in socialisation and the fortnightly Austudy payments that would appear if they managed to attend classes. I assumed they would be 'terminal' students: that their days in college would be numbered either by their low academic achievement, lack of belief in themselves or for the really lucky one or two, the prospect of a job.

Armed with my new key, which incidentally did not fit the lock, a pile of getting-to-know-you activities and strong resolve, I headed off to the fray! Because the key did not fit, I met Thommo. He was leaning against the wall and looked like a carbon copy of John Travolta direct from the set of *Grease*. Tight white T-shirt and even tighter black jeans peeled themselves off the wall. Thommo sneered with contempt at what he obviously considered another useless woman.

'I can pick the lock for you. Wouldn't take me long at all.'

I had no doubt as to his expertise in this area, but none the less declined the offer and sent for a replacement key. Once inside the drab classroom with peeling paint and frayed carpet matching my peeling courage and already frayed nerves, the lads took up residence in the back row, defiantly placing assorted smelly sneakers and Blundstone boots on the desks. I took a deep breath and began.

Attempting to call the roll, I was very quickly initiated into the nickname culture that was to prevail throughout the year. Thommo I'd met, but then there were his mates. Malteser, who hailed from Malta, was a tall lad with ink-black hair, wide grin and a nervous giggle. He was the basketball freak and could recite any known fact at any given time on any matter relating to American basketball.

Kenny came from a potato-farming district and his family specialty were kennebecs, hence his nickname. Once Kenny and I had reconciled our differences over his other 'gardening' habits, he would often lump in on Monday morning with a bag of potatoes.

'Dug 'em meself early this mornin'. Dad reckons this lot are better boilers than roasters,' Kenny would declare. The others would mumble something about trying to be teacher's pet and who was the old 'boiler' anyway?

Moonshine was easy . . . yes! He ran a sly grog operation from the back of his panel van in the local car park and would give me a good deal if I was interested. He would often come to afternoon lessons reeking of his hooch and wanting to sing the entire AC-DC collection. Thankfully he wasn't a violent drunk and was malleable enough for me to gently guide him outside for some fresh air.

Doc was quite aptly named as he specialised in tattoos and body-piercing. He didn't carry lunch in his black backpack but the most amazing collection of earrings, nose-rings, body art illustrations and a portable sterilising unit for his needles. He even offered mate's rates for all staff members should I care to drum up business.

Animal was the music specialist and all he did for the entire year was beat his fingers or his drumsticks on the desk. He would spend hours drumming out all kinds of exotic rhythms. Sometimes I would try to distract Animal, as his constant drumming almost drove me to accept Moonshine's offer of cheap grog just to keep me sane. I did find one thing that worked with Animal: reading aloud to the class. I set up the weekly serial and during these sessions, Animal's concentration did not falter. He would hang on every word and it was one of those rare moments of joy for me as a teacher.

During these readings to the class, I waded through some literary and some not-so-literary novels and short stories and was thrilled when Animal brought in a tatty old copy of *The Scarlet Pimpernel*. He thought the class might like to hear it. It was his favourite novel. I was amazed. (Sometimes as teachers we think we know our students. How many wrong assumptions do we make?)

A man of few words was Animal, but when he did speak it was usually on some musical tangent and to the rest of the class he may as well have been muttering in ancient Greek. I never did really break through with Animal apart from my reading aloud to him. He was never any trouble and kept very much to himself locked away in his musical world. He did have the great claim to fame at the end of the year that he had not put pen to paper – not once. Mind you, he didn't blow his trumpet on this score, but it was duly noted by the remainder of Feral Line 5. They would watch closely throughout the year and wait for him to produce a pencil or pen. I suspected Malteser of running a book on the chances of Animal actually writing something . . .

Another of the lads in my line-up was Derrick, whose real name was John. Derrick was so-called because his father worked on an oil rig in Bass Strait. He was probably the meanest looking of all the lads. He never ceased to amaze me with his hair; sometimes bright red, iridescent blue and sometimes no hair — just shaved off! He was solidly built, a result of his doing weights. There was some speculation about him taking steroids but he never admitted it and seemed to relish the attention he received as he regularly flexed his biceps.

Derrick would know how to disrupt the class in two seconds with comments such as, 'Jeez girls! Don't ya love me muscles? Ya can touch 'em if ya like . . .' Needless to say, the girls would shriek and giggle and tell Derrick what he could do with his muscles (generally speaking, what they suggested was anatomically impossible). Derrick bragged about his condom collection and was forever relating lurid tales of his weekend escapades with his contingent of female followers. Doc chimed in with, 'In ya dreams Derrick! If that's true, when would ya sleep and eat? Ya full of shit!'

For all his mean exterior, Derrick sometimes showed a gentle and protective side. This became evident later in the year when the class was joined by a mildly intellectually disabled student, Michele. Derrick did everything he could to help her. He even took his duty-of-care to extremes such as threatening 'to do ya' when she was pushed or shoved in the canteen queue. His most touching contribution was at the end of year gala ball. I was surprised he turned up but there he was . . . resplendent in a purple tuxedo with hair to match! He swept across the hall, found Michele and with great panache, invited her to dance. I was so proud I could have hugged him but I knew that was not cool.

Last but not least in the nickname stakes were the twins, Bill and Ben. I never did learn the reason for their nicknames. I suspect, however, it was their naturally bright red hair reminiscent of terracotta flower pots. Bill had the most severe stammer and eliciting any verbal response from him was often excruciating. Malteser would always be ready to step in and answer for him. I used often to wait for the baiting or the teasing, but strangely enough it never came.

The remainder of the boys used their own names, which was a relief when having to fill out the endless forms and paperwork all teachers know and hate.

The three girls were a strange and wonderful mixture. I had Sahadra, a forty-year-old Iranian mother of three who just wanted to practise her English while her husband was studying at the local university. She was a microbiologist and I shall never forget the look on her face when she entered my class . . . a fairly formidable back row greeted her with leering and muttering. When I introduced her to the class they thought Iran was Iraq and there followed a spate of Saddam Hussein jokes and mutterings about having more 'wogs' in our college. I was quite surprised they knew, albeit roughly, where Iran was on the world map. I spent much of the following weeks discussing the racial origins of all the class in an attempt to reach at least some understanding of cultural diversity. Some days I would despair of ever getting the class to gel and respect each other's differences.

My second girl was Kylie and she desperately wanted to either work with children or be a flight attendant. Most of her time involved chatting up any of the lads who had discovered women, or teasing her thickly hairsprayed fringe into the most amazing verandah. Some days that fringe defied the laws of gravity. Her other talent was the most wonderful agility to manipulate chewing gum (supposedly banned throughout the entire college) while she was speaking. I often wondered if she chewed gum in her sleep. Her vocabulary was extensive, but most of it would not be accepted in the general halls of academia. Most outbursts – and that's what they really were, short sharp staccato bursts of language – were prefaced with, 'Yeah! Waddya fuckin' lookin' at me for?' I thought this line would go down particularly well on a Melbourne–Sydney flight as Kylie demonstrated the safety features of the aircraft and some poor unsuspecting businessman accidentally made eye contact with her. It took almost all of first term before Kylie felt secure enough to drop her introductory line.

The final female in my line-up was Cheryl. I have to admit I was terrified until we found some middle ground. I'm not sure where to begin with Cheryl. When I looked through her school records they rivalled *War and Peace*. Cheryl was tall and thin with a nose that looked like it had done many rounds with Mike Tyson. She had three tattoos on her cheek and 'FUCK' tattooed across each knuckle on both hands. Although Cheryl was only twenty, she would occasionally bring to class the youngest of her three children.

Cheryl made no bones about what she did to supplement her income. She ran a mobile brothel catering to anyone who 'had the money up front'. At one stage during the year I happened to mention a pile of unpaid bills. Cheryl assured me she was always looking for a more mature woman. 'Some of the blokes like 'em a bit older, ya know.' I just had to let her know if I was interested. I was never sure whether to take the offer as a compliment or not.

Her other source of income to support herself, her children and her very obvious and sad heroin addiction, was the odd 'burg' as she called it. She knew roughly where I lived and told me I need not worry as she didn't touch mates' places. Once again, I wasn't sure if this was a positive comment. She missed class a couple of times because of court appearances for breaking and entering. Cheryl would roll back into class and discuss her exploits as if they were a natural part of life. I guess for her, they were.

With this amazing collection of students, I somehow made it through the year. My terror turned to tolerance as I came to understand some of the horrendous backgrounds and life experiences these students had endured. Mostly the intended syllabus went out the window (literally on one occasion), and we worked together on basic literacy skills and attempting to improve their self-confidence and self-esteem. They all became experts at caring for an eighteen-month-old baby and assisting Cheryl when she was 'hanging out for a hit'. They learnt to love and devour Iranian pastries, were shocked to learn of Sahadra's arranged marriage and they supported Animal when his rock group produced their first CD.

I did lose some of my class members as the year rolled on. Thommo went for an extended stay as a guest of Her Majesty, Malteser went back to Malta to visit his grandmother. Kenny told me that in fact Malteser was wanted for drink-driving offences. 'His old man shipped 'im out to his granny so he wouldn't have to pay the fines.' Doc just left one day with no explanation. Maybe the body-piercing business was booming.

I gained one student, Nigel, who was clean-cut and impeccably dressed as opposed to the black jeans and Megadeth T-shirt brigade. As the pecking order had already been established, poor Nigel copped it.

'We're not having a fuckin' poofter in 'ere.'

'Sit 'im over there with the girlies!'

When they found out Nigel was an accredited Australian Rules Football umpire, the climate changed dramatically. He was set upon for autographs of famous football stars and given friendly advice about wrong decisions he'd made during his last footy match.

By the end of the year, I realised that I had done the learning and probably not much in terms of traditional teaching. At the Feral Line 5 end of year barbecue I thought about Roethke's words as the sauce squirted over the sausages:

> *So much of adolescence is an ill-defined dying,*
> *an intolerable waiting*

*a longing for another place and time,
another condition.*

I still hear about some class members from time to time. Malteser came back and did a bricklaying apprenticeship; Kylie completed a TAFE childcare course and is working in a childcare centre; Kenny is back on the family farm growing potatoes; Nigel works in a local bank and Animal plays gigs on the pub circuit. As for Thommo, Doc, Cheryl and the others, I'm not sure but I do hope they have found a place to be content, somewhere.

ANTONY

Peter Cox

I've known Antony all his life . . . all twenty years of it. He used to live four doors down my street, but lives and works in Melbourne now. That in itself is a minor miracle.

I couldn't help but meet him and get to know him well. Life in our small country town is like that . . . closeness. Only eighty residents and I know almost everything about the private lives of my seventy-nine neighbours, and they know all about me. Some may find that invasive, even threatening, but I find it supportive.

Antony was born with severe physical disabilities.

Every weekday morning, at 8.35 am sharp, the community funded minibus would pull up in front of Antony's house, honk its tinny horn, and wait patiently for Antony to hobble out his front door. Off to Special School. If the weather was fine he would often be waiting on the footpath, eagerly clutching his school bag, an indelible broad smile and a bubbly greeting for a passer-by. As I walked past on those mornings, heading for the train station, we shared a common bond. I was off to high school. I don't think he distinguished between the roles of teacher and student: he was off to his school and I was off to mine.

Like a lot of non-thinking people, I had assumed that because Antony had severe physical disabilities he must also have a degree of intellectual disability. As if one affliction automatically produced the other. After all, those callipers and crutches were evidence of a physical disability, and his lack of literacy seemed to provide evidence of the other. Or did it?

Antony loved to bring home a whole bag full of books from Special School, but it was immediately obvious to an observer that he could not read the printed words. He was illiterate; it had even been suggested that he was incapable of ever learning how to read. Mum and Dad seemed to have accepted that advice and come to terms with it. But he liked to hold up his books, just like everyone else, stare at the pictures and pretend he knew what the words meant. He knew most of the stories off by heart and could be very convincing — unless you knew him well. But he began to develop a peculiar technique of 'reading' by bringing the book right up to his eyes. So close, it rested against his nose.

At ten years of age his eyesight had deteriorated to partial blindness. The regression had been gradual, masked by a welter of other more pressing, more obvious disorders. Perhaps today this creeping blindness would not go unnoticed for so long a period, but twenty years ago it was not uncommon in country areas — where specialists and facilities were non-existent — for many disorders to go undiagnosed.

As if Antony did not already have far more than his fair share of afflictions, his eyesight problem turned out to be a type of disorder the specialists could not fix. Antony had to wear 'Mr Magoo' spectacles and in spite of their unsightliness they were only a marginal help to him. Once again life seemed to have slapped him in the face, but he took the blow without a single whimper and smiled on.

I often imagine Antony and God in conversation; after God has added one more handicap to Antony's burden, that inimical broad smile would look up at God and say: 'No worries mate, I can take anything you dish out. I love life and there ain't nothing You can do to depress me.'

One Saturday morning I ran into Antony and his mum while shopping in Main Street — our only street. We chatted about many things, including Antony and his progress at Special

School. He was doing very well, according to Mum, so well that he was complaining of being bored. He needed a greater intellectual challenge. I suggested that his intellectual capacity ought to be retested, this time taking into account his near blindness. It was partly an off-hand suggestion, I had not given it much thought, but there was a faint suspicion wafting around the back of my mind. I certainly had no idea of the chain of events that my simple suggestion would put in motion.

Antony was tested again, and found to be of average intellectual ability, but his cognitive development had been considerably held back by his physical problems. His parents were so delighted with the news they shed tears of happiness, thanked me profusely, but wondered what they should do next? As the only teacher living in the town they earnestly sought my advice.

I realised that the hardworking teachers and carers at the Special School were doing all they could for Antony, but he needed more than they could offer – more than the Special School environment could offer. I recommended they try to get Antony admitted to the local primary school, but I warned them of the battle they faced in trying to break new ground.

It was certainly not policy or practice in those days to admit disabled children to regular schools. Terms like 'integration' and 'mainstreaming' had yet to be invented, let alone the concepts they represented. The disabled had their Special Schools and there they were meant to stay, that was the de facto policy. There were no Integration Aides, no official support, no extra funding for coping with a disabled student.

After a long discussion with the head teacher at the primary school, Bob Jamieson fully agreed with me that Antony ought to be in his school. Bob recognised the problems ahead but didn't shirk from the challenge: it was 'right' that Antony should come to his school, so that was exactly what he set out to achieve.

Antony was right at home at primary school. He made good progress and soon learned to read. His unbridled enthusiasm and quick comprehension impressed and amazed Bob Jamieson and his classmates. His fellow students had a huge headstart in the education race, but Antony was rapidly running them down. Antony wanted to learn – he had a passion for learning. Even the bureaucrats in the Department – those frowning, doubting paper-pushers – had to sit up and take notice of this boy's achievements.

There came a time when his age and size dictated a departure from primary school, although he was still not as adept as most of the Year 6s. The traditional move to high school was not an automatic option in Antony's case ... battle would have to be waged again, against yet another set of grey-suits with negative attitudes. I wanted him at my school. He had every right to be there.

My hard-pressed secondary school colleagues could easily have refused point blank to take on the extra burden and responsibility. They were overworked, understaffed and needed the extra trouble like a hole in the head. I had to talk fast, I had to talk long, but I found I had more supporters than doubters. Sentiment slowly tipped Antony's way, then became an avalanche of eager support. The idea of admitting a severely disabled student was new, so it took time for the concept and its implications to sink in. To my delight the staff responded to the challenge by forming a special support team for Antony, setting a trend that would be copied in other schools in the future. We worked out a special program for him (physical education was not a possibility, nor was metalwork) and were determined to make his stay a rewarding one.

I had my worries. It was not possible to predict how the teenage students – so into appearances, being cool and being macho – would take to Antony. Physically, he stood out like a sore thumb, a very vulnerable target, and it was conceivable that some of the students might decide to tear him apart. Kids can be horribly cruel at times.

Our Principal spent day after day battling the bureaucrats, who seemed to have decided that disabled kids should stay in their special schools. Antony's success seemed to threaten their paper world in some way I could not fathom. The grey-suits threw legal and bureaucratic obstacles in our path at every turn, seemingly bent on stopping our 'experiment'. Their argument was absurdly simple – and brainless. Since there was no formal written policy in place, they argued, then that legally prevented admission of disabled children to high schools. Our Principal had a simple answer for the nameless, faceless grey-suits. He completely ignored them.

The 'Antony phenomenon' is now well documented but it was a revelation to me and my colleagues at the time. In his classes there was a dramatic reduction in disruptive behaviour; attitudes and values such as consideration for others and compassion were given much greater weight; he was adopted by his classes and became the unofficial school mascot. His profound disabilities and seemingly indomitable spirit made the 'have-nots' and less academically inclined students reassess how lucky they were. Few people felt inclined to be sorry for themselves around Antony. Wherever he went he engendered 'heart' and brought out the best in us.

Overnight successes are few and far between in real life and Antony's situation was not one of them. There seemed to be a never-ending list of unforeseen problems, like access to buildings, but patience, perseverance and goodwill eventually overcame most of them. There were no special devices to help the sight-impaired; we did what we could to enlarge material but we were exploring new territory and it was plain hard work at times. Try as we did, we could not solve some minor irritating problems, but we persevered. It took two years just to iron out the major bugs.

ANTONY

I taught Antony Mathematics. I had to write everything on the board in 30 cm high letters – he could barely see the blackboard let alone anything written on it. Even from the front row the teacher and the board were an obscure blur to him. The teachers usually produced A4 sheets of notes for our students, so we enlarged them to A3 size for Antony. Even then he could only read printed material by putting his face flush against the paper – with or without his glasses. The first time he did this in class he caught his English teacher off-guard. For a moment she thought he had put his head down and gone to sleep. Whenever possible, written work was converted to oral work and it was soon obvious that his intellect and hearing were above average. And there was that fierce desire to learn.

We noted that the other students in his classes were making better progress because of the improved attitudes to learning and behaviour that his presence inspired, and the variety of teaching techniques we were forced to adopt assisted many of the able-bodied students too. The poor readers benefited from the conversion of written instructions to oral work. That gave us cause for a lot of thought about our teaching methods and their effectiveness. We were learning from Antony. He rode high over all the bumps, refusing to be impeded by his handicaps and dragging us along in his wake at times.

There came a time when Antony faced the prospect of leaving secondary school, or doing the Higher School Certificate. This was undoubtedly a daunting challenge for him, for at this level we could not cut corners with the curriculum. He would get no special consideration for his disabilities, he would be treated by the external examination system the same as any able-bodied student. Everyone seemed willing to call it a day, having made such good gains with Antony's education. Everyone but Antony. He determinedly announced that he was going to attempt the HSC.

Mum and Dad were very worried that failure at this stage

could destroy Anthony's spirit. Neither of them had gone this far with their own education, but they knew how difficult the HSC was even for good students. They sought my advice. What could I say? Antony had said it all.

I was pleased to find Antony in my Year 12 Maths class. I had a gut feeling that he was going to pass Maths: his skills were very good, his near-blindness was a handicap but not a critical one in this subject. If nothing else, his presence would boost the attitude and performance of my other students.

Our country town is certainly short of resources but we are rich in spirit. By rallying community support we managed to find a sponsor who provided Antony with a computer which helped him complete written work at home. Another generous sponsor gave the school a TV camera and monitor, so that work written on the board could be magnified onto the screen on his desk. The devices helped him greatly, but demanding intellectual work was still a huge challenge for Antony, given his relatively late start to formal education. Even with the aid of this technology he was way behind the eight-ball.

About mid-year we were visited by a speaker who addressed the whole student body. He explained that he had been confined to a wheelchair by muscular dystrophy. I thought he looked just like Antony-on-wheels. The speaker explained the disease and its consequences, though many were immediately obvious. At the end of his lecture Antony turned to me and, in all seriousness, remarked that he 'felt sorry for people who were disabled like him'. He asked me if I knew of some way to help the visitor.

Antony worked doggedly. Although we could not criticise his attitude, we were not expecting too much quality work from him, and some of his first efforts were below par for Year 12. Our expectations were not high. At least when exam time eventually came around, he had already faced so much adversity in his short life that he had no intention of becoming nervous about something as trivial as a few exams. We wished him well . . . and started to think of what we could say to ease the pain when the results came out.

When the Year 12 exam results were published in the daily papers there were tears of joy streaming down a thousand faces. Parents, teachers, students, friends, we all read – and re-read – those wonderful passing grades. Hardly believing what we saw. Hearts swelled with unconfined pride and joy. Antony was the least excited of us all: he knew he was going to pass, so why get excited?

Every now and then a teacher has a victory – they are usually few and far between. Every now and then I think of Antony and I walk just a smidgen taller, I smile, and I tell myself 'I done good'.

Mars Bars and Lawson

Lyn Chatham

'Luke, where's your folder?'

'Umm. Dunno. But it's okay, cos I've got everthin' in here.' He reached into his black zip-up jacket and took out an exercise book.

'Is that really a good idea?'

'Yeah, well, me pack got nicked. An' a folder's too big.'

'Alright. Have you got a pen?'

'Nuh. Had one, somewhere.'

I gave him one. He was sitting up the front by himself. Not like Alistair, who had to plonk next to someone to get him through the session. The someone was usually Brett.

I flicked through the roll looking for the right page. A tap started splashing.

Alistair was the one sitting closest to it.

'Alistair, was that you?' I said.

'Me? Nuh.' He looked disgusted with me for asking.

'Well, shut it off, please.' He jumped up and turned it off. I knew it was him, but I let it go.

Alistair, ADD and taps in the same room was really asking for it. I thought those things had all been turned off. It would've been simpler if my special group didn't have to be in an ordinary Science Room. One with no carpet, too, so that chairs and tables joined in the talking much of the time.

There was a sudden grind.

'Back in a mini, Sue, just goin' to the toilet,' Luke said, as he pushed his table forward and hurried out.

Brett smiled and looked at me knowingly. Luke had been

very pale. He was often very pale. Sometimes he reminded me of a Catholic schoolgirl from the 1960s, with his shiny brown hair pulled back in a severe ponytail. I gave out some photocopies.

'Everyone, can you have a go at these fractions? I'll give you twenty minutes.'

They got going on it, with Brett helping Alistair. Luke came back and sat down quietly.

When the bell went I asked Luke to come into my office, to talk about his task for Oral.

'Are you eating okay?' I said as we sat down.

'Not really.'

'Well, what have you had today?'

'Just a Mars Bar.'

'Mars Bars are not enough,' I said quickly. 'You do know there's a free breakfast on at the canteen?' He shook his head. 'It's from 8.30 to 9.00. You need to get some structure in your life, you know,' I said more gently.

'Mmm. But I've had a bad week. Actually – ' He paused for a moment. 'I nearly did meself in.'

I tensed. It was the first time I'd ever heard a student say those words.

'Anyway, it was me birthdey on Tuesdey and I got real down.' He moved around in his seat. 'Me mum didn't ring, neither did me sister. And I had this big barney with me mate in the house. See, I sold him stuff but he reckoned the stuff was bad, and I should give the money back. But I couldn't, cos I'd spent it. I bought these.' He pointed to the black jeans he was wearing.

I was trying to slow my heartbeat down. 'Do you feel okay now?' I said.

'Yeah, yeah.' He looked me in the eyes steadily and I believed him. 'Y'ever thought how beautiful a gas ring is?' he went on. 'A real fat circle of blue light. Magic.'

I said that I'd never noticed. I swallowed and relaxed my shoulders. 'Do you want to talk to Brian, the psychologist, about things?'

'Nuh.' He got up and walked around. 'I left home when I was twelve, yer know. I was on the streets for a while, then I was down at St B's. Actually, I got involved in the Peer Support Program there and I was gettin' a wage n'all. Then the fundin' ran out.'

'That's great you were working,' I said.

'But now, I don't wanna see do-gooders any more. Cos they don't actually know yer, if yer know what I mean.' I nodded. 'But I don't mind talkin' to you. You won't tell anyone about the dealin' will you?' he followed up.

'No, I won't,' I said quietly. My brain was in rapid fire, trying to make excuses for him. It could be just dope – I mean, who wasn't smoking, these days? Even some teachers were. And cigarettes were more addictive than all of that stuff. I'd have to talk to one of the staff about suicide, though. I'd heard somewhere that if someone mentions it, you shouldn't ignore it.

'What was I gonna ask you?' he said. 'Oh yeah, that's it. Do you wanna read me Jim Morrison book?' He reached into his jacket and took out a small black and yellow covered paperback. 'He is so cool! And there's not many of these ones around. It's special, from America.'

I nodded. 'Okay. Some of my friends were right into the Doors, when I was your age,' I said. I looked at the first few pages. 'You know, this'd be okay to do a review on for your Reading task.'

'Really? Great. The way he writes is unreal.'

'Well now, about your Oral task? Zoe said you wrote a really good song on a Lawson story in Drama.'

'Yep, the story's called "That There Dog o' Mine". Good story. About a shearer and his best mate. His kelpie.'

I was surprised at his enthusiasm. I thought there'd be a better match-up than a nineteenth century writer, writing about the bush, with an ex-street kid living in an industrial city.

'Right, well, Zoe said you could do a monologue of the story for me. But you have to promise me you'll be here on the day we set. Because I have to book the video for that session, and I want to take the tape to Moderation. And, of course, you know you need this Oral subject to get the Level Two Certificate.'

'Well, I'd be pretty nervous,' he said hesitantly.

'I know. But you'll be right,' I said.

'Okay.'

So we had a deal. 'Well, get out your diary,' I said.

His diary was small and black. He mumbled something about 'little black books'. I realised that my feminine-looking student was really quite masculine. We agreed on a date and he flipped over a week of pages and wrote in the time, 11.00, under Friday, 10 November.

'So Luke, barring getting run over by a bus, you must be there. Right?'

'Yep, gotcha.'

'Okay. And you need to come to class to practise before that.'

He nodded.

At lunchtime I talked to Karen, the Welfare Coordinator, about Luke mentioning suicide. She said it'd be best to speak to Brian the counsellor – but he wouldn't be in for three weeks. Great.

Luke didn't come to class on Monday. Well, it was the day straight after the weekend. When I went to my pigeonhole at recess there was a phone message in it: 'Luke Crocker says he'll be in class on Friday'. But he wasn't. He rang me at lunchtime and said his boots were soaked from the rain yesterday and he didn't have any others.

On the tenth, the other kids were allowed to stay home to finish off work. But the one who wasn't allowed to do that wasn't there. He turned up at ten minutes past eleven.

We started taping. It was going fine, his accent sounded just right for an old bushie, and he sort of looked the part with his op shop man's hat. Suddenly he shook his head and waved at me. I pressed the stop button. He started pacing up and down.

'I don' know, I just lost it,' he said.

Too much of something has killed off some short term memory, I thought.

'It's all right,' I said. 'We can stop any time you want. We'll do it in dribs and drabs. But I'll need some kind of sign to stop the tape.'

'Umm, what about if I bend over and me hat falls in me hand,' he said.

'Good one!' I said.

He sat down and jigged one hand on his leg for a few moments. Then he stood up and said, 'Right'. We did a bit more. It was all right until he tripped on the word 'pupped' in the line 'that there dog was pupped on the track'. This time he didn't hang around. He was out the door with the hat coming to rest on the floor.

I'd been so flexible with him all the way along and now he'd run out on me. Literally. His acting was right on the button — that's what made it so frustrating. I walked over and looked out the window. Nothing was moving on the basketball courts. It must have been five minutes later when he did come back. He walked in quickly, half smiled at me and said, 'It's okay' and sat down. He didn't say where he'd been — to have a cigarette, go to the toilet, or to walk out the gate. And I didn't ask. To see him come back through that door was enough.

When I started the tape this time, he stayed right till the end. When we'd finished, I went over to him and grabbed him on the arm.

'See, see what you can do.'

'Phew,' was all he said.

We watched his performance. Luke had a quizzical expression on his face.

'Not bad.' He nodded at me.

I laughed. I don't know why he came back. Maybe he didn't want to let me down. Or maybe he knew he had a real opportunity to get a piece of paper that showed something to the establishment out there. He might've just really believed in the dog who the shearer said was 'a better Christian' than he was. I realised then that I really liked Luke. He'd never been rude to me. And he talked to me straight, not like he was trying to put one over me. As for that talk about doing himself in, I told myself things were all right now.

One week later at Moderation, everyone was saying how clever I was to bring a tape to the session. And how Luke's acting was excellent, making it such a moving study of an old man's love for his dog. I felt pretty good. Luke ended up getting his certificate. And I'll never bag Lawson again.

An Inquiring Mind

Vic O'Callaghan

I

Monday mornings in primary schools have a certain air of expectancy about them. With the weekend behind me I awaited the creative skills and energy of four hundred students to initiate me into yet another week. Being an Assistant Principal of a primary school was no place for anyone thirsting for a predictable day's labour.

I sat in my office, my index finger searching for the day's date in my diary. The excited cries from the playground grew more audible as the multiplying feet pounded the concrete outside my window. I was about to make a phone call when there was a faint knock on my door.

'Come in.' The doorhandle turned yet the door remained closed.

'Come in and don't bump into the furniture.' I thought my last remark would produce a slight snigger, as I had fallen over a chair during the school assembly on Friday.

I stood and walked to the door. In the doorway were two girls from Year 6: Vanessa and Michelle.

'Come in girls,' I said as I ushered them toward the two vacant chairs. 'How can I help you?' I asked as I sat down at my desk.

Vanessa looked at Michelle. Their eyes met.

'Who wants to speak first?' I asked.

Vanessa took a quick breath.

'Mr O'C, we ... we want to talk to you about something important.' I leant forward and nodded.

'You know how you always say that if we have something we need to say to you, you will always listen.'

'Yes.' I glanced towards the door. It was open.

'A boy on the bus has been asking us to do things,' blurted Vanessa. She immediately turned to Michelle for assurance. Michelle sat looking straight at me.

'What kind of things?' I asked quietly.

'He asked us to let him touch our breasts,' said Michelle.

'And other things,' added Vanessa.

Both the girls before me were twelve years of age. They were intelligent, athletic and fun loving. I had taught them a number of times during the year. I remembered them from my sessions during Book Week and when I had taken their class for Drama earlier in the term.

'What school does this boy come from?' I asked, immediately assuming the young man was a student from a nearby high school.

'He's in our class.' The girls replied in unison.

God no! I thought to myself. 'What is his name?'

I felt strange asking this question. I was somehow hoping that the girls had forgotten the perpetrator's name. There, I had branded him. It always seems easier when an anonymous person is branded.

'Terry . . .' Vanessa stopped mid-sentence. Again she looked at Michelle.

'Terry Phillips,' replied Michelle calmly. Her voice had a determination that seemed beyond her years.

'From what you've told me, Terry was suggesting something quite inappropriate. Did Terry do anything while you were on the bus?'

'He did it to Vanessa,' answered Michelle.

'He did?' I was momentarily lost in the story. 'He did what?'

'He touched her and he asked her.'

'So, that's what he did eh?' I was stalling for more than time,

I was stalling for the glimmer of an idea. I paused for a moment.

'Can you tell me what he asked of you, Vanessa?'

Vanessa again looked to Michelle for support.

'What do you mean, Mr O'C?' asked Michelle. 'What does "ask of us" mean?'

'What did he ask you to do?'

'Sex,' said Michelle. It was as though she was answering a question in class and was hoping in all hope that she was getting the answer right.

'That must have been . . . difficult for the both of you.' I had always highlighted the great gift of our sexuality when teaching about human reproduction. In the clinical space of the classroom, it was easier to talk of dignity and respect. This was the other side of discovering and learning. On the playground, on the buses and behind concrete walls it had a confronting edge.

'Is there anything more you want to tell me?' Both girls shook their head. 'I want to thank both of you for coming to speak with me about this matter,' I said. 'I know how difficult it has been to come and speak with me. I think you are both honest and courageous young ladies. I'll talk with Mrs Ross about this and we will be speaking with Terry Phillips.'

'What will you do, Mr O'C?' asked Vanessa. 'Will I be in trouble?'

'What do you mean be in trouble?' I asked. 'You haven't done anything wrong, Vanessa. How could you be in trouble?'

'He said we would be in trouble if we said anything,' said Michelle.

'I want to reassure both of you that you are in no trouble at all. The person in trouble is Mr Phillips.' Michelle and Vanessa looked at each other. 'I mean Terry Phillips.'

They both smiled. It was at this moment that I realised just how much trust these two young girls had placed in me. Coming to talk with me about sexual behaviour had meant going outside their cultural sphere of understanding. I was an adult. I was an authority figure. In many ways I was portrayed by those who stretched and tested the limits as the enemy.

As I closed the door behind them, I heard whispering as Michelle and Vanessa walked hurriedly down the hallway. I turned and reached up to the folder entitled 'Protective Behaviour Policies'. I'd been to a number of inservices on this subject, but all the material I had read was related to adults as perpetrators. I went searching for a section on peer abuse.

II

After finding little information in the folder, I sent out a couple of runners to the playground in search of Terry Phillips. I wanted to speak with him as soon as possible. Five minutes later there was a knock at my door.

Terry Phillips had an open and vibrant smile. He had the kind of face that was always ready to please. My only dealings with Terry had been when I was asked to be the arbiter of rough play. Twelve-year-old boys are notorious for thriving on the release of energy.

I silently ushered him to a chair.

'Terry, I have been speaking with two of the students in Year 6, and they have told me of something that happened on the bus last week.' Terry's eyes widened. 'Do you know of anything happening on the bus that I should know about?'

'No.' Terry paused as if in deep thought. 'No. I . . . I haven't seen anything.' He then looked up at me. 'I haven't done anything wrong, Mr O'C. Honest I haven't.' There was a plaintive edge to his voice.

'Did I say that you'd done anything?'

'No. But there's usually trouble on the buses. I reckon there's a lot goin' on on those buses that shouldn't be going on.'

'You know Vanessa Grimer.' I watched Terry's eyes as he

heard me mention Vanessa's name. An instant of full alert, then the smile.

'You know I do, Mr O'C. She's in my class.'

'The very same, Terry,' I said as I eased into the next sentence. 'Vanessa has told me about an incident on the bus last week.'

'Incident. I don't know anything about any incidents.'

'Some girls from your class, including Vanessa, have come to see me about something they say you did and said.'

'Mr O'C, some of those girls don't like me.'

'Who doesn't like you?'

'Rosemary and ... Michelle and ... a few like that.'

'Terry. I want you to listen to what I have to tell you,' I said as I straightened slightly in my chair. 'The girls who spoke to me said that you touched them deliberately and asked them to do things of a sexual nature.'

Terry's face went almost white. He stared at me as he struggled for breath.

'Mr O'C, I didn't do anything. I didn't touch those girls. I don't know anything about what they're talkin' about.'

'They said that – '

'I didn't do anything to them girls. I didn't say anything to 'em. They're lyin', Mr O'C. They're out to get me 'cos I won't go around with 'em.'

'One girl said you touched her.'

Terry held onto the arms of the chair and almost lifted himself from the seat.

'I didn't do anything, Mr O'C. Honest.' His eyes were reddening at this point. 'I don't know how ta convince ya.'

'You don't have to convince me, Terry,' I said quietly. 'I'm only in search of the truth.'

'Why?' he said as his eyes swept across the floor in wonder. 'Why have those girls made up these lies?'

Just then there was a knock at the door. It was Anne Dobson, coach of the swimming squad.

'I've been looking for you everywhere, Terry.' Anne turned to me. 'What's he doing here? Didn't you remember the bus should've left ten minutes ago?'

'Oh no!' I said as I swung round in my chair. 'The State Finals.'

'Have you finished with Terry?'

'Yes, sure Anne.' I turned to Terry. 'I'll see you when you come back tomorrow, Terry. Good luck with the swim.' I almost choked over my good luck wishes. Whether Terry had been propositioning the girls or not, the brief interrogation had given his adrenalin an early start for the finals. It was probably the worst start he could have experienced. I should have remembered today was the day of the finals. Terry was our only entrant. He'd come to school because his parents hadn't organised any transport for him to the pool.

III

'Being noticed as female during puberty is uncomfortable enough,' said Julie Ross as I poured more coffee into my mug. 'But being propositioned at twelve years of age is another story.'

Julie was the school Principal. She was a person who was passionate about children learning. She reminded me of a protective lioness. 'Safety is as important as food when it comes to children learning' was one of her few maxims.

'I'm not sure if the girls noticed how uncomfortable I was,' I said as I looked out onto the playground. 'It's bloody difficult trying to take care of these kids and to know exactly where they are developmentally.'

'And as well as being sensitive to each of them, the stories conflict,' added Julie as if she knew what I was thinking.

'Bloody boys,' I said as I turned away from the action outside. 'I don't remember this type of thing when I was in primary school.'

'Well, it was high school for me. But you must admit that girls are maturing earlier these days.'

'Now come on, Julie,' I said as I went in search of a non-existent biscuit. 'The human race hasn't suddenly evolved that fast.'

'Almost forty years of evolution is another age you know.' I caught Julie's smile. 'It still doesn't excuse young Phillips, though.'

'As I said, he swears he didn't do it.'

'You mean he says the girls are making it all up?'

'He says it's all lies.'

'Who's lying?'

I didn't answer. I turned and watched the kids on the playground again as they ran and laughed, twirling and searching for the best play they could experience. I caught sight of Michelle and Vanessa sitting among a group of their friends. Everyone else in the group was animated.

'This is a serious accusation, you know.' Julie was standing beside me.

'I wouldn't know how serious it was if they had remained silent.'

'You kept the door open during the interview?'

I nodded as I gazed into the playground.

'You're uneasy about it, aren't you?'

I looked at her. Julie had never been this direct with me in the two years we had worked together.

'It's just that both stories are so plausible. The girls have come and told me of an incident that was difficult to recount, and young Terry seems so honest.'

Julie turned to look out over the playground. 'Young Terry.' I caught her eye as she turned towards the sink. The endearing use of the word echoed in my mind.

'This isn't a male protective thing, you know,' I said defensively. Julie lifted her eyebrows and smiled as she left the staffroom. Her ascent to silence made a poignant statement. She knew she was leaving me with a bundle of facts and a mixture of feelings that would keep me from many of the trifles with which I often occupied myself.

Ten minutes later I felt as though I was being moved by the current of events to have my head placed firmly in the grip of a vice. A hurried assembly was arranged for nine o'clock. The playground was abuzz with talk of Terry Phillips. He had set a State record for the 200 metres freestyle.

IV

He stood there holding the shield high above his head. Everyone clapped and the three cheers resounded and then floated over the sports oval. Heroism has a mystical appeal. Even though it exists ever so briefly, the birth of the hero points and lifts the ordinary towards the heavens. Terry Phillips loved it. I could see the adulation fire its intoxicating effect as he accepted the pats on the back from his peers. Everyone else wanted to touch him and feel a part of the moment, while it lasted.

I waited until classes had moved off and everyone was involved in the slide and close manoeuvring of getting into class. I reached through the throng and tapped Terry Phillips on the shoulder. He turned and saw me. New red blood evaporated his smile. I was the last person he wanted to see.

'Congratulations, Terry,' I said. 'Can you come with me now?'

'Sure Mr O'C,' Terry replied. His confidence returned as he spoke and oozed and splashed about the hallway, as the others in his class continued to congratulate him and marvel at his deed.

Back in my office Terry shifted in his chair, his eyes glancing around the room. It was as though he was searching for something. He seemed to be waiting to be rescued.

'I've spoken to Mrs Ross, and she says we should get you and the girls to talk this matter through.'

'Do you think I did it?' His question startled me.

'It's not a question of what I think, Terry. It is a simple question of who did what.'

'You know I didn't do it.'

'As I just said, what I think or believe doesn't matter.' I was beginning to resent the reversal of roles. 'I want you to give me the names of boys from your grade who go home on the same bus as you.'

'Wayne Thompson and Chris Jones.'

'Chris only goes to the railway station.'

'I didn't do it, you know, Mr O'C.'

'Give me the names of some of the boys who travel home with you on the bus.'

'Michael Simpson and Roberta Lacey.'

'I thought the name was Robert Lacey.'

Terry placed his face in his hands. He was beginning to cry. 'I didn't do it, Mr O'C. Ya gotta believe me.'

I got up and opened the door. Julie stood there with Michelle and Vanessa.

'Come in, Mrs Ross. Hello Michelle. Hello Vanessa.' I indicated where each was to sit.

'We won't take long here. I just want to establish the facts so that each of you knows exactly what the other is saying.'

I noticed Vanessa was breathing quite heavily. Michelle sat silently as Terry looked around the room.

'I wonder if I might say something, Mr O'C?' inquired Julie. 'Vanessa and Michelle have told me their version of what happened on the bus last week, although it seems a little different from what you told me. Apparently it happened more than once.'

'It didn't even happen once, Mrs Ross,' said Terry. 'I didn't do anything to Vanessa.'

The room had gone quiet. With all classes beginning the day, the playground was in its serene mode. I saw two starlings hopping from the empty bread crates outside the canteen. The school flag offered itself to a zephyr that unwrapped it briefly into life. I noticed Julie staring at Terry. She seemed distant and deep in thought.

Then suddenly she continued. 'Vanessa tells me there was a lot of push and shove.'

I turned and looked at Julie. 'Push and shove' was a euphemism for light-hearted play. Vanessa was looking at the floor. Though her breathing had steadied, she was still unable to look at me. Michelle looked towards the ceiling. I wanted to begin questioning the girls again, but I was aware the agenda had changed.

'Push and shove happens a lot on the buses, doesn't it, Mrs Ross?' I turned to Michelle. 'Is there anything you want to say to me, Michelle?'

Michelle shook her head slightly.

'I think it might be a good idea for everyone to go back to class,' I said as I stood and opened the door. 'Mrs Ross, I'll take these young people back to their respective rooms and then call in to see you in your office. If that is okay?'

Julie nodded as I ushered Michelle, Vanessa and Terry to the door.

V

'What did those two say to you?' I asked Julie as I entered her office. 'There's something going on here.'

'Their version of events was quite different from the one you recounted to me,' said Julie. 'I was given a sanitised account of normal action in close quarters as happens on our buses in these days of budget constraints and bureaucratic number crunching.'

'Do you mean Michelle didn't tell you what was said and done?'

'Why do you say Michelle?' asked Julie. 'Didn't you say it was Vanessa who was propositioned?'

'Yes, she was, but it was Michelle who was the stronger of the two. I believe she gave Vanessa the confidence to come forward and speak to me in the first place.'

'Michelle said almost nothing. She mumbled something about rough play and rough stuff and then said Vanessa knew more about what went on than she did.'

'Someone's got to them.'

'Well, there is a lot that could have gone on that we don't know about,' said Julie. 'I can only go by what I was told and by the demeanour of the girls. I hate to say it, but they seemed almost contrite.'

'It may have looked like contrition, but the two girls I saw were cowering in fear.'

'What do you mean by that exactly?' Julie was a keen one, she did want things to be as exact as they could be.

'Phillips is a standover merchant. He has something on those two. I wouldn't be surprised if he hasn't got something on a good number of other kids in the school.'

'I know what you're getting at. I have seen it happen before like this. You must admit, it's a bit like knowing what people are doing under the covers. You have to be at the end of the bed to be able to prove what went on.'

'In this case, maybe we have to get under the covers.' Julie reached for the phone. 'I'll get someone to relieve you from your class for the next day. It may take a while to sort this out.'

It was almost recess when I sent a message to Year 6 Green for Terry Phillips to come to my office. I wanted to keep him away from the rest of his cohort during recess and lunchtime.

Separation for a period of time would test his confidence.

I spent the next fifteen minutes talking with Terry about his family. I knew that he lived with his mother, but I didn't know how his father fitted into the picture. Terry said that his mum worked at the nearby university as a clerical assistant and that his dad was interstate all the time on business.

In the period between recess and lunch, I spoke with the school secretary. Yes, Terry's mother sometimes appeared at school functions, but his father hadn't been seen for eighteen months or so. I asked to see Terry's file.

I searched through reports and letters and then came across a letter that had been replaced in its envelope. It was addressed 'Confidential, Mr Peter Carrick, Acting Principal'. Peter Carrick had replaced Julie for a time when she was ill. As I read the neat handwriting, the life and times of Terry Phillips became clearer. I walked into Julie's office.

'Did you know that Reggie Phillips is in prison?'

'No, I certainly did not,' said Julie quite indignantly. 'What did he do?'

'An assault and battery, about two years ago. It's all in this letter from Janice Phillips to Peter Carrick.'

'Peter certainly didn't say anything to me about it. This is unsatisfactory, you know.'

'I bet it wasn't very pleasing for the poor coot who copped the hiding.'

'How long will he be at the governor's pleasure?'

'Another two weeks, then he'll be heading home.'

'She's kept so quiet. Poor woman.'

'Poor bloody kid.'

'Have you spoken to Terry about this?'

'Not yet. I'll see him again at lunchtime.'

Julie stirred her coffee and drank the last drop. 'We simply don't know the pressure the kids are under when they come to us. I can't take it all in sometimes. Where is the fairness in things such as this? Why do the young have to be visited by violence and separation so often?'

'I'll try not to talk to Terry about his dad,' I said.

'How will you handle it now?'

'I'm aiming at relieving Terry of some of his burden.'

Julie nodded and returned to gaze out at the trees that edged the playground. She seemed to be taking solace from the beauty that surrounded us.

VI

The lunch bell rang as Terry appeared in my office.

'Sit down, Terry. We need to sort this out, mate.'

'Mr O'C, why won't you believe me? I didn't do anything to the girls. Even Vanessa says it was rough and tumble.'

'Yesterday morning, Michelle and Vanessa came to me and told me of something that had happened on the buses. I believe them, Terry.'

It was like a physical blow. Terry's eyes swelled as they had the previous morning. He gripped the arms of the chair and pleaded with me. 'I didn't do it. You've gotta believe me. How many times do I have to say it?'

'You've only got to tell me the truth once, Terry. Just once.' I leant closer to him and said in a gentle voice, 'I'm going to call your mother.'

This was the first time I noticed any trace of fear in his eyes. Fear is a common commodity in schools. The subculture has an abundance of intimidation and fear of exclusion. This wasn't a fear related to peer activity, this was real and powerful.

'Don't call my mum! Please, don't call her. She'll kill me.'

'Why would she want to kill you, Terry?'

''Cos of what I've done.'

'She won't kill you, mate. No one is going to hurt you in the least.' I leant closer and said slowly, 'Look at me, Terry.

Look at me.' I paused as he lifted his head towards me. I nodded my head and said, 'Say it to me. Say it to me, Terry.'

'Yes. Yes.' He was weeping. 'I did it to the girls and I did ask them what I shouldn't of asked them. I didn't mean to hurt 'em. I didn't want to hurt 'em.'

NEVILLE

Pino Saccaro

Sometimes I wake up in the middle of the night and I think of him. The red hair and freckles. The four foot, six inch body. His incredible bundle of energy. He was irrepressible and fearless.

If there was someone on the roof collecting tennis balls, it was Neville. If a redhead had been seen shoplifting, we instantly suspected Neville. When there were rocks being thrown at cars or windows were broken, it was not difficult to know where to turn. Once, in Year 7, a police van returned him and a friend to the school. Curiosity had got the better of them and they had visited a brothel. The ladies made them a drink of lemonade and then called the boys in blue.

Neville had many of the qualities I lacked. As a young and inexperienced teacher I was shy and introverted, while he was confident and outgoing. He was his own person with an inherent emotional honesty about him that I could not help but admire. Had he been a character in a movie, and not my student, I would have cheered for him.

Unashamedly and openly, however, I wished that he would be absent in my PE classes. But he never was. He never missed a class. I would wait for the barrage of abuse when a decision went against him. It was like watching, waiting, for dynamite to explode. The javelin, shot put and discus were lethal weapons in his hands. I banned archery when he tried to shoot an arrow at someone's foot. Many times I sat him out, yet he held no grudges. He would be back the following lesson to wish me good morning and then proceed to give me hell.

Neville copped plenty also. Some of the senior students tried to swat him like a fly. They never succeeded. Secretly I admired his spunk, his spirit, his resilience. He just came back for more.

In a funny kind of way he bonded together all those teachers who taught him. There was almost a feeling of *esprit de corps* in combating a common enemy. The teachers who taught him shared a knowing look. We called him 'Neville the Devil'. As a Year 8 he was hell. As a Year 9 he was simply uncontrollable.

It was the second week of term and already he had established himself. Neville was caught trying to extort money from one of the junior boys. Although Carl, the boy he was extorting from, was not actually small – he had the somatotype of a Sumo wrestler – such is the power of psychological dominance. Besides, Neville had mates.

Neville and his mates were given a 'final' chance. A green suspension form was waved in front of Neville.

'Next time you step out of line.' The Principal dangled the form and Neville looked suitably impressed.

It was not surprising to hear about Neville that week. The Year 9 coordinator was in full rhetoric.

'I came around the corner of the lunch shelter and guess who I found with a cigarette in his mouth?' There was a pause for effect. 'Neville. He quickly tried to hide the smoke between his legs.'

'So what's happened?' I asked.

'He's on his last chance,' said the coordinator.

'But wasn't he already on his last chance?'

'Yes, but that was for extorting. If he smokes again he's out.'

The green form was dangled in front of Neville. Again he looked suitably impressed.

The next day during lunch Neville's presence was felt again. Marion the cookery teacher retold how Neville had proceeded to try to set fire to the cookery room. An extinguisher quelled the flames.

I had Neville after lunch. He'll be a little more subdued today, I thought. On the contrary, he was more hyperactive than usual. I tried to assert myself.

'Neville, one more mistake and you'll be going up to the Principal. I've heard what you've done today. Another incident is not going to help your case. I am referring to the fire in the cookery class.'

'Did Mr Wilson tell you about the scriber I tried to steal in Sheetmetal?'

'No.'

'Was it the fight I had in Art?'

'No.'

'Was it the door I kicked in during Maths?'

'No.'

'Did Mr Considine tell you he caught us smoking again at lunchtime?'

'No! Forget it, Neville.' Was this happening? The boy sure did have a full life.

During the next two weeks Neville caused us considerably more headaches. Once he came in to the class and was a little more subdued than usual because he had been concussed in the weekend's football match. After the class I went into the change rooms and found a hole in the wall where Neville had kicked his foot through the plaster.

Neville was finally expelled when he told the Principal to get fucked. The fact that he had told all the other teachers to get fucked at least once meant little. No one says that to the Principal. The buck stops there.

Sometimes during lunchtime we would discuss Neville. What would come of him? Most of us figured he would do well. He was intelligent, bright and energetic. School could not harness his sense of adventure. So it was with shock that we were greeted with the news about Neville. It was the beginning of the school year. Marion, the Cookery teacher, came into the staffroom.

'Have you heard about Neville?'

During the summer holidays in his usual energetic, cavalier style, Neville had dived into a shallow lake and broken his spinal cord. He would be a quadriplegic for the rest of his life.

I was incredulous.

'It's true,' said Marion. One of her reliable students had told her.

'It was bound to happen,' said the Woodwork teacher. 'Still, you wouldn't wish it on your worst enemy.'

Neville was a rogue, but a lovable one. Now he was a quadriplegic. We all wondered how he would cope. The two pictures of him contradicted each other – a dynamo and a cripple. It seemed so incomprehensible.

Maybe he will show his spirit and come through it. Even in his wheelchair I hope he is still giving people hell. I wish him all the best.

Sometimes We Forget!

Ron Skidmore

It had been a hard day. Mondays are always bad but when you are greeted in the car park by a deputation of angry Grade 6 kids arguing over a game of cricket, the day can only get worse. My impersonation of Solomon settled matters as usual, but the kids didn't look happy as they sauntered away and I knew that I hadn't heard the last of it. With an armful of books I wandered into my classroom to prepare for another day at the chalkface.

Three-quarters of an hour's preparation is never enough. I jumped as the bell screamed and rushed out to morning assembly. As I did so I saw a mother approaching. She had that determined look on her face that teachers fear. I tried to ignore her. The last thing I needed was another parent complaint to start the week off. No matter how hard I tried I could never do the right thing in some people's eyes.

She intercepted me as I reached my class. I kept my back to her as I attempted to organise the kids into something resembling a line. It was always a battle. They would rather just stand and chat about the weekend. So I wandered around coaching and at times physically moving the kids into the correct position. When I had my grade into what roughly resembled a line I became aware that the mother had not taken the hint. She was still standing behind me.

I turned and said, 'Good morning, Mrs Wilson. Can I help you?'

'Yes, Mrs Edwards, I just wish you to have this.' She handed me a letter and walked away. Another complaint! I get a copy and no doubt she's off to hand one to the Principal. I stuffed the letter in my pocket. I'd read it later.

I turned and faced the front. The assembly started. The drone of the Principal waffling on was not doing my headache much good. Luckily, after ten minutes it started to rain and we all had to rush inside.

With as much noise as a buffalo stampede my grade crashed inside, talking all the way. My grade is a pretty good bunch really. They're noisy but full of life. Never boring, that's for sure.

Once inside the week started as usual. Demands from the office for the cash book to be sent up. The battle with the normal kids over weekend homework. The same old kids with the same old lame excuses. Then there were the lunch orders, book fair forms, absence notes, the attendance roll, medicines to be kept in my drawer. On and on it went into vocab work, literature studies and an introductory Maths session on place value. Boy those vacant stares didn't really instil much confidence.

I was saved by the bell at 11.00 am and sprinted up to the staffroom to grab a cup of coffee and then outside to do yard duty with bumbag in hand. The rain had stopped but it was cold and I forgot my coat as usual. The wind whipped through my thin satin shirt and the complaints from the kids never stopped.

The boys from the morning encounter were at it again and I had to march two of them up to the office after a punch was thrown. Then it was into the sick room to clean up a bloody knee and wipe away a few tears.

Monday crept on.

Discipline problems, forms to fill out for the office, a parent interview at lunchtime, a rushed sandwich in Room 6 at a quick PD meeting, up to production practice and then into line at the photocopier to run off a last-minute idea to finish off my first lunchbreak of the week. A normal day that brought about the same level of excitement as usual.

After Technology studies and Science all the Grade 6s were involved in the Buddy System. It was my turn to organise the activity and in all the rush I had forgotten to prepare. I grabbed a box of chalk and made it up as we walked out. I had the older kids use the coloured chalk to trace around the preps on the brick walls near the assembly area. The kids loved this. The younger kids then had to draw things in their body shapes which showed what they were like as people, and the older kids wrote the words. Each Grade 6 child had their own little buddy and it was cute seeing them look after the preppies.

After an hour or so they had all finished their masterpieces, out there for all the community to see, and we set off back to our rooms to pack up. High fives and smiles everywhere as the little kids said goodbye to their big buddies.

When we got back to the room a few parents were waiting and they all had to have a little word to me. I smiled and answered their questions, trying to pull myself away so I could make sure the room got cleaned up before the bell. I didn't want to be rude so I kept talking to them until the bell went. The room was a mess of course, so I picked up all the papers after the kids had left and rearranged the desks and chairs so that the cleaner wouldn't be mad at me.

When the room looked alright I collapsed into my chair. Then the announcement came over the loudspeaker that the staff meeting was going to commence in two minutes. So it was into another meeting to discuss next week's fete, inter-school sport, teacher appraisal and the PD activities that were coming up in the next few weeks.

After the meeting the Principal asked to see me in her office. A complaint had been handed in to her. A mother was not happy with the way I was treating her son. His homework was too hard and he was not happy in my grade. I wanted to yell at her that little Jimmy wouldn't work in an iron lung, that he was a vicious bully who dominated the class and brought other kids down. That he was smart but couldn't care less about learning and that he had no respect for me as a person. But I didn't.

We talked about ways to help Jimmy. We set up a program to build his self-esteem and to cater activities that would interest him. We talked about my grade organisation and my failings and we arranged a telephone interview with the mother. She didn't want to talk to me face to face because she said she would punch me.

By five o'clock it was all over. I dragged myself out to my car and flopped into the seat, started the engine and drove home.

When I pulled into my driveway I had had enough. It had been a hard day and I had tried my best. I couldn't believe that teaching could be so hard. I just wanted to give up. As I sat there, though, I felt something in my pocket. It was the note the parent had handed me in the morning. I took it out and looked at it. I ripped the top off angrily and there I sat, in my driveway, in the pouring rain, with darkness approaching . . . and in the depths of despair I read the note:

Dear Jenny (and whoever else is involved in the Buddy System),
Just wanted to share a warm feeling with you that we've got from the Buddy System.

Mary's middle name, Wendy, was chosen because of her paternal grandmother, Wendy Wilson. Mary was very fond of both Granny and Grandad in Ireland, and last year was a sad one for us with both my husband's parents dying within two months of each other. Mary came with us to Granny's funeral, but we felt the second trip was just too much to expect of her.

It's taken Mary weeks to finally find out and remember her Grade 6 buddy's name, and we've been quietly and warmly smiling whenever we hear it. Mary never stops talking about her buddy. The buddy's name is Wendy!

I know that this is all pure chance, but we're so glad — thank you all. To us it feels like Granny is still there, looking after our child.
Thank you very much.
Yours sincerely,
Liz Wilson

I folded the letter slowly and put it back in my pocket, collected my things and walked up to the front door. My husband had been watching me through the window, wondering why I had stayed in the car so long.

'Are you okay?' he asked as the door opened, with a worried look on his face.

'Yes I am,' I said.

'Then what's wrong?'

'Nothing, nothing at all.'

I placed the letter into his hand, walked inside and flopped on the couch.

Another day finished and only four to go.

NOTES ON THE CONTRIBUTORS

Susie Armillei

Reunion at the Star Hotel
Susie Armillei was born in Tasmania and worked as a Maths/Science teacher for four years before retraining as a Teacher of the Deaf in the 1980s. She has since taught at the innovative 'Claremont Project', the first integrated bilingual bicultural education system for deaf children in the world. She lives near the beach with her husband David and a fat, white cat.

Greg Bogaerts

A Fine Line
Greg Bogaerts is a Newcastle writer, who has had many short stories published in journals and magazines around Australia. He is 43 years old and has taught English in state and private education systems in NSW. He is now self-employed as a tutor, which gives him the time to write. He is working on a trilogy of novels about Newcastle entitled, 'The Coal River Collection'. He is married and has two stepdaughters.

Lyn Chatham

Mars Bars and Lawson
Lyn Chatham has taught in Melbourne and Geelong. She is an ex-secondary teacher who now works in Adult Literacy and Training. Lyn is co-author of *Fun and Fantasy*, a booklet on Process Writing, and has written for *Idiom* and had poetry published in *Famous Reporter* and *Yellow Moon*.

Peter Cox

Antony
Peter Cox has taught Mathematics and Science in Victorian secondary schools for twenty-five years. He has recently taken up writing after a long illness forced his retirement from teaching. Peter has won a number of minor awards in literary competitions and has had a dozen stories published in literary magazines. He is currently working on a murder mystery.

Laura Deriu

Lesbeans
Born in 1963 to Italian parents, Laura learnt English in a St Kilda playground before graduating from the University of Melbourne. Currently, she teaches at Methodist Ladies' College, and has taught at Geelong Grammar School and 'Woodleigh'. She has published various educational articles and short stories, and has had several plays performed, including *The Gasman's Coming*, *Hatecrime*, and *Truth or Dare?*

Sheila Duke

The Lesson
Sheila Duke has been teaching ESL for nineteen years, eight of which have been at the Southside Primary Introductory English Centre in Canberra where she is currently teaching. She has written various articles for magazines and newspapers as well as a teacher's guide to the countries and customs of students with non-English speaking backgrounds, *Bridging the Gap*, which is being published by Macmillan in 1998.

Rhodes Garwen

The Wasp in the Soccer Socks
Rhodes Garwen is the Special Education Co-ordinator at Chevalier College, NSW. He has an abiding interest in story telling and writing. Rhodes finds it successful in stimulating students at both ends of the learning spectrum. He lives on a farmlet in the Southern Highlands with his wife Roslyn and their four dogs.

Helen Gordon

If No One Cares for Me
Helen Gordon MEd (Studs) Dip. Teach. Lib. was for thirty years a NSW Teacher-Librarian and was most recently employed at Maitland Grossmann High. She now works if it appeals, editing, proof-reading, writing reviews and her views, but generally more appealing are travel, reading, film, fitness, friends, gardening and making marmalade.

Kathryn Harrison

Choose Your Own Adventure: Don't we All
Kathryn Harrison works as an English and History teacher at Golden Square Secondary College in Bendigo, Victoria. She lives in a big yellow house on a twenty acre block with her husband Paul and daughter Isabella. Kathryn loves reading and writing and hopes she brings to her students a love for both.

Maree Herrett

To Ms With Love?
Maree Herrett began teaching with the NSW Dept of Education in 1976. In 1986, she moved into the Catholic schools sector, after a number of

years of part-time TAFE teaching, and is now Senior English Co-ordinator at Santa Sabina College, Strathfield. Maree has had feature articles published in *The Bulletin*, and has an MA in Creative Writing.

Gordon Holder

Why Do I Keep Teaching?
Gordon Holder started teaching after a career change. He worked in government schools and the private sector in Australia before taking early retirement in 1993. Gordon now combines teaching adult literacy with travelling and studying classical guitar. He lives in Cumbria, UK.

Lyndall Hough

Acting Up
'You probably won't remember me but you used to teach me in . . .' After thirty years in teaching Lyndall Hough hears this phrase a lot. She recently moved from the classroom to a full time writing career and is employed as an educational writer. She has published short stories, poetry, advertising copy, articles for newspapers and journals and recently a text book, *In Fact, Reading and Viewing Factual Texts*.

Peter Howe

The Three Microphones
Peter Howe is a father of five who has taught in western NSW, Sydney, Wollongong and the NSW South Coast. He believes that public schools are the single most important force for good in Australian society and that teachers are heroes on the frontier between good and evil, hope and despair.

Russell James

The Great Greasy Pig Chase of 1967
Russell James has been a teacher in Victorian state and private schools for more than thirty years. He has co-written and edited several legal studies text books for various teachers' journals. Currently he is combining teaching with writing for *BMW Magazine*, *Move Magazine* and *Golf in Victoria*.

James Johnson

The Pole
James Johnson began his teaching career in 1958 at 19, sweeping the floor and emptying the toilets of a leased hall in the Victorian Mallee. Later on he taught at a couple of Melbourne primary schools, a tech, adult evening classes, and several secondaries concluding with 5 years as a principal at a country one. He found his name on a jumper in a school lost property basket, and after several lunch-time announcements assumed its owner no longer wanted it.

Susan Lane

Walls and Bridges
Susan Lane was born in Sydney and studied at the universities of NSW and Wollongong. Susan has worked as a bus conductress, teacher, filing clerk, counsellor, and researcher, and has had short fiction and non-fiction stories published in anthologies and magazines. She lives on the south coast of NSW near the beach.

Sharyn Lawrence

Archery Delinquents
Sharyn Lawrence has been a teacher for eighteen years and is currently teaching creative writing through distance education to post-secondary students. She lives on a small farm in Tasmania with her son, three geriatric horses and some beef cattle. Archery is not one of her hobbies.

Bev McGregor

The Key
Bev McGregor has been writing for more than ten years and is author of eight children's books and numerous magazine articles. She has a background in teaching and librarianship, but has worked as a swimming instructor, medical clerk, employment officer and supervisor in a girls' remand centre. Bev has taught in NSW, Malaysia and Canada and is currently travelling around Australia with her husband.

Graham McLennan

Red Corner, White Corner
Graham McLennan moved from journalism to teaching in 1980. Since then he has been a medieval history teacher at Hawker Secondary College, ACT. He has written numerous newspaper feature articles as well as historical research published in a variety of formats. Graham has also lived and worked in the UK, and the USA. His hobbies include painting water colours and drawing.

Christine Melican

Write for Life
Christine Melican began teaching twenty-five years ago. As well as teaching she has been enriched by living in a Christian community,

working for a large welfare agency, being a schools consultant for a publishing company and, with her husband, raising their children. She is passionate about teenagers and teaching English. Her dream is to soon have the time to complete all her unfinished writing projects.

Jean Mrozik

Rubicon
Jean Mrozik retired as principal of a metropolitan high school in 1986 after a 43 year career as a secondary school teacher. She has had various short stories published in literary magazines and anthologies here and overseas and is currently working on a novel.

Vic O'Callaghan

An Inquiring Mind
Vic O'Callaghan is married to Liz. They live in the Blue Mountains west of Sydney with their two sons. Vic taught in primary education for seventeen years. Over the past three years Vic has written two books, *The Jesse Tree*; *The Bower Bird's Nest* and a number of articles. One of Vic's treasures is the window at the back of the family home where numerous birds of the mountains can be seen feasting and flying. 'It's a bit like a playground.'

Joy Price

How Yellow Changed to Gold
Joy Price was born in Wellington, New Zealand, in 1932 and educated in Manchester and Blackpool. After migrating to Australia in 1949, she began a teaching career spanning 45 years and taught English in high schools in Sydney and the ACT, and was also a Careers Adviser until her retirement in 1997. Joy has written special high interest courses

(Career English, P-Plate English) for use in ACT schools for non-tertiary students doing English and Careers units.

Wendy Ratawa

A Place for the Living
Wendy Ratawa was born in Swan Hill and trained as a secondary art teacher in the 1950s. After three years in Bendigo, she spent thirteen years in Fiji where she married Rev. Peceli Ratawa. They have three sons. After returning to Australia, Wendy completed an MA in ethnomusicology and settled in Geelong. She now writes short stories mainly on feminist issues.

Pino Saccaro

Neville
Sicilian born Pino Saccaro migrated to Melbourne when he was five. He has worked as a physical education teacher for seventeen years, the last seven teaching refugee children.

Pino is an avid freelance writer – his articles have been published Australia wide in newspapers and magazines. He has travelled the world but calls Australia home.

Ron Skidmore

Sometimes We Forget!
Ron has been a teacher for twenty-one years. He began writing three years ago and his histories have appeared in various publications. Ron is a single parent living in Berwick, Melbourne; a sport lover and Western Bulldogs fanatic. Ron spends most of his time ferrying his two sons around town or jotting down idle ideas for another story.

Michael Small

Her Master's Voice
Michael Small has taught English in England, Sweden, Canada and Australia. Among his numerous publications are *Her Natural Life and Other Stories*; *A Resource Book for Studying Film as Text* (with Brian Keyte); and *Unleashed: A History of Footscray Football Club* (with John Lack, Chris McConville and Damian Wright).

Don Smith

Slippery the School Mascot
Don Smith has lived and taught in remote Queensland for over twenty-five years. In that time he has faced many unusual experiences including floods, plagues, fires and droughts. Since the events described in this story, Don has focussed on helping children appreciate the importance of preserving our natural heritage. He is currently living in Brisbane with his pet python Snappy Tom and two giant huntsman spiders Mr and Mrs Lazybones.

Susan Utting

Out of Uniform
Susan Utting was born and educated in Melbourne, but bred in northern Victoria. After studying Arts and Education at Monash, she taught in suburban and country primary, secondary government schools and further education institutions for twenty-five years. Susan has three children and teaches at TAFE near her farm at Shady Creek where she attempts to produce grosse lisse tomatoes and prize winning pumpkins as well as the odd short story.

Helen Wakefield

The Hill School

Helen Wakefield trained as a primary and Art Teacher in the 1960s and has taught in Scotland, Japan and in state and private schools in Victoria and NSW. Helen has had work published in the Young Victorians' Quilts Project, *The Fabric of the Mind* and in *Computer Usage in Education*. She has written numerous short stories, poetry and prose over the past twenty seven years.

Linda Wells

Kultitja

Linda Wells is originally from Melbourne. She has lived in Central Australia for 10 years. She is the single mother of a Warlpiri child, one of the outcomes of falling in love with a unique group of children. Linda is currently working in Adult Education in Alice Springs.

Edel Wignell

He's Our Boy

Edel Wignell is a freelance writer, former teacher. She taught in primary schools in Victoria and in London for eight years and at a Teachers' College for seven years. She has about 50 stories for children and short stories, features, scripts and verse for adults and children in more than 80 magazines, newspapers and radio programs. Edel lives in Melbourne with her husband Geoff.

Roseanne Wildman

Feral Line Five

Roseanne Wildman was born in Tasmania in 1951. After graduating from Launceston Teachers College and the University of Tasmania,

Roseanne taught Year Three to Twelve from west coast mining areas of Tasmania to inner city Sydney. Teaching has been punctuated by fruit picking, banking and writing.

Robby Wright

A Winter's Tale
Robby Wright is currently teaching in the NSW state system. She has recently completed her Masters degree, writing a thesis on the travel writing of Paul Theroux and V.S. Naipaul. Robby is now hoping to spend more time on other writing and is researching a biography of Germanicus.

Robert Yen

Best Before March 1
Robert Yen teaches Mathematics at Ambarvale High School in outer south-western Sydney. He writes regularly about his teaching life and experiences in 'Mr Yen's World', a column in *Education*, the NSW Teachers Federation journal. He also enjoys writing maths textbooks in the little spare time he has.

Amanda Tattam

Amanda Tattam was born in London and educated in four schools in Melbourne. She has eleven years experience as a reporter and editor, including six years in London. Amanda writes on education, health, social affairs and industrial relations for numerous publications and was the editor of the bestselling anthology, *From The Heart – True Stories by Australian Nurses*. Amanda lives in Melbourne.

MORE BESTSELLING NON-FICTION AVAILABLE FROM PAN MACMILLAN

John Marsden
Secret Men's Business

This is the most urgently needed book of our time.

Where Steve Biddulph's best-selling *Raising Boys* talks to parents and teachers, *Secret Men's Business* talks to young men themselves – in the way that only John Marsden can. It sets out, in direct honest language, the things every young man needs to know . . . and the things young men aren't being told.

Young men who read this book will learn how to be strong, how to be honest, how to confront their fears. They'll understand how to deal with men and women, parents and teachers, male friends and female friends. They'll get a sense of the integrity that every true man needs.

They'll find ways to resolve problems without being destructive or self-destructive.

They'll have their questions about sex answered . . . in clear, straightforward language.

With *Tomorrow, When the War Began* John Marsden wrote the most powerful novel for teenagers ever published in this country. Now he has written the most powerful non-fiction work ever made available to young men.

Walter Mikac
with Lindsay Simpson
To Have and To Hold

On 28 April 1996, Walter Mikac lost his wife, Nanette, and two daughters, six-year-old Alannah and three-year-old Madeline. They were shot dead, along with 32 other innocent people, during the Port Arthur massacre in Tasmania.

To Have and To Hold is Walter's tribute to Nanette and the girls, and their uniqueness. Walter recounts their early life together, their love for each other and the years of happiness they shared – all of which have sustained him through grief.

He tackles with courage and honesty aspects of bereavement that are rarely acknowledged. After having the love and security of a family, he is now a single person confronting an unknowable future. He has also found himself thrust into the media spotlight, his grief exposed for the world to see.

Through the issue of gun control and the establishment of the Alannah and Madeline Foundation, Walter has channelled his energy into ensuring that their lives were not lost in vain – a commitment that was sparked by meeting the parents who lost children in Scotland's Dunblane massacre.

Walter Mikac is an ordinary person who, through no fault of his own, has been put in an extraordinary positon. Coping with the unimaginable loss of his family has led Walter down a spiritual path of discovery – one of hope and belief that the circle of life continues. His grace and dignity in the face of tragedy have inspired a nation.

'You come away from *To Have and to Hold* with a renewed faith in the human spirit – nobody could remain untouched by this book.'
THE AGE

Daniel Petre
Father Time
– Making Time for Your Children

How are men supposed to work hard and have time to enjoy their children? Daniel Petre, who has experienced first-hand both fatherhood and corporate success, has written a great how-to for busy fathers.

Father Time is written for fathers by a father, and shows how just a few simple changes in the way a man approaches his work and his relationship with his children can result in a much more fulfilling and happier life.

The father of three young daughters, Daniel Petre is an extremely successful businessman. As Managing Director of Microsoft Australia and subsequently a Vice-President at Microsoft's corporate headquaters in Seattle, Daniel has been at the forefront of the emerging information age.

Daniel is now Chairman of PBL Online, a subsidiary of Publishing and Broadasting Ltd, as well as being a board member of a variety of government and commercial organisations.

'Brilliant, readable and revealing. One day we will live in a different world, and this will be one of the books that made it so.'
STEVE BIDDULPH

Athol Moffitt
Drug Alert
– A Guide to Illicit Drugs for Parents, Teachers, Everyone

ESSENTIAL READING FOR EVERY PARENT

Drug Alert is for every person concerned about illicit drugs and their effects on young people.

In clear and simple terms *Drug Alert* lists the street names and side effects of all the commonly used illegal drugs in Australia, and contains all the informations parents need to discuss the dangers of illicit drugs with their children.

'The drug problem is a very real social problem for the whole community to address and I commend Mr Athol Moffitt for his important efforts in educating the community about the dangers and risks of illicit drug use.'
THE HON. JOHN HOWARD, PRIME MINISTER

'My fifteen-year-old daughter Anna left the house one Saturday night to spend the evening with friends. She never came home. If only I had been able to read *Drug Alert*, maybe things would have been different. From a mother who will never see her daughter reach eighteen, get married or have children of her own, I urge everyone to read this book.'
ANGELA WOOD

Dr John Irvine
WHO'D BE A PARENT?

'Dr John Irvine is a child-respecting, parent-understanding person with vast experience. He genuinely likes children, and artfully combines laughter, joy and practical help. When the going gets tough, this book will help you feel you're not alone!'
STEVE BIDDULPH

Parenting is the most important job we'll ever do and yet children come without a manual – or a money-back option!

Who'd Be A Parent? is THE must-have manual on how to raise good kids and solve the inevitable behaviour problems in non-violent ways that are easy to understand and easy to use. Every chapter is written in Dr John's unique style to help parents not only see the lighter side of coping with kids, but to help families use more playfare than warfare in their approach.

Who'd Be A Parent? is the foremost parenting book in Australia today. Comprehensive and practical, it is written by one of the most experienced and well-known practitioners and authors in this field, Dr John Irvine.